Additional Praise for *The* [...] *Electronic Marketing f[...]*

"I'm an e-millionaire thanks to the Internet [...] n
Tom Antion. The only marketing I do is on th[...] d
when they phone me they only have two questions. p[...] e
already sold after having read the content on my site."

Gloria Star
Image and Etiquette Consultant
http://www.gloriastarr.com

"Tom Antion is one of the Electronic Marketing geniuses of our time. He is wise, tested, proven, productive, and profitable and wants to show you how to be the same. He has helped our business enormously."

Mark Victor Hansen
Author, *Chicken Soup for the Soul, One Minute Millionaire*
http://www.MarkVictorHansen.com

"Thanks to Tom Antion's help we did $250,000 in product sales with about three-quarters of that coming through sales from our e-zine."

Chris Zimmerman
http://www.drzimmerman.com

"Tom Antion's book *The Ultimate Guide to Electronic Marketing for Small Business* has been nothing short of a life saver for my Internet business. It is the most comprehensive book on Internet marketing available. Using his upsell techniques, I have turned a routine $65 book order into a $120 order time and time again. His section on e-books is worth many times the cost of this book. I converted a number of my printed titles into e-books and noticed a staggering 35 percent increase in sales. I sold my first downloadable e-book 25 minutes after it was uploaded to my shopping cart!"

Dr. Dicken Weatherby
http://www.BloodChemistryAnalysis.com

"Tom Antion's book has saved me over $40,000 in Web design costs and has earned me over $100,000 in product sales."

Jim Gillespie, PhD
Advanced Real Estate Sales Coaching
Jim@RealEstateSalesCoach.com

"I took Tom's suggestion for a special sale and advertised it to my e-mail list. It resulted in more than $22,000 in orders in only two weeks. And I didn't have to pack a suitcase, go through security, or get on a plane."

Joan Stewart
The Publicity Hound
http://www.PublicityHound.com

"Since purchasing Tom Antion's book and *following his strategies,* I have easily doubled my income. In the last two weeks, I've made $7,500 from Internet leads! I have another $8,000 deal about to close that just came from an Internet lead.

"Tom Antion has created an easy-to-apply system that gets results. I strongly recommend Tom's products and services to anyone interested in running a successful online business!"

Ruben Gonzalez
Olympian, Keynote Speaker, and Author of *The Courage to Succeed*

"Tom's ideas helped me NET over $14,200 on my very first teleseminar and more since then. The ideas flat-out work!"

Art Sobczak
President, Business By Phone Inc.
BusinessByPhone.com

"Tom Antion's information taught me how to start my own e-mail newsletter. With it I have sold over $100,000 of products and services over the Internet. Thanks for the information and direction."

M. Tewart
President, Tewart Enterprises Inc.
Mtewart@tewart.com

"When it came to Internet marketing I knew nothing. Tom Antion taught me about search engine optimization, web page design, e-books, and hundreds of essential tips that have increased my business by over a million dollars a year."

Lewis Harrison
www.chihealer.com

"I'm very cautious about who or what I endorse. I can tell you that without a doubt, I think Tom Antion is the BEST in the world at what he teaches! Following Tom's advice, I have saved at least $20,000 to $30,000 in Internet mistakes and I expect to add at least another $250,000+ in additional revenue. If you want to make serious money on the Internet, then you must listen to Tom and follow his strategies!"

James Malinchak
www.Malinchak.com
www.CollegeSpeakingSuccess.com

"Tom taught us to do teleconferences and that alone has been worth about $50,000 to us so far."

Dr. Van K. Tharp
Coach for Traders
www.iitm.com

"My monthly Internet sales have doubled since I began taking Tom's advice. Thank you, Tom!"

Lois Carter Fay
Success Secrets of Women Entrepreneurs
http://www.WomenMarketing.com/success.htm

"With guidance from Tom's Internet strategies, my book started hitting bestseller lists within three weeks of its publication by HarperCollins."

Judge James Tamm
Author, *Radical Collaboration: Five Essential Skills to Overcome Defensiveness and Build Successful Relationships*
www.RadicalCollaboration.com

"Tom opened my eyes to the critical importance of online marketing. With very little technical knowledge, I have since created an e-book, written an online course, and began a mentoring program. As a result, my database has doubled and I have created an extra $8,000 in sales that I never would have made through regular marketing. Listen to what Tom has to say and do it!"

Michael Licenblat
Resilience Expert
Melbourne, Australia
http://www.StressManagementSuccess.com

"Thanks to Tom Antion, I managed to get myself out of the 'rat race.' He opened a whole new world of possibilities for me! Last year I made $50,000 from a one-page website! Now that I know the formula to making money on the Internet, life will never be the same again."

Ernesto Verdugo
http://www.SeeingWithoutGlasses.com

"My product sales have increased by 50 percent online and I am now building a business that is an asset that makes money while I sleep and gives me a future exit strategy and pension. Thanks, Tom!"

Frank Furness
www.frankfurness.com

"It only took me 15 minutes to tweak my website with one idea of Tom's that resulted in $5,750 in fees plus product sales! But that's not all. I got my site listed number one in most of the major search engines for more work in my own backyard, which has resulted in even more qualified leads that come in every week! Tom is spot-on with ideas that WORK!"

Rick Butts
www.rickbutts.com

"I cannot tell you how much you have changed my life. I'm now doing what I have dreamed of. I am a retired police officer, on a disability retirement. I bought your book and read it all. I put up my first web site at www.hotdogbook.com and it sells all over the world! I now have three other sites, www.eagleceremony.com, www.1861Reenactors.com, www.TacticalTalk.com and I'm making lots of passive income every month. You have taught me a lot, and you are an honest and genuine business person. Thanks."

Mike Chilton

"Tom Antion saved me thousands of dollars in programming fees by showing me how to simply create a blog myself in only 4 minutes. He saved me 6 months of waiting to get listed with most of the search engines including yahoo. He saved me over $5,000 in future web designer fees by showing me how simple was better. The investment in his book pays back tenfold."

Dr. Jamie Fettig

"In May 2004, at age 63, I knew very little about Internet marketing. I'm a syndicated columnist for the *Orange County Register* in southern California, writing about finding love after 50.

"As a result or your information, I am now generating $5,000 each month from Internet sales and that is mainly profit. You taught me to create repeat profit, year after year. And the best part, I've just touched the tip of the iceberg, my profits are going to grow dramatically as I fine-tune my operation.

"Tom, very simply, without your leadership, none of this would have happened."

Tom Blake
www.findingloveafter50.com

"Thanks to you, I started an electronic newsletter on sewing tips and techniques in November. My web host just informed me that my website now has the second highest amount of traffic of all of the websites they host! They wondered how I did it in such a short amount of time on my limited budget."

Susan Wigley
http://www.paragonpatterns.com

"I was a little skeptical at first. NOT NOW! As I implemented the insider secrets from Tom's book our sales increased an amazing 102 percent over the previous month! (No, this is not a sales pitch and I have not received any compensation.) Sales were up another 30 percent the following month.

"Has it been worth it? Beyond my wildest dreams! It's amazing watching the orders streaming in."

Fire "Captain Bob" Smith
www.eatstress.com

"Tom's techniques have permitted us to move into new markets with amazing effectiveness and profitability. As speakers and consultants, we have doubled our fees in the past six months, and launched into new arenas, including highly desirable and profitable web-based seminars and e-publications. We have stopped doing work that was less profitable and focused on opportunities that permit us to earn far more. Tom is a marvelous mentor. He has assisted us in making our dreams come true and can do the same for you."

Chris Brigham, MD
www.brighamwalker.com
www.brighamassociates.com

"Tom's information transformed my life and my business. I have developed electronic products that provide an additional revenue stream to my speaking and writing business. Each week customers deposit a steady income into my bank while I am focused on the other services I supply to my customers. Listen to Tom—his message is always bang-on (!), current, practical, and makes you steady money."

Julie H. Ferguson
Author and writing coach for teachers, students, writers, and speakers.
Beacon Literary Services
www.beaconlit.com

The Ultimate Guide to

Electronic Marketing for Small Business

The Ultimate Guide to

Electronic Marketing for Small Business

Low-Cost/High-Return Tools and Techniques that Really Work

Tom Antion

WILEY

JOHN WILEY & SONS, INC.

Published by John Wiley & Sons, Inc., Hoboken, New Jersey.
Published simultaneously in Canada.

For general information on our other products and services please contact our Customer Care Department within the United States at (800) 762-2974, outside the United States at (317) 572-3993 or fax (317) 572-4002.

Wiley also publishes its books in a variety of electronic formats. Some content that appears in print may not be available in electronic books. For more information about Wiley products, visit our web site at www.wiley.com.

Library of Congress Cataloging-in-Publication Data:

Antion, Tom.
   The ultimate guide to electronic marketing for small business :
low-cost/high-return tools and techniques that really work / Tom Antion.
      p.   cm.
   Includes bibliographical references and index.
   ISBN-13 978-0-471-71870-3 (pbk.)
   ISBN-10 0-471-71870-X (pbk.)
   1. Telemarketing—Handbooks, manuals, etc.   2. Small
business—Management—Handbooks, manuals, etc.   I. Title.
   HF5415.1265.A45 2005
   658.8′72—dc22

                                        2004028307

Printed in the United States of America.
10 9 8 7 6 5 4 3 2 1

To my girlfriend Kay Hubin
and her entire family who have been there and
supported me through thick and thin. These people
are the best quality people I know on earth.

Acknowledgments

I'd like to thank the following very special people: My editor Matt Holt who definitely is the person who made this book happen. Deborah Schindlar who watched over the details so every part of the process came out correctly. Tamara Hummel who made sure I knew what I was doing when I submitted this mass of paper so it could be turned into something coherent. Nancy Land who put up with my ignorance about the editing process. My agent . . . Oops. I didn't have an agent. So thanks to me ☺. Imal Wagner who is keeping me in the news. Kay Hubin who kept me nourished and who always worried about my health while I kept my nose stuck into the computer for 16 hours a day. My assistant Jocelyn Holman, who jumped and got me things whenever I needed them. Leah West quickly got photos and graphics ready and her appearance on the scene has been a Godsend. Corey Rudl for getting me started on the right path many years ago. Alex Mandossian for teaching me many conversion techniques. John Reese for being one of the truly good guys and probably the most brilliant Internet marketer I know. Mark Victor Hansen, the *Chicken Soup for the Soul* guy and his staff, Lisa, Michelle, Jodi, Mary, Pat, and Richard, for exposing my expertise to thousands of his followers. Terry Brock who keeps me up to date on cool gadgets. Rick Butts for always being an advocate. Wade Thomas for teaching me what I know about domain names. Jason Saeler who expertly handles any problems that come up with my websites and Harold Hingle who handles many of my clients with kid gloves. Chris Davies who always has a brilliant idea for me every time I see him. Perry Marshall for teaching me to become an expert at Google AdWords. Bill Harris for teaching me his awesome customized autoresponder technique. Rob, Cliff, and all the folks at KickStartCart who provide great service to me and all the users of the cart. Jimmy D. Brown for teaching me about viral marketing. Angela Adair Hoy for all her help with e-book information. Mike Stewart the "Internet Audio Guy" for all his great tips on recording audio yourself. Sam Silverstein and his lovely wife Renee for their extremely good service duplicating CDs for me. Richard at Lyon Recording for his awesome service duplicating audiotapes. Armand Morin for producing all his great software for Internet marketers. Jonathan Mizel for teaching me how to use pop-ups correctly. Rick Raddatz for helping me with my unblockable pop-ups. Dan Poynter for teaching me so much about product creation. Gary Smith for taking care of all my web video. Yanik Silver for teaching me a ton about affiliate marketing. Janet Hall who trained lots of my students in Front Page and who handles my shipping for me when I'm on the road. All my publicity buddies, Alex Carroll, Joan Stewart, George McKenzie, Rick Frishman, Dan Janal, Steve and Bill Harrison, Mitch Davis, and Paul Hartunian. Gayle Carson for running our association so efficiently. All the people of my mentee/joint venture program who keep me on my toes and learning new and more powerful techniques. All my affiliates who keep making money for us. Milt and Susan Saunders for giving me such a great deal on their home when I was looking for a location for my Internet retreat center. Maggie, the dog, for sitting in her chair next to me and making me smile as I slaved over the edits for this book. Dad who is doing electrical work on the pearly gates for molding me into what I am today and Mom who has given me a strength that is impossible to describe. If I forgot you, I'm sorry. Just know that I love you and it's only because I'm working on this at 3:00 A.M.

Contents

5   Product Development   206

About the Author

Tom Antion is an internationally acclaimed expert in Internet Marketing for small business. He is a full-time professional speaker who has been featured on major news media worldwide including the Canadian Broadcast Network, The Australian Broadcast Network, Associated Press, The Tokyo Today Show and hundreds of radio, television, and print outlets across the United States.

Tom was the chief spokesperson for CBS Switchboard.com in their Main Street Online program. Switchboard is one of the largest and most heavily visited websites on the Internet. Tom consistently makes large sums of money while sitting in front of his computer, which gave him the idea for his infamous Butt Camp Seminars (http://www.antion.com/buttcamp.htm). Where you can "Make more money sitting on your rear end than going out and working for a living."

Tom's low cost/no cost website techniques have helped thousands of small businesses around the world. One of his websites cost only $650 to create and received "Best-of-the-Web" honors in *INC.* magazine beating out sites that cost millions to produce.

Tom was starting offensive guard for the West Virginia University football team where he earned his bachelor's degree in psychology. Always seeing the light side of things, Tom says he got his clinical experience in psychology in the six years after he graduated when he owned a nightclub just outside Morgantown, West Virginia. The ultimate entrepreneur, Tom has never had a job. Starting from scratch, he owned five apartment buildings and a hotel before he graduated from college.

Tom is the author of the only video seminar of its kind, The Wake 'em Up Video Professional Speaking System (http://www.antion.com/speakervideo .htm). This training course is considered the standard for training professional, or aspiring professional speakers in the art of speaking and the science of marketing professional speaking and training services.

Tom is also cofounder of http://www.NetAim.Info, the Internet Association of Information Marketers.

Quick Start Overview

Whether you perceive yourself as a local business or you already sell world-wide, there will be something in this book for you.

Let me give you a quick start overview of some of the big things you are going to accomplish with this book:

- As a small business owner, you will be learning to use the Internet to sell your existing products and services.
- You are going to learn how to create even more income by selling other people's products and you are going to have an army of other people selling yours on a purely commission basis. This is called *affiliate marketing.*
- You are going to learn to look for other ways to make passive income with your website and database by joint venturing with others, selling ad space, making money when someone leaves your website, and lots of other ways to give you a much greater return on your web investment.
- You are going to learn how to acquire powerful websites for virtually no investment that look great and represent you well professionally.
- You are going to learn to evaluate those that are helping you to see if they know what they are doing.
- You are going to learn the psychological sales process of a website so your site sells.
- You are going to learn the value of having a great shopping cart system that automates your business and sells more to the same number of people.
- You are going to learn the methods of getting high rankings in search engines.
- You are going to learn guaranteed ways to get top rankings by using pay-per-click search engines.
- You are going to learn how to build a massive e-mail database of people who want to hear from you. This database will be extremely valuable to you because it is virtually cost free to reach customers and prospects over and over when you have something to sell.
- You will learn the latest techniques to reach your customers and prospects through the Internet without fighting the e-mail spam filters.

- You will learn how to use your website to reduce your customer service costs.
- You will learn to create digital and physical products that compliment and promote your existing product line that you can sell over and over again without keeping any inventory. You can even give them away as a form of Viral Marketing.
- You will learn how telephone seminars can directly bring you in tremendous cash flow or indirectly promote your products and services.

You will learn tons more along the way, but I just wanted to give you a little preview of what you are going to accomplish. That will help you when you get a little bogged down now and then trying to learn this stuff.

I can assure you that my students who consistently apply the knowledge in this book are making more money on the web than they ever dreamed they could.

Good luck and let's get started!

Tom Antion

Introduction

The reason I got into this Internet Marketing stuff was because of statistics. I had a website for two years and didn't even know that statistics were being kept on the site. When I saw them for the first time, I almost fainted. Only 400 people had come to my website in two years . . . ouch!

I had fought with my web designer over that two-year time period about updates taking forever, or more likely never being implemented at all. My *Wake 'em Up Book* was out a year before the webmaster got it on the site. The depression and shock that I felt was the best thing that ever happened to my career.

Now I get many thousands of visitors per day to my websites and earn over a million dollars a year in Internet-generated income.

I had to learn many things to make this happen. You need to start somewhere and consistently work at it to keep people coming regularly to your site and keep the numbers building.

I am not a tech guru. I just studied the simple techniques that either I can do myself, or I can farm out to some professional who does it all the time. The more you do yourself, the cheaper this whole deal is going to be. You can call or e-mail me for recommendations of people who can do things you don't want to do yourself.

Website . . . Ya Gotta Have One

Everybody tells you that you must have a website, but hardly anybody tells you how to really have one that kicks, brings in new customers, and automatically sells more to your existing customers.

What happens is you spend a fortune getting someone to design a website for you and then you sit there and wait for the money to roll into your bank account. It just doesn't work like that. You need to make a commitment to actively manage your website operations and supervise, or completely control, the marketing efforts of your site.

By using this book, you can develop a successful small business electronic marketing system. I recently attended a small business association meeting and it was very evident that there were only a handful of us who knew these techniques and tricks and had successful websites.

If you think that something is a little bit over your head, I don't want you to worry.

I have put "What You Need to Know" lightbulbs just after sections that might be a little confusing if you are a beginner. I'm not expecting you to be able to do everything in this book . . . that would make you a "techie." You must, however, know what needs to be done so you can make sure it gets done.

What You Need to Know

 You don't have to know everything or even anything technical to make a lot of money with electronic marketing.

Watch Out for Electronic Artists

I want you to be prepared because many of your web designers and technical people driving old Ford Pintos will argue with you and try to talk you out of doing some of the things mentioned in this book. Always remember, this book came about because people making extremely large amounts of money taught me how to do it and I'm making extremely large amounts of money with the same techniques. Exactly how much money are your web designer and techie friends making by actually selling things on the Internet?

You need to make sure that you don't get stuck in the typical trap of paying for a beautiful design of a website that nobody comes to . . . and more importantly, you need to make sure your web visitors stay and buy your products and services. The "Pretty Website Syndrome" is the most common problem I see. Many people are website designers because it is so easy to become one. However, very few know the marketing techniques I'm going to cover in this book.

You have to make sure your designer or web person knows how to do these things. If he doesn't, you need to educate him or get somebody else. It's that simple. I know you bleeding hearts out there are thinking, "Oh, but my web designer is so nice and the site looks so pretty, I couldn't possibly find someone else as nice." I hate to be the one to tell you . . . nice is important, but nice ain't going to make you any money in this specific aspect of your electronic marketing efforts. I can virtually guarantee that your web designer doesn't know what is in this book. Maybe 2 percent at most might know some of what's here. Maybe a tiny fraction of them know more. What are the odds that one of these few select people is currently working as your web designer?

It's relatively easy to design your website, but putting in the appropriate marketing elements is not so easy. If you fall into the "Pretty Website Trap," it's going to cost you a lot of money. If you want to stick with your current designer, then get another copy of this book to educate him or her.

Designers who haven't come to my Butt Camp generally don't like me because I expose them for what they are . . . electronic artists. Designers who come to my Butt Camp usually end up loving me before they leave because I have just put them into that tiny, tiny, percentage of people who can both design and market a website properly. That makes them VERY valuable.

Learn from the Best

I'm also going to be telling you about a consultation I did with Corey Rudl, who sells over six million dollars a year on the Internet. I have a website that brings in good money. . . . I've earned as much as $50,000 by sending one e-mail that drove people to one of my sites . . . and this guy ripped me to shreds. I'm going to tell you what I found out during this consultation, and all the improvements I've made to my sites because of what I learned from him. It cost me $640 to talk to this guy for an hour (now it's $1,280) and I'm going to share the concepts he told me so you too can use them on your website.

Remember—I'm not a techie. I just know where to click to make money. I'm hoping I can be a model for you to just go out and do it! I will tell you that learning how to update my website myself is by far the best single investment in time and money I made in my entire business career. It took a month and a half part-time with no help to learn how to update the site. With the update method I teach, that time can be reduced to a few hours of training.

Three-Pronged Attack

I'll be teaching you my three-pronged attack of electronic marketing in this book. You'll make the most progress the fastest if you move ahead on these three prongs concurrently.

The Three Prongs

In Prong One, you create and market a killer website. That will entail creating it properly so that the marketing aspects are worked into the design of your site. You will learn many electronic methods of promoting the site along with all the traditional off-line methods. You will create the proper sales atmosphere on the site to maximize your return on investment. You'll also learn the electronic mechanics of making your website an automatic sales machine that not only sells directly, but drives people to your brick-and-mortar store if you have one.

Prong Two is all about e-mail list building and responsible e-mail marketing. This is where the money is. Savvy companies large and small are using this extremely cost-effective method to reach out to their customers over and over. This creates more loyal customers and keeps their company name at the top of their customer's minds. The customers on your e-mail list who hear from you regularly are the ones who pull out their wallets and buy. You can also make really quick special announcements and sales that fill in slow times at your store. A regular e-mail magazine that gives good tips about using your products and services will establish you as the expert and the one to call when someone needs what you have to offer.

Also in prong two is blog and RSS technology that allows you to reach your prospects and customers directly through the Internet and bypasses e-mail filters. Savvy small business owners are capitalizing right now on this inexpensive technology and also using it to plan for the future in case e-mail becomes ineffective.

Prong Three concentrates on product development and delivery and all the ways you can sell your knowledge electronically. You'll learn how to make downloadable products and e-courses that have no cost of goods sold. You'll learn how to make high-profit CDs, audio, and videotapes, and how to handle the order fulfillment process.

Most small business owners have no idea how e-books, pamphlets, CDs, DVDs, and e-courses could create demand for their existing products and services. By reading this book, you will be far ahead of your competition and you'll be able to tap this very lucrative source of promotion. Also, if you simply want to have an Internet business and you don't know what you're going to sell, information products have the least risk and highest return of any other product line.

If ever you feel like you are getting confused or lost, revert back to the three prongs. You're either working to make a great website, getting more people on your e-mail list and in your database, or developing more things to sell or give away to your target market.

One Page Websites

This is an entirely new method I've developed to make very low cost websites that sell digital products. These sites can be developed in a matter of days for almost no cost once you have your basic shopping system in place. Just three of these sites are going to gross over $100,000 this year with a total investment of less than $1,000. How many other projects do you have under development in your business that produce that kind of return?

You'll read about this and the exact technique I use to create these low cost sites in my "White Paper for One Page Websites" that follows.

Mac versus PC Debate

I couldn't care less what kind of computer you prefer to use. What I will tell you is that all the cool, cheap, and free software to be a prolific Internet marketer is created for the PC. So you can be a Mac holdout if you want, but you are seriously impeding your Internet marketing operations.

A band-aid you could use is Virtual PC for the Mac. I've never heard anyone rave about how great it is though. Keep in mind you can buy an outrageously fast marketing PC for $350. I make more than that selling two multimedia CDs, so consider keeping your Mac, but getting an inexpensive PC and putting it to good use making money.

A Little Info about This Book

This book includes all the links you need to help make your electronic marketing efforts kick into gear. I've also included a special web page where I'll post updates and new and exciting e-commerce developments as I learn about them. Thus, you can keep up with the latest and greatest developments between major updates of the book (http://www.UltimateGuideToEMarketing.com). Your user ID is tomantion and your password is ultimate1.

This book has tons of information from the most dynamic field in existence today . . . the Internet. Don't be surprised if you go to a link and it's not there, or something has changed. That's the nature of the beast. Please send me a note and I'll post it on the updates web page.

I've attempted to give you many resource choices on every topic I cover. This is not because I want to confuse you, but because, as I just mentioned, some may close down before you get to them. You should always have a couple from which to choose.

Research any site you do business with carefully, and don't forget to read the fine print. Some of these relationships take considerable effort to set up, and you want to be sure you can live, for a while at least, with the deal you make.

I can't vouch for every website I reference. Use them at your own risk. Everything changes so fast, that something good one day could be bad the next. However, I will tell you if I've used a service and how it worked out for me.

Also, if you are relatively new to Internet stuff, sometimes you will see a web address listed at the end of a sentence and it will have a period just after it. If you type the address into a web browser, make sure you don't include the period at the end or you'll never find the web page you're looking for.

Please e-mail me with your comments and concerns regarding web marketing and I'll try to post answers on the updates page.

One Last Important Tip

This book has so much information you might tend to skim over some of the points, checklists, and ideas. That's okay for a quick first read of the book. But don't forget to go back and pay attention to the details!

Here's a $500,000 example: In Chapter 1 I talk about Electronic Ways to Get People to Return to Your Website. One of the ways mentioned briefly is to compile "What's New in Your Industry" information so people come back to your website to find out what's going on. This saves them time, so it should work pretty well in getting them to return to your site.

A guy I heard about in California took this one simple idea, expanded it and now makes a substantial amount of money. He spends about three months of the year researching the changes in California tax law. He compiles all the changes into a big binder and sells it for a large amount of money to California CPAs. He then puts on high fee seminars for CPAs who want live explanations of the laws. In the report I read he makes about $500,000 in roughly six months time and takes the rest of the year off!

Think past the surface ideas you find in this book and relate them to what you do or what you would like to do. It's very likely you could hit on a big winner.

How to Create a Small Business Website That Kicks

Websites

This is the "dummies consultation" on how to create a small business website that kicks. The one thing you have to know is that the web is rapidly changing. If I had written this last week, I might have learned something this week that makes it a little bit different. Many of the things I am going to tell you are broad-stroke principles that don't really change that rapidly. When you put some effort into what you read, you can expect to get some returns on it for quite a while, so you don't have to worry about it changing every two seconds.

As soon as I make such a statement, something major will change, or I'll learn something new that will help you, so I'm setting up an update web just for you that will have all kinds of new tips and tricks. Visit http://www .UltimateGuideToEMarketing.com and register to get all the new tips and tricks as soon as they come about.

Benefits of a Kickin' Website

The benefits I have received by putting effort into my website, electronic magazine (e-zine), and electronic marketing are many. Let's look at some of them.

Benefit 1: More Money

You will have more money by learning the information in this book and doing some of the work yourself. The time I spent learning how to do my website updates is the best single investment I have made in my business to date.

Previously I was going to networking meetings and paying $35 to shake hands with a bunch of people who had no clue as to what I did, and frankly couldn't care less. Now I reach people around the world who want to know me, and for a lot less money and time.

Benefit 2: Increased Product Sales

Going online and doing it correctly generates many product sales. If you've read some of my past e-zines (http://www.antion.com/ezinebackissues.htm), you may remember that the combination of my electronic magazine and website brought in about $25,000 in a couple days while I was just sitting here.

Benefit 3: Goodbye, Expensive Information Kits

I cannot remember the last information kit I sent out since I designed a killer website. Many people have hired me directly after looking at the website and seeing the credibility I have established on the site.

Benefit 4: Sayonara, Printing Costs

I do a lot less printing since I have the website. When someone wants to have something sent to them, I tell them I'm simply going to send them the same thing that is on my website and almost all of them take the website option. They get the information quickly, make their decision, and hire or don't hire me. I don't spend a nickel on them.

That's at least four major benefits from having your own website. Let's consider what you can do to develop your own kickin' site. The first thing you need to consider is a name for your site; this is extremely important to your success.

Developing Your Site

There are many different levels of Internet knowledge among the people reading this book, so I'm going to start out on a basic level. Advanced Internet and web development people can skip to Search Engine Strategies on page 13.

For those of you who are new to this subject, I suggest spending a little time every day at http://www.newbieclub.com. Since I'm self-taught when it comes to computers, I missed a lot of the basics that can be found at the Newbie Club.

> **TIP:** Don't buy anything there until you finish reading this book or e-mail me for an opinion. I may have better options for you.

Should You Have Your Own Domain Name?

This is a question I get all the time. A domain name is antion.com. You don't want to get something like Geocities/ImTooCheapToGetMyOwnDomain-Name/joeblow.htm even though it's free. All your promotional efforts will be wasted if Geocities makes some small change. People won't be able to find your site anymore. If you have your own domain name, you can move and be hosted anywhere, and people will still be able to find you through all your promotional efforts. In addition, having your own domain name gives you greater credibility.

For now, check out domain names using the free tool available at http://www.KickStartDomains.com. You can purchase domain names there, too.

> **TIP:** Here's an up-to-date reference on buying and selling domain names: http://hop.clickbank.net/?powertips/open4sale.

Want to find out who owns a site so you can make an offer to buy it? Go to http://www.whois.sc and http://www.whois.org. These sites also show the deleted and expired domain names that are available.

Subdomains

Having keywords in your domain name can be very helpful in getting you high rankings in search engines. What if you can't find a regular domain name with the keywords in it that are beneficial to your business? Get a variation of the domain name and then add subdomains as needed. For instance. I couldn't get publicspeaking.com so I got http://www.Public-Speaking.org, which has great keywords for my business in the domain name. If I wanted to I could now add humor.public-speaking.org and storytelling.public-speaking.org and so on.

Your web host will advise you on making subdomains on your site. (Some don't have them available so check first.)

> **TIP:** Here's a great article on using subdomains: http://www.webmar-ketingplus.co.uk/seo_positioning/tutorials/subdomains.html.

What Name Should I Use?

It's better not to use your own name. If I had to do it over again, I would not use my name as my main site. I would still have http://www.antion.com but I wouldn't have developed it as deeply as I did. In fact, I just bought three other domains that include important keywords in the name:

http://www.dynamicspeaking.com

http://www.greatspeaking.com

http://www.speak4money.com

The highest ranked one I've got is http://www.Public-Speaking.org. (Notice: It's got a major keyword phrase in the domain name.)

If anybody knows my name, they will easily be able to find me on the Internet. I want the people who never heard of me to be able to type in something in the search engines and find me.

How Much Should It Cost?

When registering your domain name, you can easily find websites that charge $15 per year or less. One place is called http://www.KickStartDomains.com where $15 is the actual fee for the domain name. A lot of people that have contacted me are paying $200 or more because they don't know how to fill out the form. If you pay anything above $15, you're paying the company to fill out the form for you and submit it.

> **TIP:** You can easily check if a domain name is available. Visit http://www.KickStartDomains.com and type in the domain name. If the name you want isn't available, you can see who owns it by visiting the "who is" link and then making the owner an offer. I bought http://www.dynamicspeaking.com for only $119. So, don't feel that all is lost just because the domain name you want is not available. Make an offer and see what happens.

> **TIP:** Make sure your name or your company name is listed as the administrative contact for your website. Some people will do everything for you including listing "themselves" as the administrative contact. This gives THEM total control of your website. You'll be stuck dealing with them every step of the way, and if you want to move to a different host, they may make it very difficult or even impossible for you to do so. In effect, they own your website. And it will be even worse if they go out of business and disappear.

I get asked all the time, "Once you have the domain does that name automatically go up on the web?"

The answer is no. You can find places that "park it." This means if you just get the name and you're not ready to use it, you can store it somewhere for almost nothing. When you're ready to use it, you have to pick a Web Hosting Service. There are thousands of those around. However, you can park it for almost nothing if you buy it now. Later, it may not be available.

Here's a general rule about domain name selection: If someone has to remember it or if you are saying it on the radio or printing it somewhere, you want the shortest most memorable dot-com you can get. If people only have to click on it because you do a good job of search engine positioning or you are driving traffic to the site with pay-per-click search engines, then any domain name is okay. Having dashes in your domain name is okay and is actually better for search engines like http://www.Public-Speaking.org.

What Is an ISP?

ISPs are the companies that give you an e-mail address and access to the Internet. That's about it. This does not necessarily mean they host websites. That is called a *web hosting service.* In some cases, they do both functions, but not always. There are thousands of ISPs you can read about at the links listed next. You might want to ask a few questions before you pick an ISP.

Some ISPs may give you website space, but you must be sure you can use your own domain name. Look for ISPs at:

http://www.isp.com?antion
http://thelist.Internet.com

Monitor your Internet connection speed:

http://hop.clickbank.net/?powertips/absolutefy

What about AOL?

AOL is its own online network. You have to pay to use it, although you can send e-mail "to" AOL members at no charge. AOL has all kinds of features and web pages that are only available to AOL subscribers.

I would not recommend using AOL to do serious Internet business. It is simply not set up for it. Trying to send large amounts of e-mail through AOL will more than likely get you kicked off of their service.

Another important thing about AOL is that if something goes wrong at AOL, which is not unheard of, all the members are cut off from the Internet. If you are depending on your Internet operations to bring you business, you certainly don't want that to happen to you. AOL is simply not designed for the commercial applications we're talking about in this book.

What Is a Web Hosting Service?

This is a place that has one or many computers that store your website and make it available to the Internet. Your website is housed on a *web server* that is basically a specialized computer.

Web hosting services typically have many more services than a simple ISP. You can get e-mail through them, some provide you with shopping carts (that are usually pieces of junk), web authoring software (again very low level software), statistics, automatic backups, and tons of other things that are website related.

The problem with web hosting services is that in many cases they go through a continual porpoise cycle, that is, they provide really good service so all their customers who brag about them, and they get a good rating in an Internet magazine. Then they get a rush of new websites to host and everything slows down because they don't have enough computer space and tech support to handle the surge in business. As a result, your website slows down, and you can never get anyone on the tech support phone. Six months later, they start to improve and add new equipment and hire more people and everything is fine again until the next rush.

Avoid freebie hosting and hosting offered by your ISP (they do too many things and have too much demand on their bandwidth to do a super great job at web hosting). Get good solid hosting because you will be crying big tears if your site loads as slow as molasses or never loads at all.

Picking a Web Host

Here is a checklist of points to consider when selecting your web host (you may not understand some of these terms yet, but you will by the time you finish reading this book):

- ✓ If you are using Microsoft Front Page to create your website, do they have Front Page Extensions installed to make all the different parts of Front Page work?
- ✓ Do they give you autoresponders?

TIP: You'll learn all about what these are later.

- ✓ Can they handle multimedia and CGI scripts? Do you have full access to the cgi-bin? You may want to have things like Real Audio and Real Video. Or you might want to put some custom functionality in it, like a "recommend me form," or something like that. If they can't handle it, you can't have it on your website.
- ✓ How about backups? Do they have a reliable system? How often do they back up? How long will it take to restore your site from backup if something goes wrong?

TIP: This doesn't relieve you of the necessity of doing your own backups.

✓ What statistics packages do they make available to you? Do they just have a bare bones package, or maybe none at all? Do they make really advanced packages available? Do they have "real-time" statistics? Is there a monthly cost for the advanced packages? Do you have access to the "raw server logs"?

✓ What kind of connection do they have to the Internet? Do they have superfast T-1 or T-3 lines or something slower?

✓ Are there limits on file transfers? Will you have to pay more soon after you sign up and your site starts getting busier?

✓ Do they have secure server capability for your e-commerce efforts?

✓ How much space do you get? How much does extra space cost as your website grows? My site has grown to nearly 300 megabytes in 2.5 years.

✓ Do they provide web-based administration. This allows you to operate your server from a web page with no technical experience.

✓ Do they have complete e-mail services like Pop 3 mailboxes and the newer IMAP? Do they give you unlimited e-mail aliases?

✓ Do they require a long-term contract. Avoid them if they do. What will you do if their service is poor?

✓ What is their uptime? A good web host should be up and running 99.9 to 100 percent of the time.

✓ Is their tech support any good? They should have support by phone and e-mail 24/7. You might want to test them out on this before you sign up.

✓ Watch out for ripoffs. You should never pay extra for autoresponders, e-mail aliases, CGI bins, statistics, and POP mailboxes.

You can find a directory of web hosts at http://www.webhostdir.com.

Changing Web Hosts

This is usually a massive pain in the neck if you have a complex website, and only a very large pain in the neck if you have a plain website.

Why would you want to move? Well maybe the web host has old and slow server computers, or maybe they have a slow connection to the Internet. Maybe they can't handle Front Page websites, CGI scripts, and streaming video. Maybe they are just jerks and never return your calls or e-mails. Whatever the reason, think long and hard before you make the move and plan for disaster. Here are some tips to help you reduce the size of the pain that you are definitely going to suffer:

✓ Don't quit your old web host until the new site is up and running perfectly.

✓ Before you do anything, make sure your new hosting service can do what you want it to do. If moving a complex site is a massive pain in the neck, then doing it twice would be considered massive, colossal, and you're-a-big-dummy-for-not-checking-the-new-place-out-first pain in the neck.

✓ You must make sure you have a copy of every single file that will be transferred to the new web host both on your hard drive and backed up to a floppy, zip drive, or CD. This list of files could include graphics, text files, web pages, and whatever else you have cooked up that is included in your website.

✓ You must stay organized. Match all of the directories and folders on your hard drive to the ones you have on your website. Example: If you have a folder for "images" on your website, then make a folder of the same on your hard drive and keep all your images in that folder.

✓ Once you have your entire website organized on your hard drive and backed up, then upload the files to the new host.

✓ If you have forms, CGI scripts, secure servers, shopping carts, and similar advanced functionality, someone (probably not you, unless you are a techie) must make the appropriate coding changes to get everything working again.

✓ Test everything thoroughly over a couple of days and have some of your friends test things, too. Make sure everything is working perfectly before you actually make the switch.

✓ After you're thoroughly satisfied that everything is working properly, go ahead and authorize the new web host to make the changes needed for the Internet world to find you at your new home. This step could take a few days and you may have some down time on your site while the change is occurring. Be prepared for the fact that you will probably not get much cooperation from the host you're leaving. Get the new host to advise you on the steps you need to take. For security purposes, you might have to jump through a few hoops to get the change made.

Dedicated Servers

Dedicated servers are designed to give you more control of what happens with your web hosting. You have a complete computer "dedicated" to doing your bidding. Now this doesn't mean you buy a computer and put it in your basement. In fact, you will probably need a technical person to help you operate your dedicated server, which will be located in a hosting service somewhere.

When your hosting fees for individual websites exceed the cost of a dedicated server, you might want to start thinking about getting one.

What You Need to Know

 You have to have a name for your website. You have to have some way to access the Internet when you are at home and also when traveling, and you have to have a really reliable place to store your website so the world can see it. Getting a dedicated server gives you cheaper web hosting when you have many websites.

How Do I Make a Website?

There are lots of ways. I'm only going to concentrate on one method that I know works. I used to try to get people to do their entire website from scratch because they could save the most money. After seeing the results of this advice, I have totally changed my mind. Almost all of those sites look homemade, which doesn't represent you well professionally. Here's the method I now use. The people who follow these six steps usually have fewer headaches and actually stay motivated because things get done quickly:

1. Search the web and find pages you like and generally try to get the feel of what is already out there in your industry. Bookmark and save these pages in your favorite places so you can get back to them easily.
2. Get a plain paper tablet and start a diagram. What will be on the home page? What buttons (navigation system) will it have to lead people around the site? What content will it have?
3. Start collecting keywords you think will be appropriate for your site. These are words that someone might type into a search engine or directory when they are trying to find the service you offer. You'll learn very specific techniques for finding keywords later.
4. Get a professional to design the basic look of your site and handle all the technical details of getting the site up and running on the Internet. This will save you an enormous amount of frustration. I recommend, without reservation, Saeler Enterprises in Tucson, Arizona: http://www.saeler.com. Jason is very familiar with the way I do things and makes a special effort to please the clients I send. Another recommendation is http://www.HaroldHingle.com.

    Your website should be created to allow you to update it yourself if desired. I highly recommend this. Your ability to add page after page after page of content to your site will have a direct correlation to your ability to use many of the techniques taught in this book.

TIP: For this to work smoothly, your site should be created in the program you plan on using to update it. Don't worry if you already have a website that needs to be redone. The major web authoring programs can import it and convert it, if necessary.

5. Purchase and install a web authoring program on your computer (see discussion that follows).
6. Learn the basics of the web authoring program. You can do this while your site is under development. I strongly suggest having some telephone coaching, or better yet, some tutoring at your office, both to help with the basic install and to teach you the simple things you need to know for updating your site.

After you have the basic site up and running, you need to know how to do four simple things to start. How to:

1. Add a new page with all the navigation buttons from the last page.
2. Add text.
3. Make a hyperlink.
4. Add a graphic.

These four things are done over and over again and can really make your site grow into a force to be reckoned with on the web.

TIP: You can learn this in about an hour working with a coach directly or within a couple hours on the phone.

As you get more comfortable working on your website, you will start to learn a little bit more about how to use tables to keep things firmly in place. You'll learn a little bit about HTML (the behind the scenes coding language of the web) to help you make little improvements here and there to your website.

TIP: When you are ready, see Chapter 7 for some basic HTML tutorials.

During this step, you'll also be getting used to the idea that making a web page is not like printing something on your printer. When you create a document to print on your laser or inkjet printer, you pretty much know exactly what it is going to look like. Items you've put on the page are exactly where you saw them on the screen. Web pages are different. They can look completely different depending on the web browser used, such as Internet Explorer, Netscape, and AOL. As you create pages for your site, you want to check how they look in those different systems. You might even ask friends with older or newer versions of the different browsers to tell you how it looks to them. You may be very surprised at what they see.

Here's an Internet tool that will help you if you don't feeling like running all over town to see what your site looks like: http://www.anybrowser.com.

Here's a quick tip on picking fonts for your website. In most cases, you want to use standard typefaces like Helvetica and Times Roman that are installed on virtually everyone's computer. That way you can be sure your text looks about the same everywhere it's seen.

I highly recommend that you purchase the book *The Non-Designers Web Book* by Robin Williams (Berkeley, CA: Peachpit Press, 2000). You'll learn many details to turn your site from an amateur hack job into a polished, professional-looking, and functioning site.

And don't try to get too fancy. It will hurt your sales! You'll find out why later.

Website Authoring Programs

Get a highly supported professional program. That way you'll always be able to find someone who knows how to use it when you get in a jam.

Website authoring programs are designed so you don't have to write all the HTML code from scratch. In fact, you don't have to write any at all if you don't want to, although learning a little as you go along is a good idea. Here are three options:

1. Microsoft Front Page (http://www.microsoft.com/frontpage): This is the program I use. You can pick up this product as a stand alone program for about $150, or it may actually be already included if you use some versions of Microsoft Office.
2. Macromedia Dreamweaver (http://www.macromedia.com/software/dreamweaver): Dreamweaver is a much more complicated program that excels in really advanced web creation techniques that are counterproductive for the purposes of this book. (keep it simple!) It's harder to learn and it's quite a bit more expensive, too.
3. Adobe GoLive (http://www.adobe.com/products/golive/main.html): This program is available for both the Mac and PC.

For help with any of these programs, simply type in the name of the program and the word "tutorial" in any major search engine (for example: "Front Page Tutorial").

WHAT YOU NEED TO KNOW

 You probably need a web designer to start off your site with the least amount of hassle. You need to pick a web authoring program, so you can make updates yourself. The program you pick should be well supported around the world and match the one your web designer is using. My suggestion is Microsoft Front Page.

What Is a Search Engine?

We are now going to cover some details on page design and search engine marketing. First, I'm going to tell you about some of the programs I currently use to manage search engine marketing. Since these are always subject to change, be sure to check the updates on my site regularly. I'll also give you a list of reference materials and books I use to increase the number of visits to my site.

Dealing with search engines is the biggest pain in the neck you will face when designing your website. Why is it a pain? Because you need to integrate strategies in the design of your site so that search engines can find your pages. It shouldn't be an afterthought. You can put a lot of work into making your website beautiful, but it's all for naught if no one sees it.

A search engine has electronic robots or spiders that go and look for information on the web, including your site. Some of the strategies to get those robots and spiders to do what you want. Some of it may be on the edge or slightly controversial. We're going to avoid spamming the search engines at all costs. There are two kinds of spamming and they're both bad. Most people have heard of spam e-mail. That's where you send bulk e-mail to someone who has not agreed to receive it. Spamming a search engine is a little different, but the consequences can be just as severe. See the following section for techniques that are not permissible with search engines.

Spamming a Search Engine

- Don't make your text the same color as the background of the site in an effort to hide extra keywords. Just making it the same color can get you banned, even if you aren't stuffing in extra keywords. They'll even nab you if you use a text that is just slightly different in color from the background.
- Don't use a keyword or keyword phrase over and over again in your keyword META tags, anywhere on your page, or in any HTML areas.
- Don't stuff a bunch of keywords way down at the bottom of your page where you think no one will click on it. The search engine spider police will get you.
- Don't create a highly optimized page to get a high ranking and then switch the page on your server to another one.
- Don't use automatic redirects. If you have a legitimate reason, use javascript and make the redirect time as long as possible (none of this is recommended if you want to get high rankings).
- Don't submit the same page over and over again or try to trick the engines by simply renaming the same page.
- Don't submit nonsensical sentences that are stuffed with keywords.

- Don't submit more pages per day than a particular search engine allows.
- Don't put too many keywords on any one page (you'll learn about this later).
- Don't put a tremendous number of transparent GIF files on the page with the same alt text. When using transparent GIFS, don't put the height and width tags.
- Don't put multiple title tags in your HTML code. This used to work, but alas no more!

Search Engine Strategies

I'm going to give you the strategies I use, although I don't totally depend on them. I have managed to reach the number one and two positions on Alta Vista and Google by using a certain keyword. That means I am more likely to get an increased number of visits to my site. It's been a struggle to do this, but I made it and it is paying off. You do have to keep at it, though.

> **TIP:** In the last paragraph, I used the term *visits* instead of the term *hits*. I need to tell you that the term hits means absolutely nothing. An interesting definition of HITS is "How Idiots Track Success" ☺. A *hit* is a file downloaded from the Internet. So if you visit a page that has 10 graphics on it, your visit counts as 11 hits—one-page downloaded and 10 graphics. If the page has 20 graphics, your visit would count as 21 hits. So, you can see hit totals are meaningless. If you hear somebody bragging about the number of hits on their site, look a little further.
>
> The number of hits (files downloaded) can determine how much it costs to host your website. Be very careful about where you host your site. Ask them about their costs for going over your allotted amount of web hosting usage.

I define the terms *individual* or *unique* visitors as individuals that have come to my website. *Page views* is defined as the number of pages they actually visited.

One person visiting your site would be a *unique visitor*. That means that a person has come to your website. If they came back a day later (or some other time period that your statistic package is set for) that would be two unique visitors, although it's the same person. Although these numbers will be close to the actual number of people that visit and the number of pages they look at, it's not exact.

> **TIP:** For a really comprehensive discussion visit http://www.webtrends .com/support/hits_views_sessions.htm.

The other term *page views*, is when somebody actually downloaded a whole page, including the graphics. The web automatically downloads the page to their computers when they visit a site (you do the same when you visit a site). It does not mean they looked at it, but it means they "pulled it up."

What You Need to Know

 Don't let anyone talk you into trying to cheat the search engines. It could get your website banned. Don't be impressed when someone tells you how many hits they got.

Keywords: The Critical Component

There are two critical methods used by search engines to find pages. The first is by *keywords,* and the second is *metawords* or *META tags.*

An extremely critical part of this whole mix is the keywords and keyword phrases you select that match the services and products you offer. A keyword is the term someone uses when they look for information. What they type would be the *keywords* that the search engine uses to look for the information.

If you kill yourself designing your site based around certain keywords that you think are great, but the searcher uses other keywords, then they'll simply find your competition who did a better job of picking out keywords.

Each page of your site may have different keywords associated with its content, or you could have a site that has every single page optimized to the same keyword. The important thing is that it must be the *right* keyword or your site will never be found.

For example, let's say someone goes to the search engine Google and types in the keyword phrase "presentation skills." Google has cataloged millions and millions of pages, so they can find the pages on the Internet that are most relevant to that particular keyword phrase. Their goal is to return the proper list to the person who is looking for information on "presentation skills."

What Makes a Good Keyword?

General keywords are not very useful. Here's why. Let's say you are a professional speaker and use "speaker" for your keyword. Go ahead and try typing it into a search engine and see what you get. For the most part, you get information on stereo speakers. Yes, some public speaker related stuff comes up, but using a general keyword like that gives you incredible competition fighting for the top 10 results. And that competition isn't even from other public speakers. It's mainly from stereo speaker companies. Yes, you should use the word, but it should not be number one on your list. There are much smarter words to use.

Let's say you sell office furniture and you're based in Los Angeles. Some keyword phrases for you to use would be "home office furniture," "used office furniture," or "discount office furniture."

You could add the city name to any of these keyword phrases to make them more specific. There will be less people typing this in, but they will be highly targeted people who are more likely to be interested in your site. The only exception to this is if you use a keyword phrase so specific that no one is using it.

Okay, okay, I hear you saying, "But Tom, we sell office furniture all around the country or the world. Using this technique would eliminate me from all business other than in Los Angeles." No, it won't! Here are some more keyword phrases that might make you start getting the idea: "office furniture San Francisco," "office furniture Seattle," "office furniture Las Vegas," "office furniture New York."

"WAIT A MINUTE TOM. I'M NOT BASED IN ALL THESE AREAS!"

Tom's answer: "So what?" When someone finds one of these pages in a search engine, the top of the page could read, "Special Discount to Buyers in the Las Vegas Area" or something like that. You make a special deal for these people. The Las Vegas people won't know or care that you make the same deal for someone in Miami or San Antonio. Remember: We're playing the search engine game here. Someone searching for office furniture in San Francisco is never going to see the page that says office furniture Detroit. You'll at least get a shot at the business even if they aren't in your home city.

Regional Keywords

People in different parts of the world use different terminology for the same product. Where I come from, they use the term, "pop." In other areas of the country they might use the term "soda." You can seek out and use these alternative keywords by checking with friends or colleagues from different parts of the country. You can do the same for other countries as well.

Where to Place Keywords

I'm going to give you lots of places where keywords can be put on your page. That doesn't mean that every page you create will have keywords in all of these places. You can put too many keywords on the page and do yourself more damage than not having enough.

One of the main places that a search engine looks for the keywords is in the "Title Bar" of your web page (Figure 1.1). The title bar is usually a blue bar across the top of each one of your web pages. It is also the link that someone clicks on when they receive the results of a search, and it is also the text used when someone "bookmarks" your site or puts it in their favorite places.

Figure 1.1   Title Bar

Many people put their name in the title bar or use "home page." All of this is meaningless. What you want to do is put keywords in the title bar.

> **TIP:** Go though your website and make sure each page has keywords in the title bar. Using keywords in the title bar tells someone what's on that page. If you look at my home page, for example, http://www .antion.com, it does not say, "Hey this is the big shot professional speaker Tom Antion." My keywords in the title bar say "presentation skills," "speeches," or "public speaking." Use something relevant to the search engines and your topics. The title bar is weighted very heavily when the search engine is looking for the page.

The next place you want to put keywords is near the top of the page, within the first visible screen if you can. Why? First, you don't want people to scroll too much on your main pages. You want it to pop up and give them the information. Second, search engine spiders read your page from the top down. Therefore, you need to put these keywords above any graphics that you have, especially because the spiders have a tough time with graphics. If you go to my home page, http://www.antion.com, you'll see that I specifically write text at the top of the page so I can stuff keywords in there (Figure 1.2).

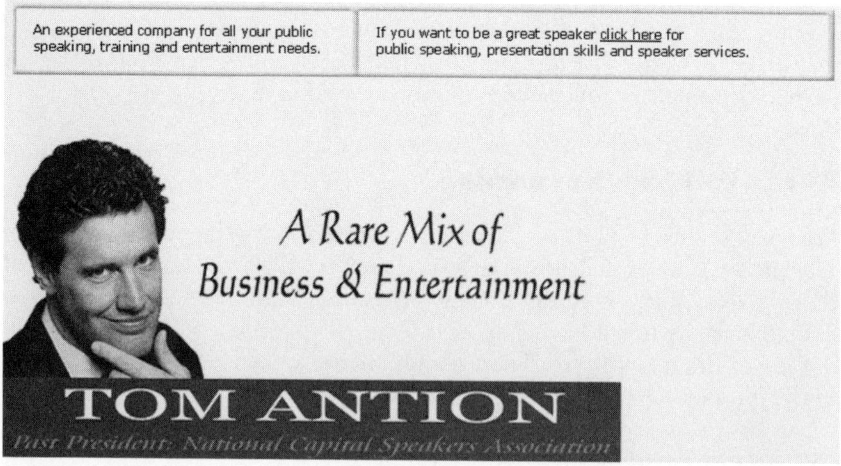

Figure 1.2   Keywords in Text at the Top of the Page

When I say "stuff," I'm not saying spamming or cheating. I made up two little sentences and put them near the top of the page to direct people to different parts of the site, but I used keywords in them.

Don't forget to put your keywords in the text of your page, especially near the top and toward the front of paragraphs. This can increase your *keyword prominence,* which is yet another factor many search engines look at before they give you a high ranking.

You can put some keywords near the bottom of your page, too, so the search engine sees a theme to the page.

Keywords in Graphics

Another place you could put keywords, which many people and web designers don't know about, is in the alternative description of graphics. This is also called the *alt description* for short. Sometimes you see little descriptions come up when you run your mouse over a graphic. It might say "JPEG 2000 bytes." You can take every graphic on your page and, instead of it having a worthless JPEG label, you can use keywords. If you do this, don't put your keyword a hundred times in a row. That is spamming and you will be kicked out of many search engines when they catch you. You can hide keywords in the alternative description of your graphics, for example:

```
<td width="50% ><img src="tompho.gif"

alt="Presentation skills, speeches, professional
speaking, humor, exciting speeches for large
meetings." Width="398" height="206"></td>
```

TIP: If you work with the government, the alt description of graphics must fall within its guidelines of usability for sight-impaired persons. A sight-impaired person has software that will read these alt descriptions to tell them what the picture or graphic is, since they can't see it. It's not a bad idea to combine keywords with accurate descriptions so that any sight-impaired person can use your site.

Search engines are getting so sophisticated now that you want to take advantage of any little boost you can get to beat the system. You can also name your graphics with keywords. Instead of making the file name of a photo "joe.gif," you would name it "presentation-skills.gif." Anything you can do to boost yourself without spamming is a good idea.

Keywords in Link Text

Anchor text is the actual clickable part of a link. Putting keywords here gives you a boost in the search engines. The closer you put the keyword to the front of the link the better. For instance—Public Speaking Tips is the link or anchor text even though the link actually takes people to antion.com.

Keywords in Heading Tags

Heading tags show the search engine that particular words are to be emphasized on a page. They run from <H1> to <H4>, <H1> being the most prominent. You can use multiple heading tags, but I wouldn't use more than one of each. You can use the <H1> tag toward the top of the page and then maybe use <H2>, <H3>, and <H4> on the subheading as you go down the page.

For instance your <H1> tag might look like this at the top of a page.

Public Speaking: How to Use Humor in Your Speech

Your <H2> tag would be on one of the subheadings and would appear smaller:

Public speaking is great for your career.

Your <H3> might look like this:

Public speaking doesn't have to be hard.

And your <H4> tag would appear the smallest:

Public speaking sometimes makes you nervous.

Summary of Keyword Placement

Keywords can be put in:

- Title tag
- META description tag
- Keyword META tag
- Heading tags
- Alt description text
- Naming of graphics
- Link text
- Body text

Finding Keywords

How do you find out what people are using for keywords when they find your site? This is where you get into the field of statistics. Statistics are another thing that your ISP might provide for you. You should ask your ISP, "Do you provide a statistic package? If you do, what does it tell me?" Statistics tell you what hours of the day people are coming to visit you, where they're coming from, and how long they stayed there.

The more sophisticated programs have the keywords that people typed in and the search engine they used. These are critical pieces of information. The most advanced programs tell you this and a lot more. Verify exactly what you get in the way of statistics before you sign up with a web host.

If your own service provider does not have the kind of tracking you need, there are other companies who will do the tracking for you. Here are some paid and free places to get statistics. I use the first one, but you can check out some of these other places:

http://www.clicktracks.com/entrypoint.php?a=46673

http://www.idstat.com/counter/index.html

http://www.statpak.com

http://www.extremetracking.com

http://www.webtrends.com

The keywords you find through your statistics package are great to have. The only drawback is that you are getting only those keywords people are typing in that actually find your site. What are the keywords people are typing in that don't find your site? If you find out what those keywords are, you can design pages in your site that are optimized for those new keywords.

One of the best tools for finding other keywords is a free tool at http://www.Overture.com (formerly goto.com) called the *Keyword Selection Tool* (see p. 33). It can be found by visiting Overture.com by clicking on "advertiser center," then clicking on "tools," then clicking on "keyword selector tool." Don't be surprised if this method doesn't find the tool. It is so popular that Overture moves it around frequently, so it doesn't get overrun with usage.

This tool gives you all kinds of variations for terms that people are actually using. If you can't find it anywhere, then Overture may have shut this down as a free service. The way to get around it is to sign up as an advertiser and put up a $50 deposit. Believe me, it's worth it to get to use this tool.

There is another site (http://www.Wordspot.com) that has both a paid and a free service. In the paid service, you can enter your keywords. They will search the Internet and find out where those keywords come up and how often they are used. With that information in hand, you design your site and specific pages in your site around specific keywords because more people type them in.

You can also take a free trial at http://www.wordtracker.com, another service that has tools to help you pick the best keywords for your product or service:

> Here's an e-book that will help you with WordTracker: http://hop .clickbank.net/?powertips/wtmagic
>
> Here's a tool to help you find keywords for niche markets: http://hop .clickbank.net/?powertips/renio
>
> Here's another great program to help you find keywords: http://www .xybercode.com/ezGaffurl.php?offer=powertips&pid=1

Using these tools can keep you from wasting effort and money. A client of mine wanted to build his site around the keyword "Value Added Selling." I found out for him that no one was typing that phrase when they were looking for "sales training." Knowing this saved him a great deal of time and money.

Want to see exactly what people are typing into the Internet right now in real time? Visit http://www.metaspy.com.

Google's pay-per-click program called "adwords" will also help you pick keywords. You have to sign up for their program before you can use their tool.

If you find a keyword that applies to you that doesn't get searched much, don't discard it. Always keep in mind two things: (1) the big target theory and (2) time management. Work on your most popular keywords first because obviously they will bring in the most traffic the fastest. After you have worked on the most popular words, start making pages based on the words that are not as popular. People are still typing them in all around the world, and they add up to increased, targeted traffic.

An opposite theory is to work on the less popular keywords first because it's easier to get high rankings on them since the professional optimizers your competition is using most likely will try to work on the more popular key-words. This gives you a better chance to get good results quickly even though it won't mean massive amounts of traffic.

> **TIP:** When you get a list of terms from the keyword selector tool, high-light the entire list including all the numbers next to the terms and copy it. Paste the list into your word processor so you can work on the list and eliminate any terms that don't really apply to your business. For instance, if you put the term *training* into the keyword selector tool, you'll come up with a list that includes "potty training" and "dog training."

It is very difficult for you to be totally objective when it comes to your own site. It's hard for you to know what people sitting at their computers in the middle of the day, or the middle of the night, will type in to find your service. Remember—don't put your name as a main keyword unless you are a celebrity!

Counting Keywords

You can use the "page critic" function of Web Position Gold to help you with this, but I have found another tool for quick and dirty analysis. It's called the *Keyword Density Analyzer* (http://www.grsoftware.net/search_engines /software/grkda.html). It checks the keyword density (ratio of keywords to total number of words on the page) instantly and saves me lots of time.

Ethically Spy on Your Competition's Keywords

Here's a great idea. Why not let your competition do lots of work for you and you reap the benefits? You can find out what keywords your competitors are using by opening their websites in Internet Explorer browser. After the site you are spying on is open, click on "view," then click "source."

A window will open, and it will show you all the behind-the-scenes HTML coding of the site. This most likely will include the keywords that site is using to try to grab traffic.

Some very sophisticated webmasters can hide this information from you or even feed you false information, but that is very rare. For the most part, you will see what words they are using.

Just because you find these words don't assume the webmaster for the site you are looking at knew what he or she was doing with them. Your job is to look for words that you may have overlooked and take them to the Overture keyword selector tool to see the popularity of the keywords you find.

Here's another great spy tool to find out what your competition is up to: http://hop.clickbank.net/?powertips/seospider.

Ethically Spy on Your Competition's Traffic

While you're busy spying on your competition you may as well spy on their traffic. Although there are lots of factors at play, you might be better served by emulating sites that have lots of traffic.

One way to check on traffic is to use the free Alexa toolbar (http://www .Alexa.com). You can download and install this toolbar in seconds. It will tell you how much traffic a site is getting and also its rank among all the other sites it looks at on the Internet. You can compare your traffic to another site, and you can even look at an archive of how websites looked in the past.

Don't forget to take your competitors' e-mail addresses out of your database so they don't see what promotions you're sending out.

Avoid Frames on Your Pages

The frame is the fixed part of your web page while the rest is variable. Why shouldn't you have frames? Search engines have a tough time with them. They're supposed to be getting better, but you're safer not having them on your site because the last thing you want to do is make it tough on a search engine.

Don't let your designer talk you into having frames. They are only interested in the look of the site. None of the top marketers in the world who are actually making money and getting top search engine rankings use frames.

Usability of the Website

One of the biggest mistakes beginners make is haphazardly throwing their site together without evaluating how a typical user would navigate through the site. You must pay attention to this, or you will frustrate your visitors, and they will promptly leave.

Although I don't think our government knows too much about selling things on the Internet, they have an entire website that is devoted to usability of websites: http://www.usability.gov.

Also check Jakob Nielsen's site out. He's really into usability and has some really great articles: http://www.useit.com.

Accessibility of Website to People with Disabilities

One consideration you should not ignore is the accessibility of your website to persons with disabilities. The following link will give you some food for thought: http://www.access.pdx.edu/workshops/myths.html.

What You Need to Know

 You need to put a great deal of effort into locating keywords that apply to your products and services. These keywords need to be worked into the design of the site. Most designers don't know about this. You must demand that they either learn, or you should find someone who does have this kind of knowledge. If you don't, it is unlikely your site will be found by someone searching for your product or service. You can ethically spy on your competition's keywords. You also can't let fancy designers talk you into design elements that will hurt your chance of being found.

Multiple Domains

While we're on the topic of keywords and domains, getting more than one domain (website) is another strategy. It gives search engines a bigger territory in which to find you. I personally bought:

http://www.dynamicspeaking.com

http://www.greatspeaking.com

http://www.speak4money.com

http://www.public-speaking.org

http://www.public-speaking.net

http://www.wedding-toasts.org

http://www.wedding-speeches.org

http://www.InstantEulogy.com

As you can see, each domain name has a keyword or keyword phrase in it. The domain name is not the heaviest weighted area that a search engine looks for, but every little bit helps.

Another benefit of this is that I can use many of the same side door (see next section) pages over again (with minor changes to the pages because exact duplicate pages are frowned on) on those sites, but since they have a different domain name, they're considered different pages. Let's say I have 200 pages on my website. With three domain names, I have 600 pages (200 × 3) all attracting traffic and sending them back to my main site.

A third benefit of having a domain name with keywords in it is that it helps you out in the very important directory listings. You don't want to give directory editors any excuse to put you in the wrong category.

My multiple domain strategy at this point is to have many of the other domains feeding traffic to one sales site: antion.com. You could have all the sites selling their own products if you wanted.

Also, multiple domains in your control are great for manipulating inbound and outbound links that contribute to your link popularity as we'll see further ahead when we get into link trade strategy and megalinking.

Some people think that another domain means an *alias* of the same site. This is incorrect terminology. An alias is part of an e-mail address. For instance, I could have orders@antion.com or customerservice@antion.com. "Orders" and "customer service" are the aliases.

TIP: I used to let anything at antion.com come through, but spam is so bad now I only let very specific aliases come to my inbox.

Another point of confusion is that some people think that having another domain name that forwards visitors to the same place is a side door.

This is called *pointing* and is not what we are talking about here. You must have a separate domain actually hosted somewhere for this particular side door technique to work. If the search engine sees that the domain is just "pointing" to another domain, it will not index a complete new set of side door pages.

Modern Day Side Doors

A *side door* (splash page, gateway, doorway) page is tuned to a specific search engine in an effort to get you a high ranking in searches.

My friend Steve Epner explains this best: Many magazine publishers put out the same magazine but use different covers to please different markets or to test which cover gets the most newsstand sales. *TV Guide* is aggressively doing this (not to mention selling more *TV Guides* to collectors, but that's a different story).

I look at side doors as different covers on your website designed to please a particular search engine. Each page is designed to have just the right number of words in the right places to get a high ranking in a particular search engine.

The reason I call this section "modern day" side doors is that in the old days you could put up pages that made no sense in an effort to "fool" the search engines. Today, this will get you banned from the search engines. Modern day side doors must be readable by the public.

There are links on the page that direct the visitor to your home page or to other subpages of your site. You can have hundreds of these side doors for a single website, each one custom-tailored to suit different search engines. (Once you create these side doors, you can change them slightly and use them on other related websites. This multiplies the value of your work in creating the pages in the first place.)

How does this work? Let's say there are 100 words on your homepage and 5 of them are keywords. Therefore, you have a 5 to 100 ratio or 5 percent of the words on the page are keywords. This ratio is called the *keyword weight* or *keyword density*. Maybe the old Alta Vista search engine loves 5 to 100. Maybe another search engine doesn't like that; they want a 7 to 100 or 7 percent keyword density on a page.

You create individual pages that have the right keyword density and submit them to the search engines. (You'll see how to submit them later.) Basically, you have many different covers to your website. You could end up with hundreds of these pages as you continue to develop your website. By doing so, you give the search engines a bigger target to try to hit.

Also, it's important to have many different pages on the same topic with different keyword densities. When the search engines change what they like about a page to give it a top ranking, some of your pages will reduce in ranking and others will improve. Since I have so many of these pages out there, I don't have to sweat the search engines that much.

Side doors can be housed on your main website or on a different website under your control. They are just different content pages that, when found in a search, allow someone to click to your homepage or another page in your site.

TIP: In the old days, these side doors used to be created generically with a template. You just put in any old words and the right number of keywords and submitted them to the search engines. You would have put an *automatic redirect* script on the page so the person clicking on the link listed in the search results would never even see the side door page. They would be automatically "redirected" to your real website.

This will not work anymore for two reasons: (1) The search engines are looking for template pages and refusing to give them high rankings, and (2) the search engines are looking for any pages that have an automatic redirect script and refusing those pages high rankings because it knows that the page is a "fake" designed to beat the system.

Side door pages now must appear to be a normal page in your site. I think it's dangerous to use an automatic side door generator like you would find in older versions of a program called Web Position Gold (although this is still a great program to own for other web promotion tasks as you will see later). Search engines are pretty smart and have a tendency to ignore pages that appear to be automatically generated. And don't even think about using a redirect script. You can find Web Position Gold at http://www.webposition.com. Just don't use the page generator (unless you know what you're doing) or automatic submitter (you'll see why soon).

TIP: You can automatically generate pages if you really know what you're doing and have the appropriate software. Those of you sophisticated enough to do this already know what software to get.

Robots.txt

Sometimes you will not want certain engines to look at certain of your side door pages. You may also not want other pages that you have created for certain clients to show up in search engines. You can avoid this by placing a robots.txt file in the HTML code of your web page that tells certain robot spiders from the search engines to simply ignore your page. There is a good

article explaining this more advanced technique located at http://www
.1stsearchranking.com/robots.htm.

What You Need to Know

 Side doors are content-rich pages added to your website to give
you a better chance of being found. Besides having good information, they are constructed with just the right number of keywords
to please search engines. They should not be automatically generated unless you really know what you're doing because search engines may ignore them.

Creating Side Doors

I previously used the Web Position Gold program for creating side doors, but
now I simply make articles or mini articles and make sure they have the right
keyword density for the particular search engine.

> **TIP:** Making a really fine-tuned side door page is somewhat tedious and
> time consuming. What I do is go for volume instead of extreme fine
> tuning. I create a ton of pages with a keyword density of between 2
> and 8 percent. This is pretty much the range in which modern day
> search engines work (this doesn't mean you won't find keyword den-
> sities outside that range). The idea is that if there are less than 2
> percent of the words on the page that are keywords, then the page
> isn't really that relevant to what the searcher was looking for. If
> there are more than 8 percent then it looks like you are trying to
> spam the search engine. With enough pages out there, even when
> the search engines change what they like about top ranking pages, I
> can still have a certain percentage of my pages ranking high some-
> where. When one page drops out of favor with a search engine, an-
> other one at a different keyword density picks up. This really
> smooths out my search engine ups and downs.

Web Position Gold

The program Web Position Gold does more than one thing. It actually has
seven different functions. I don't recommend all of them, but I still highly
recommend the program.

First, the Reporter is a very handy tool you can use to tell where you show
up on all the major search engines for particular keywords. It is a very handy
thing to keep track of how you're doing. Because there is so much delay on
many of these search engines when you make a change today it might be a
couple weeks or more before something happens. It is hard for you to keep
track of it. Web Position Gold does that for you.

The Scheduler function allows you to set the program to run the above report automatically at regular intervals such as once or twice a week.

I do not recommend the Page Generator and Submitter functions. As explained previously, template side door pages have fallen out of favor with the search engines. I'm never in favor of automatic search engine submitters for the following reasons:

1. It is too easy and common for the search engine to refuse automatic submissions, and
2. If they do refuse the submission, you are virtually never notified that the submission was refused, so you sit around waiting to show up in the engines when your pages were never actually submitted.

TIP: Just when I say "never," a new submitter program comes out that submits very slowly. It's called Search Engine Commando.

The Web Position Traffic Analyzer can be helpful if you don't have a really sophisticated statistics program, and the Upload Manager helps you put side doors on your website (but you don't use it if you are using a program like Front Page).

The Page Critic is one of the most valuable parts of the Web Position Gold program. It will analyze the top sites that come up in a particular search and report back to you what you need to do to give your page the best chance of getting in the top 10.

I concentrate on the Reporter and the Page Critic functions of Web Position Gold. Those two parts of the program more than justify the cost of the entire program. Don't let it worry you that you aren't using some parts of the program. This is typical of many programs. They usually have many more functions than you'll ever need or want to use.

WHAT YOU NEED TO KNOW

 There are programs that help you automate the tracking how well you are doing. There are many programs and companies on the web that specialize in helping you get high rankings in search engines and directories. You don't have to do it all yourself, but you do need to understand what needs to be done.

Basic HTML Structure

Behind your web page is a hidden language called HTML, which is the language of the web. Until programs like Microsoft Front Page were developed to make it easy to create web pages, web designers had to do programming behind the scenes.

You need to know a little about the behind-the-scenes area of your website even if it is just to check up on your web designer. Web pages need to have the following basic structure:

```
<HTML>
<HEAD>
<TITLE></TITLE>
<META name="description" content="">
<META name="keywords" content="">
</HEAD>
```

Some search engines may totally ignore your page if it has unusual HTML tag sequences. Don't worry if this doesn't mean much to you now. Later, you'll learn how to check every page of your site by looking at the HTML code.

TIP: There are other types of web pages like asp and php. No doubt that there will be many more ways to make web pages in the future. All you need to worry about right now are plain old HTML pages and be wary if some techie tries to talk you into some higher level, newer, and cool way of making web pages. It just could be that the search engines will not index your pages.

Use META Tags

Before I talk about this, let me give you an analogy that might help you understand what HTML coding is. Have you ever been to the theatre? What you see on stage is the actors, the furniture, the scenery, and so on. Behind the curtain is all the rigging that makes the play work. What you see on stage is analogous to your web page. What you see behind the curtain is analogous to the HTML code. Your browser (most likely Internet Explorer or Netscape) interprets all the crazy looking HTML code from "backstage" and makes it look like a web page.

So, now that you know what HTML is, let's look backstage and see how META tags apply to your site. META tags are being used less and less, and you certainly shouldn't depend on them to get high rankings. However, you should know how to use them as long as search engines are still using them.

If you want to see some samples of META tags, open your browser (either Internet Explorer or Netscape) and click on "view." Then click on "source" in Internet Explorer, or "page source" in Netscape (Figure 1.3). A new window will pop up and you can look at all the behind-the-scenes HTML pro-

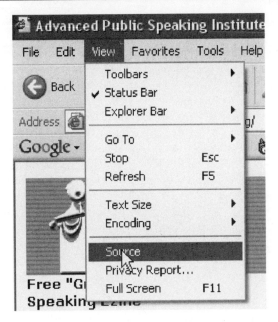

Figure 1.3   Click on Source for a Backstage View

gramming of just about any web page. You can also see the META tags of other web pages if they have them.

> **TIP:** The <TITLE> Tag should be the first thing after the <HEAD> area of the page and then comes the "description" META tag and then the "keyword" META tag.

SAMPLE META TAGS

```
<HEAD>
<TITLE>Customer service training</TITLE>
<META name="description" content="Customized customer service training at your
location by the person who 'wrote the book' on customer retention">
<META name="keywords" content="customer service speaker, training, trainer,
client retention">
```

Description META Tags

These META tags are a place where you can put a description of your web page and your keywords. On the search engines that use these META tags, when your site comes up in search results, it will have the description that you wrote, which is really nice because that means you can control what's being said about your site and entice people to click on your link.

You should do your best to write descriptions that are compelling. It would be a shame to come up as number one in a search but have no one click on your site because your description was so poor. Search the web to see descriptions of other sites. Try to evaluate the techniques they use to entice you to click on their link. Incorporate the same techniques when writing the descriptions to entice people to click on your link.

The concept of site popularity is another reason having compelling descriptions is becoming more and more important. Some search engines give a boost in the rankings to sites that are clicked on more often (i.e., the rich get richer). Let's say your site starts out as number five in a search. After a week, 100 people clicked on your site and 600 people clicked on the site that was number six in the original rankings. The number six site will now pass you up for a higher ranking because it was clicked on much more than your site. This sends a message to the search engine that the number six site was better than yours.

Don't try to beat the system by constantly clicking on your own site. The engines are too smart for that, and you'll get caught and banned.

If you don't have description META tags when the search engine spider comes to visit, it would crawl down your page from top to bottom. If it saw a graphic or some goofy stuff and could not interpret it, you get nothing. The person that's sitting there at his or her computer thinks to him- or herself, "Well, I'm not clicking on that site because I don't know what it's about."

That's one type of META tag (description) and they're very simple to create. In fact, there are sites out there on the Web that will create your META tags for nothing. Therefore, you can go out there and type META tag generator into a major search engine and follow their instructions. Then all you have to do is cut and paste what they give you into the HTML (behind the scenes view) of your web pages.

Free META Tag Generators

There are many places on the web that will generate META tags for free. This link is one of them: http://www.anybrowser.com/MetaTagGenerator .html. The new version of Microsoft Front Page makes the META tags easy for you.

Keyword META Tags

Then there are the keyword META tags. You should not put the same word in there over and over again because that is spamming and many of the search engines are catching on to this. If they do, they'll kick you out totally and could black ball you from the search engine. They are getting strict about this, so be careful!

In addition, some sneaky devils out there put Tony Robins in their META tags. I've even seen and heard of people putting the phrase, "endorsed by Tony Robins," which is fair if Tony Robins has actually endorsed you. If you are just using his name to get visitors, you can be sued over that, and there is plenty of case law on that issue. It is definitely cheating.

One good trick is to put common misspellings in the META keyword tag. Many people are tired, in a hurry, or just can't spell that well and end up misspelling words. If you have the misspelling in your keyword tag, there is a good chance your page will come up in the search. You can use the Keyword Selector Tool at Overture.com or one of the other keyword tools to help you find the most common misspellings of words.

You probably don't want to have these misspellings on the visible page because people might think you are not too smart.

Unlike the description META tag, the keyword META tags are totally behind the scenes. The public does not see them, but the search engine spiders do. This is the area where you place your appropriate keywords and their synonyms. Some search engines only want your synonyms and will penalize you for putting your main ones in that area.

> **TIP:** This is another reason search engines are such a pain. Everything is changing all the time.

In general you should use the plural version of keywords. One example is using "dogs" as a keyword instead of "dog." If someone searches for the word "dog" when you have used the word "dogs" they will still find you because the word "dog" is included in the word "dogs." But if you use the word "dog" and they search for the term "dogs," it's likely you won't be found because the word "dogs" is not entirely included in the word "dog." This trick will not work for a word like "company" because the plural word "companies" is spelled completely differently.

Worrying about this is becoming less important because search engines are getting smarter all the time and can recognize word stems, but it never hurts to use the plural.

Some people confuse a META search engine with a META tag. A META search engine is a search engine that will do a search of many different search engines. For example, a search at http://www.Askjeeves.com (Figure 1.4) searches many other search engines for you and reports the findings to you all at once. You can also use simple queries if you prefer, such as, "How do I build a deck?"

So, let's not get several issues confused here. META search engines simply search many other search engines at once for you. That is a totally separate issue from META tags that are parts of your web page.

Figure 1.4   Example of a META Search Engine. META Search Engines Search Many Search Engines at One Time: This One Allows You to Type Questions instead of Keywords

WHAT YOU NEED TO KNOW

 There are some important areas behind the scenes at your website. You have to make sure the proper keywords are there. You also have to make sure a very good description of your website is there so people will be compelled to click on your site rather than someone else's site when they see it in search engine results.

Buy Your Way to the Top with Paid Search Engines

There are certain search engines where you can actually guarantee yourself a first place position. This is commonly known as pay-per-click or PPC. One of the most prominent of these search engines is http://www.Overture.com.

When you do any kind of search there, you can jump through a few of Overtures little hoops to see the advertiser's maximum bid. You might see $0.13, which means that the website owner was willing to bid up to 13 cents on a keyword. When that keyword is used in a search, their site comes up high. If you bid 14 cents on the same keyword, you beat them and your site comes up higher than theirs in a search for that keyword.

Typically, in pay-per-click search engines, you write the description the searcher sees when they type in a keyword you have bid on. The beauty of this is that you don't pay unless someone clicks on your description "ad," hence the term "pay-per-click."

Overture still must supply search results even if no one has bid on a keyword. You might even get a number one ranking if you have an obscure keyword or keyword phrase. So, you don't have to bid anything to be listed in Overture, but if you want to guarantee a top ranking on a particular keyword, then bidding is the way to go.

When you use Overture.com, real people review your keywords to make sure they land on pages in your site that are relevant to what the searcher was searching for. If the keywords don't match the content of the page you are sending the searcher to, you will not be allowed to have your ad show. In Overture.com, this can take from several days to as much as a week.

Keyword Selector Tool

Overture.com also has a cool function to help you research different keywords. It will also tell you how many times a keyword has been searched on the Internet. It is called the keyword selector tool. If I put the word "presentation" in, it comes up 945 times. That means that in the last 30 days people searched for the word "presentation" 945 times on the search engine Overture.com and its affiliates. It also shows all of the variations of the word "presentation" and how many times they were used in searches in the past 30 days. Keep in mind that the numbers only reflect searches done on Overture.com and their affiliates.

In the search I did, I noticed one of the variations, "presentation skills," came up only 206 times. That tells me that the term "presentation" is searched four times more than "presentation skills."

How do we interpret this, and what do we do about it? The people searching for "presentation skills" are more targeted and are obviously looking for a particular thing. The people searching for "presentation" could be chefs searching for food presentation. If I create pages in my site based only on the term "presentation," I will probably pull in more traffic. Admittedly, some of the traffic will be the chefs who will probably leave my site immediately or never click on me in the first place, but a percentage of the people will want what I have to offer.

What about the fact that the term "presentation" is included in the phrase "presentations skills?" Won't the people searching for "presentation" find the "presentation skills" page? Not necessarily, since there are lots of factors at play. What you need to keep in mind is that you should use any excuse to create additional pages in your site that provide a bigger target for searchers.

Overture has deals with other major search facilities. If you are willing to bid high enough to stay near the top of their rankings, Overture puts you as a "sponsored or paid listing" on these other search engines. This is a quick way to get a high search result on other search engines, especially Yahoo who now owns Overture. Sometimes staying in the top five at Overture is good enough, but staying in the top three is the most important now.

The keyword selector tool is also wonderful for checking if a keyword or keyword phrase you think is great is being used by anyone. It's very discouraging to kill yourself getting a high ranking on a keyword that no one uses.

Go in there and play with Overture until you find a keyword that suits your topic area.

Overture.com is the largest and most successful paid search engine to date. They are always making deals to expand their influence. All the search engines and directories are changing so fast that this book would be out of date overnight if I tried to get too specific. That's why you should bookmark http://www.searchenginewatch.com and http://www.searchengine-news.com to keep up on the latest developments. They'll also send you a regular e-zine to make it easy to keep up.

Google Adwords

Google has its own pay-per-click program. It's run a little differently than Overture. Google's Adwords program actually rewards you for writing better advertisements to go with your keywords.

Most people say that Google's rise to dominance in the search engine arena was because of their obsession with giving searchers relevant searches (i.e., when you put search terms into Google's search engine, you get results you can use).

Google carried this obsession to their pay-per-click program. They actually reward you for writing descriptions that get more people to click on your ad. They figure if more people are clicking, you must be writing ad descriptions that are relevant to what the searcher was looking for.

For instance, if you and I are both willing to bid up to $1 per click for a particular keyword, and you write a better ad than me that gets more people to click on it, you will pay less for your clicks. This is really important! You might only have to pay 10 cents per click while I'm paying $1 per click. Or, looking at it another way, you could get 10 times as many visitors as I get for the same amount of money.

Google Adwords program is one of the main tools savvy marketers use to test ideas. The reason is that when you use Google Adwords your ads can show up on the Internet in as little as 15 minutes—almost definitely within a couple of hours. This means you can test ideas quickly to see if anyone is interested in your idea. One of the main rules of successful marketers is that they want to test quickly with the least effort and expense. Time is definitely money, and you don't want to spend months or even years developing a product or writing a book only to find out that no one wants it. Google Adwords can give you some good information quickly to help you make the decision whether to proceed with a project or not.

You should make every effort to become an expert in the use of Google Adwords. I suggest specific books that totally focus on Google Adwords so that you can really learn the nuances of getting the most from the program. Perry Marshall has a great primer that you can download immediately at http://www.1shoppingcart.com/app/aftrack.asp?afid=133415.

Business.com

I have had good preliminary success with http://www.Business.com in their pay-per-click program. At Business.com, you get an account rep who helps you formulate your ad and find the appropriate places to put it. You can't really hype things up as you can in Google and Overture. Test it out and see if it pays off for you.

Are paid listings worth it? It depends. You will certainly get more traffic if you have a high placement, but whether it's worth it or not depends on your ability to turn those visitors into paying customers. I didn't have any luck with the expensive keywords that were sometimes as much as $3 per click. Terms like "motivational speaker" and "professional speaker" got clicks, but no speaking engagements. I dropped those terms in favor of many more 10 to 60 cent keywords that get people to sign up for my e-zine and buy my products. I'm sure I'll be able to convert a good percentage of those people into sales.

Bid Tools

Keeping track of all your bidding can be a hassle and can lose you lots of money if you lose track. I speak from experience here. There are programs that help you keep track of your bids and keywords, for example:

http://www.clixGalore.com/PSale.aspx?BID=4953&AfID=79282&AdID=547

Google AdSense

This is as good a place as any to show you the flip side of the coin of a particular pay-per-click search engine. You'll see throughout this book that I want you to make money when people are coming to your site and also when they are leaving your site. Google's AdSense program helps you entice people to leave your site, and you get paid when they do.

When you place a pay-per-click ad with Google, it shows up on the Google website, and it also shows up on other people's websites.

Example: You sell dog collars. You purchase a pay-per-click ad from Google to promote your dog collars. When someone types in your term "dog collar" your ad shows up on Google's results page as a *sponsored listing*.

What you may not know is that your ad is also showing up on many other websites related to dogs. A visitor to a page of dog humor on my website might be shown an ad for your dog collar. This is because I joined Google's AdSense program and put a small piece of code on my dog humor page.

By putting the code on my dog humor page, I am telling Google to go ahead and show any pay-per-click ads they think are appropriate for my dog humor page. If someone clicks on the ads, I get to share the click revenue with Google.

Google might show dog food ads, ads for dog leashes, or just about anything they think would make sense to show on a dog humor page. Sometimes you may not think what they are showing makes sense for your page, and you do have a "very limited" say in what kinds of ads should and shouldn't show.

Good Deal or Bad Deal?

Most top marketers will tell you that if you are the person paying for the clicks, you don't want your ads showing up on these pages that are supposedly related to your ad. (Google's advertisers finally realized this, so Google is trying to improve the situation.) The conversion and click-through rates from these ads are notoriously low. They are so low in fact that Google will not kick you out if your ad falls below their normal cutoff point of 0.5 percent click through.

When you are the person placing the pay-per-click ad, you can turn off this function (it's called the *content network*) so that your ads only show on the Google website and other search facilities where Google has relationships. This is called the *search network*. Also, when you turn off this function, your ad will only show when someone is actually searching for the term you bid on instead of your ad showing just because someone visited a related page.

If you are a website owner and have pages that are getting traffic, you look at the Google AdSense deal from an entirely different perspective. Since you are on the receiving end of the money, you want to place ads on pages of yours that aren't critical to selling your stuff but that can bring in money when other people click on the ads.

For example: I do have a dog humor page at http://www.antion.com/humor /speakerhumor/dogs.htm. I don't really care much about this page and the other humor pages I have. They are just a service to the speakers who do business with me. Pages like this are great places to put affiliate links to other companies *and* the Google AdSense program.

You can see some of the Google generated ads. Google actually ignored the dog humor on this page and made most of the ads speaking related. Do I care? Not that much unless I am losing lots of sales of my speaker products, which I'm not.

It took me about two hours to figure out how to use the program and put up the links. With the checks I've been getting from Google for my share of the clicks, I figure my time was worth about $500/hour and that's only if the program runs for a year. If Google keeps the program running, I'll keep getting paid.

So, if you are paying for the clicks, don't let your ads be shown on "content pages." On the other hand, do participate in sharing in the revenue from other advertisers that don't know any better than to let their ads be shown on low click-through/low conversion pages.

Here's the link to the AdSense program: https://www.google.com/adsense.

Here's a link to a book that will help you figure out Google Adsense: http://hop.clickbank.net/?powertips/1insider.

Some Pay per click search engines are:

http://www.Overture.com

https://adwords.google.com/select

http://www.Business.com

http://www.payperclicksearchengines.com (list of over 600 pay-per-click search engines)

http://www.epilot.com

http://www.findwhat.com

http://www.kanoodle.com

http://www.cleansearch.com

All kinds of deals are emerging from search engines and directories that involve having the website (advertiser) pay. Some of the deals are pretty obscure. Again, keep in touch with http://www.searchenginewatch.com and http://www.searchengine-news.com for the latest news.

WHAT YOU NEED TO KNOW

 You can start getting highly targeted traffic immediately from pay-per-click search engines if you are willing to pay for each lead.

Submitting Sites to Search Engines

I either do this myself, or have someone do it for me. You submit each page of your website that you want to be seen. Some people, and even some search engines, say, "Don't submit each page." As long as I am only submitting an occasional page here and there, I go ahead and individually submit important secondary pages from my websites. You can decide if you want to bend the rules a little bit.

The big search engines are not going to know or care about it. Eventually their spiders will hit your homepage and find some of these pages themselves anyway, but you just can't count on it. Therefore, if you create a page that's important to you, go to the search engine and find the "add URL" page. It might say "add a page," "suggest a site," or something similar (Figure 1.5). You simply type in the URL of the page (URL is your address to the page, e.g., http://www.antion.com/speakervideo.htm) and hit submit. That way you know it's in there. You'll have to submit the page separately for each of the major search engines. That will give you a much better registration response time, and you'll be sure that the page is listed for each of the search engines.

For a current list of the biggest search engines, visit http://www.searchenginewatch.com.

If you have many pages to submit, take all of your pages, link them to another page, and submit that page. You might even get a higher ranking because of this. This main page could be your home page or a page you call a site index. The theory is that if the spider finds you first instead of you submitting the page yourself, you could be ranked higher. The jury is still out on this, but it certainly helps you get away from spamming the search engine by submitting more pages per day than they allow. Many of the search engines are asking you to only submit one page per domain per day. This method, which is also known as a *hallway page,* allows you to submit only one page. But since you could have it linked to many pages, you would be in effect submitting multiple pages under the guise of one page.

Don't fall for all the *auto submit* offers you either see on the web or receive by e-mail. Some offers say "we'll submit your site to 2,000 search engines for $29.95." What you'll really get is 1,990 pieces of spam e-mail from all the worthless search engines they submit you to and nothing from the few engines that you really wanted to get into. Why? Because many of the top search engines won't accept automatic submissions. So just make sure you type in your page(s) and submit them to each major search engine yourself. . . . You'll be happy you did.

Go to the important search engines (that you identify on http://www.searchenginewatch.com), find their "add page," and bookmark it. It's a fast

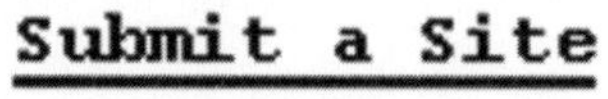

Submit a Site

Figure 1.5   Sample Submit Link

cut-and-paste thing to put in your address so that you can submit your pages. I advise you to do it regularly. Don't go for months at a time and leave your website static. Change something on the page and resubmit it. However, if you're getting a high ranking, don't resubmit it. If the search engine has changed what it wants to see in a page to rank it high, you might actually go down in the rankings.

It's important to know if and when you fall off the ranks. I'm number one right now on Alta Vista, but tomorrow this listing could disappear (and it will because Alta Vista is being closed down). If I was not checking it regularly, I would never know it and hence would not take the proper steps necessary to remedy the situation. There would be a big delay in putting the resubmission process in motion if I did not have the Web Position Gold program checking my listings for me regularly.

Paid Inclusion

Some search engines will accelerate your efforts to get into them by charging you a fee. Paying this fee does not guarantee you will get a high ranking from that search engine. It just means you will be put into their index.

One last thing on search engine strategy: I highly suggest the book *Maximize Website Traffic* by Robin Nobles (Holbrook, MA: Adams Media, 2000). Even though much of the material is slightly dated, it is still a good reference especially with regard to placement of keywords and writing titles and descriptions for your site. You might also want to take her 16-week intensive online course at the Academy of Web Specialists (http://www.academyweb-specialists.com).

For a super simple guide to better search rankings, try reading "Totally Non-Technical Guide to Better Search Rankings" at http://hop.clickbank .net/?powertips/tntguide.

There is very little free submission left to search engines. This is good and bad. It's bad because we now have to pay, but it's good because it gets rid of the riff raff who used to submit thousands of pages that just muddied the water for everyone.

Submitting Sites to Directories

Submitting a website to a directory requires an entirely different strategy than submitting it to robot-driven search engines. Remember, a real person will be looking at your website in its entirety and deciding whether it is a good enough site for their directory and where in their directory it belongs.

You don't have to worry about this too much anymore because the grand-daddy of all directories (Yahoo) has just turned into a pure search engine.

With directories, you don't submit individual pages like you might do with a robot-driven search engine. You are submitting the entire site by means of a submission form.

Directories don't care about META tags, keyword density, or much of anything that is critical in robot-driven search engine placement. But they do have a few critical needs when it comes to keywords and some other criteria you must attend to before you get accepted and receive a good placement. We will discuss these shortly.

One valuable directory site that is still free is called http://www.dmoz.org or more commonly known as Open Directory Project. If accepted in this directory, it may take three weeks or so to get your site listed. Since it's operated by volunteers, they get backlogged sometime. If you don't see it listed in the reasonable amount of time they tell you about on the site, you can then resubmit.

The reason dmoz is a really important directory is that they provide supplementary search results for many other search engines that also have directory sections. So, by being listed in dmoz, you are automatically available to many other search engines.

The procedure for submitting your site can vary between directories, so always use the latest information about the submission process listed on the actual directory to which you are submitting. Most directories will have an "add a site" or "submit a site" link somewhere on their site, usually right next to each category.

Here are some general tips to getting listed in directories:

- ✓ Make your site look as professional as possible before submitting to a directory. Remember, a real person will be looking at your site.
- ✓ Having an impressive looking logo that matches your company name appears to be important for new submissions.
- ✓ All parts of your site must be functional. No broken links or under construction signs are allowed, and make sure all images load correctly and quickly.
- ✓ For the English version of a directory, your site must be in English.
- ✓ Your site must be available 24 hours a day 7 days per week.
- ✓ Make sure your contact information is obvious on every page of your site and phone numbers and e-mail addresses are working.
- ✓ In most cases, the title on your home page must match your company name.
- ✓ Take great care to search out and choose the appropriate category for your site. This is actually where you will click on "submit a site" and submit your site directly to that category (this is called *drilling down* through the directory). It is very difficult to get your site listed in more than one category, so make sure you pick wisely.

TIP: There is no guarantee that the directory will agree with your choice. They may put your site somewhere else.

TIP: Even though directories don't really use META tags, you should still make sure that all areas of your site are consistent with your suggested category. Causing an editor to wonder about the legitimacy of your site may just make them pass on accepting your site.

✓ Don't use any "hype" in your site description. The editors of directories have heard it all and will delete your submission if they see any self-aggrandizement. For example, don't say, "Most dynamic speaker you'll ever have at your meeting." Say, "Motivational speeches for the tourist industry" or something like that. The editors may still change your description after reviewing your site.
✓ If you have a regional or international product, most directories have regional and international versions. Submit to them.
✓ Don't attempt to use automated submission tools to submit to the directories.
✓ Consider renaming your company to start with a word beginning with the letter "A." To a certain extent, the directories are alphabetical so this will allow you to be listed more toward the top, which can mean much more exposure for your site.

Do whatever you can to get into the directories because it can lead to a massive amount of traffic, and business! Also, a link from a major directory can mean a big boost in link popularity and can be very valuable to you.

Banner Advertising

We've all seen them either consciously or subconsciously. Some are animated, and some are extremely simple. They used to cost a fortune, and now they are relatively cheap. They come in all shapes and sizes. Should we use them to promote our small business?

TIP: Images are much clearer when displayed on a website.

As with many of the techniques you will learn in this book, you must test to see if they work for you. I have been against them for a long time because people tend to gloss over them. I'm now taking a new look at using banners because if done to resemble a headline that looks clickable they can be very effective. Figure 1.6 shows some examples of fake hyperlink banners.

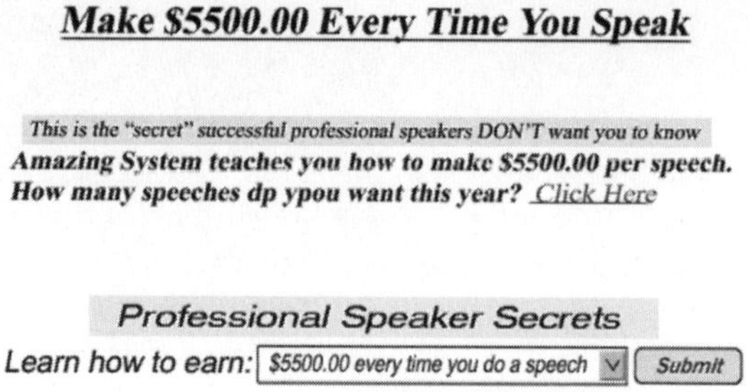

Make $5500.00 Every Time You Speak

This is the "secret" successful professional speakers DON'T want you to know
Amazing System teaches you how to make $5500.00 per speech.
How many speeches dp ypou want this year? Click Here

Professional Speaker Secrets
Learn how to earn: | $5500.00 every time you do a speech ∨ | Submit |

**Figure 1.6   Here Are Examples of a Headline Banner with a Fake
Hyperlink Underline, a Plain Text Banner with a Fake
"Click Here" Link, and a Fake Drop Down Box**

In all the examples, anywhere you click inside the area of the banner will take you to the landing page you have designated. The standard size for this type of banner is 480 pixels wide and 60 pixels high. Many new sizes are available.

If you don't have the skill yourself, you'll have to have a graphics person create your banners, or you can use one of the free banner creators that can be found online by simply typing in "free banner software" in any major search engine.

You need to do a good job of tracking your banners to make absolutely sure they are paying off.

> **TIP:** Keep this in mind: Placement on specific sites relating to your field will probably do better than banners being displayed on any random site.

Here are a few places you can buy banners:

http://www.microsoft.com/smallbusiness/products/online/bannerads/detail.mspx

http://www.valueclick.com

http://www.247media.com

http://www.fastclick.com

http://www.tribalfusion.com

WHAT YOU NEED TO KNOW

 Your site as a whole and important pages in your site must be submitted to search engines and directories. The strategy to submit to a search engine is much different than the strategy to submit to a directory where a live person will review your site. Simple banners can be effective.

Website Optimization and Graphics

When I first started doing my own website, one of my weaknesses was photo and graphic optimization. You want your website to really come up fast. People don't like to wait around for sites to load.

While high-speed Internet access is becoming much more widespread, this topic is still important. You should always think about speed of loading instead of fancy graphics and slow loading special effects.

As an absolute last resort when you do have a large photo or graphic that must be shown, put a phrase at the top of the page that loads immediately that says, "Please be patient. This page may take a short time to load."

If you just drag the corner of a picture on your website to make it smaller, it may look smaller, but it really isn't.

The whole reason to make a photo or graphic smaller is so that its file size is small, and it loads and displays fast. I thought by simply making it display "smaller" that it would also display "faster." I was wrong about that. The photo or graphic is actually the exact same size in bytes. It's only being shown smaller. While it looks smaller, the file size is just as big. You need to learn how to make the file sizes of the graphics and the pictures on your site as small as possible (as long as they still look nice), so they will load quickly. You can get a free trial of a web graphic optimizer at http://www .webopt.com.

To complicate things even more, you want the image to still look good. The bottom line is that you want the best looking image you can get that has the smallest file size.

GIF or JPEG

These are abbreviations for compression formats for graphics that help make the small file size I just mentioned. The whole idea is to show graphics that look good, but don't take long to load or send over the Internet. GIF is better when your book cover is going to be reduced to 1½ inches high on a web page and you still want to be able to read the title. JPEG is better when you have graphics or photos with continuous tones of gray or color, and there are no text or sharp edges involved.

Get Help

Get help if you can't do some of the things you want for your website. I really believe in investing in your own education. That way you don't have to depend on others, and you don't have to pay high hourly rates for things you could easily do yourself if you just knew how to do it.

The man who helped me is Darrin Graviet. I interviewed him about our topic of website optimization and graphics, and here's what he had to say:

TOM: I'm going to ask you a few questions about some of the things that you helped me do. We all want our graphics to look great. In traditional print mediums, the print is at a very high resolution. You said, "No, Tom your web graphics should only be 72 dots per inch." Can you tell us about that?

DARRIN: Well, if you have a really good-looking graphic that takes forever to load, people won't be willing to wait for it to come up on the browser. You just need as good as you can get, as fast as you can get. Speed is more of a plus to the Internet than looks are.

TOM: So, instead of using 1,200 dpi [dots per inch], which would take forever, do you scan it at 72 dots per inch, or how do you get the smaller file size?

DARRIN: Tom, if you wish, I'll go through the steps. First, you want to scan it in or develop it at about 300 dpi. That way you have enough color so that you can go into the picture, play with it, knock some pixels out, and have better control over your graphics.

TOM: All right, so scan or develop it at 300.

DARRIN: Yes. Then the second step that you want to do once you have the image in Photo Shop, or whatever you are using to manipulate graphics, is to crop all the extraneous information.

TOM: So just make it a nice tight, full frame of whatever you are showing, right?

DARRIN: Yes, get rid of any extra pixels you can because they are really killing you on the load time. Third, you want to resize the graphics to a size that you want to display on the web. Typically, what I will do is I'll open up Internet Explorer or Netscape at the same time I am working in Photo Shop, and I'll simply save it as a few different sizes and see what size I like best. Once you get accustomed to pixel dimensions, then you will be able to judge what size you want the graphics to be.

TOM: Okay, You told us something about the load time of pages and setting the height and width for all your graphics. Can you explain what you mean by that?

DARRIN: Once you've cropped and resized the image, the fourth thing you want to do is knock out as many colors as you can. Try to use the web palette index colors, which will save it as a GIF. If not, then go to JPG. JPG has a good compression and it will knock out the colors for you and then finally, no more than 72 dpi. If you don't put the tag in your HTML that actually tells the HTML the dimensions of your graphic, then your page loads twice, or more times than that. Every time it has to determine how to place a new graphic into the page, it reloads the whole page and your pages can take up to 10 times longer to load.

TOM: Okay, I know that some of our readers are beginner level and they're freaking out right now. What you are saying is that you take your picture after you've scanned it, and you put it into Adobe Photoshop or some of the other popular graphics program. Many popular programs now have an "optimize for web" function that will make your work lots easier. You either learn to reduce file size yourself, or you get your Webmaster to do it. However, you do it to make sure all of the optimization things that we mentioned are implemented so your pages will load fast.

DARRIN: What setting the height and width boils down to in real life is that if the page knows where the graphic is going, it can save the space and load the text very fast. People can be reading and having something to do while your pictures are loading. If you don't do the optimization, they will probably leave because the pages are taking too long to load.

TOM: Page loading time is why optimizing graphics for the web is important for your site. Tell us about sites that need to be very graphic oriented. Tell us about *preloading graphics* and how that little trick can help you.

DARRIN: Yes, a couple of things. Number one, you don't want to use a graphic image unless it's something that's necessary.

It must be something that is better said with an image than with a word. If you do need an image, make it as small as possible. One of the things that I do is try to put the images down low in the page so the user doesn't even see them loading. The user is reading at the top part of the page and by the time they are finished and scroll down, the images are already there.

Super Trick: Preloading Graphics

DARRIN: Another thing that you can do is the trick called *preloading graphics* and it is something that even advanced webmasters don't consider. It is so simple. Your browser has a state called *cache*. When you view a web page, it is temporarily downloaded to your hard drive. Then you go view a few more web pages, if you come back to the first page that you viewed, instead of going back to the server to get those graphics, it gets them off of your own hard drive. What you can do is trick the system into thinking that it has already seen those graphics by putting them on a previous page. I like to load the page heavy with content to stall the user.

Let's say on page eight I want to hide some graphics that I want to show on page nine. What I will do on page eight is to put the same graphics that I want people to see on page nine, but I will make them 1 pixel high by 1 pixel wide so they are actually invisible. What that does is preload the image into the visitors cache and then when they go to page nine, it shows up immediately. You're showing the same exact image on both pages. However, on page eight you show the picture at 1 pixel high by 1 pixel wide. The user doesn't even see it on page eight because of the extremely small size.

TOM: When they go to the page where you actually want them to see the graphics, bam, they'll pop right up.

Transparent Graphics

TOM: If you go to Darrin's home page, http://www.graviet.com, you see Darrin just standing there out in the middle of nowhere. This is called a *transparent graphic.* Tell us about it, Darrin, because it really looks professional and nice.

DARRIN: Well, the best way to get a transparent graphic is not by using the transparency graphic capabilities of your graphics program. It's by making the background of your graphic the exact same color as you use on your page. So it looks like I'm standing there with nothing in the background of that image, but really the background of the image is white, just like my page. I always use a white background because it loads faster.

WHAT YOU NEED TO KNOW

 If you are going to have pictures and other graphics on your website, you must make sure they load extremely fast, so people don't leave while waiting for them to load. They should also look as good as possible even though their file size is small. If you don't want to learn all the tricks of how to achieve these goals, simply hire the work out to a competent graphics person and make sure they read the previous section.

TIP: Tables are great for design purposes, but you will suffer some trade-off with search engine positioning. Anything you do to junk up your code could cost you.

Tables and Table Widths

TOM: Another thing you mentioned was table width. Tables are little boxes that you put on your website, and when you are making a table, you can pick either a "percentage" width or a certain "exact size" for them. Tell us about that.

DARRIN: Yes, there are a few different things to do with tables. Number one, I like to make sure that everything that I put on a web page views at 100 percent of the viewer's width. You go to a lot of web pages, and what you see is either a bunch of white space on the right, or you have to scroll to the right, which is even worse. It is dumb to do it that way. HTML is set up to be flexible. If you design with tables, all you have to do is tell the table to be 100 percent of the width of the user's screen. Go to my website and resize your browser. You should be able to resize it down to 600 pixels wide and still not have to scroll to the right.

In most of today's web design programs, all you do is click into the table with your mouse. Then right click, which will take you to "table properties," and you choose "100 percent width."

TIP: The 100 percent width setting is not that great for text because really wide lines of text are hard to read. I try to constrain my text especially on long sales pages so the text is easier to read.

TOM: When I first started doing this, I thought I would be cool with the buttons on my page and make them a Java Script. I found out, to my horror, that on AOL none of my buttons showed up at all. In addition, the Java Script caused troubles with some of the other browsers. Tell us about the special scripting and what that does to your site.

DARRIN: Well, if you use Java Script, you're actually cutting off a percentage of the market that doesn't have the capability of reading Java script.

TIP: This is not that big of a problem today, but you still don't want to junk up your coding.

Use Old Technologies in a New Way

DARRIN: What I like to do is use old technologies in a new way and that's the best way to make sure that people can be able to view everything that you create. I do use Java Script on my buttons, but that's because there are not many people who hire me who are using AOL to browse. Corporate environments are up to speed and have their own high-speed lines coming in, and so on.

TOM: So in other words, you have to be careful about where your market is. If you were all graphics people, you would probably have Shock Wave, Flash, and all kinds of crazy stuff. However, if your market is a consumer market, many of the people may not have the capability of seeing your fancy design, and you're cutting them out.

If you are doing any international business that we just can't make any assumptions, corporate or otherwise, as to people's bandwidth, their machinery, and software. We still have to work down to a very low common denominator.

I was in Morocco speaking and the browser was in French, and the keyboard was something I couldn't even decipher. They could just barely get on the Internet. This is a global marketplace. You also want to make sure everything is fast because they're worried about getting on and off the Internet faster because it costs them more.

DARRIN: Let me add one last thing, Tom. You were telling me that one of the problems that you had was trying to get your book jacket to be a smaller image on your page.

TOM: I could easily make it smaller, but then the text was not readable.

DARRIN: One of the things that people don't remember to do is turn off their "anti-aliasing," which is the thing that sometimes ruins your text. So, make sure you either do it yourself, or get your designer to do it for you.

TOM: Yes, and please, ask someone for help who can help you through this and teach you. It is a very inexpensive way to save yourself a lot of money because when you can do this yourself, you don't have to pay designers to do it. It is a very good investment.

WHAT YOU NEED TO KNOW

 The use of tables as a design tool is good and bad. Used correctly, they can really help align your text and graphics for a nice look. Too much use can junk up your HTML code, which hurts your chances of high rankings when a search engine spider looks at your page.

Why Does It Look Funny?

In regular word processing, if you put something on a page and print it on a printer, things print out exactly where you expect them to be. It's not the same in web page creation. Everybody is looking at your web page in a different browser, with different screen resolutions, and different default fonts. You're not exactly sure what it's going to look like. Therefore, it does take a little bit of a learning curve, and it's never going to be perfect. You just have to get it out there. You should test it in Internet Explorer, Netscape, and AOL. If the page is okay in those three browsers, then that's good enough.

Here's the link to check your site in different browsers:

http://www.anybrowser.com

Free Optimization Sites include:

http://www.gifwizard.com
http://www.netmechanic.com/accelerate.htm
http://www.netmechanic.com/GIFBot/optimize-graphic.htm
http://www.webreference.com/services/graphics

Graphic Search Engines include:

http://www.ditto.com
http://www.google.com

Graphics Optimization Software is available at http://www.webopt.com.

Many main line graphics programs like Adobe Photoshop are adding web optimization as one of their functions.

Here are some sites that allow you to create some cool buttons:

http://www.buttonland.com

http://www.freebuttons.com

http://www.web-buttons.net

Electronic Clipart and Animations

Don't go crazy with this, but once in a long while you may need a little extra emphasis. Keep animated GIFs small and please use only one on a page, or your site will look like a circus act. Make sure any "free" graphics you use are really free or copyright free. Some may actually require a small fee. Check out available graphics at:

http://www.anrdoezrs.net/click-1464114-10357251 (Animation Factory)

http://hop.clickbank.net/?powertips/fbcom

http://www.barrysclipart.com

http://www.free-clip-art.net

http://www.fg-a.com/gifs.html

http://www.gifart.com

http://www.arttoday.com

http://www.quickbanner.com (free banner and button creation tool)

http://www.Corbis.com (photographs, these are not free)

Web Safe Colors

If you stick to simple basics and don't try to get fancy, you will have no trouble with the colors you use on your website. All you need to know is that some colors look terrible and some look fine on just about everyone's computer.

I don't advocate lots of graphics anyway, so my advice is to simply get a professional web designer to make any custom graphics for you, so you won't have to worry about this issue too much.

Some people waste lots of time and money trying to match their web colors to some fancy custom brochure they have. It just doesn't work that way. Monitors cannot accurately or even consistently display colors as well as printing can.

If you really want to learn a lot about color, visit the following sites:

http://www.webdevelopersjournal.com/articles/websafe1/websafe_colors
.html

http://www.masternewmedia.org/2003/01/23/make_your_web_site
_accessible_for_color_blind_people.htm (Use this massive link to
learn about making your site accessible to color blind people.)

Readability and Text Attributes

This topic never ceases to amaze me. I guess some people don't bother to try
to read their own website, or they are just so happy to have one, they don't
care whether anyone can read it or not.

This is not rocket science. Simply make sure that you can easily read the
text on your website both on the page and in graphics. Don't let your pas-
sion for color override your common sense. People have to read your site before they buy.

Text

There's a really large and clear explanation of this topic in the book *Web Pages
That Suck* by Vincent Flanders and Michael Willis (San Francisco: Sybex,
1996). This book has lots of other very good information and I highly recommend it. They also have a sequel out *Son of Web Pages That Suck* (San Francisco: Sybex, 2002). Here's a discussion of what to look for with regard to text.

Italic

Italic is used for titles and to emphasize words. The problem is that italicized
words are really hard to read on computer monitors and look terrible. To overcome the problem on web pages, bold the ***Italic*** to improve its readability.

ALL CAPITAL TEXT

ALL CAPITAL TEXT IS CONSIDERED POOR <u>NETIQUETTE</u> (IT'S AS IF
YOU WERE SHOUTING) AND IS REALLY HARD TO READ. IT IS OKAY
FOR EMPHASIZING A WORD OR TWO, OR FOR SHORT HEADLINES.

Initial Caps

This Is When The First Letter Of Each Word Is Capitalized. Again, this is
okay for short subheadings, but not for long strings of text.

Underlined Text

This is really bad for web pages and e-books because it makes people think they can click on the word and be hyperlinked somewhere else. Please don't use underlining in web pages.

Centering

Don't center all the text on a page. It looks amateurish. Do you know why? Because it is. Headlines are okay to center.

WHAT YOU NEED TO KNOW

 You can't get so wrapped up in making a beautiful masterpiece of a website that you forget the limitations of the web. Certain colors simply won't work. People that see your page see it in different screen sizes with different browsers, different fonts, and different screen resolutions. Also, don't make formatting choices that don't work on the web.

Entry and Exit Strategies

Before we leave website optimization, a brief discussion of traffic patterns going in, out, and through your website is in order.

Entry

You might not realize that a visitor may enter your site at just about any of your web pages. This happens because, hopefully, each of your web pages is optimized to get a high ranking in a search engine. When a particular page gets that high ranking, people clicking on it go directly to the page and bypass your home page. This is a good thing because you want the person to feel they found exactly what they were looking for.

It's not a good idea to try to show them everything you have to offer in hopes they will buy it all. What you are doing is totally confusing them, as well as annoying them too. They hit your site because they were looking for something specific, and you gave them something general. When you do that, they move on to someone else's site quickly.

What you want to do is make sure that when they do hit one of these secondary pages on your site, they can still navigate easily around the rest of the site. Send a friend of yours who might not be too familiar with your site directly to a subpage of your site. Ask them to try to get around in your site.

Take their feedback and use it to make sure there is no doubt what to do when a visitor wants to explore the rest of your web.

Lead Them Around

The worst thing you can do is confuse your visitor. They will leave immediately when they start to feel lost. Most people have far too many choices on their pages. You must lead them through your site and introduce them to your information in a logical sequence and in digestible bites. And always give them a bailout home button so they can start over again if they do get lost.

You might say, "Tom, I think you're crazy. Some of the most successful sites in the world like MSN have a million choices on every page." Forget trying to compare your small business site to sites that have enough money to advertise on the side of every bus in America. The biggies can get away with things that would be suicide for your small business site.

Think about where you want your visitor to end up and what action you want them to take when they get there. Then work backwards to the most likely place they enter your site. Review each page they will encounter along the way and make sure it doesn't send them off in the wrong direction.

Exit

You may not believe it (Tom says sarcastically), especially after all the work and money you've put into your website, but people will leave your site. A good statistics package will tell you exactly where most people are leaving. This is a handy thing to know, and I'll show you some desperation tricks to do something about it later. For now, we'll try to control where people go when they leave your site.

If you own more than one website, you could put links to it on top of your exit pages and invite people to visit your other site. You might not even want to mention that it's another site that you own. This is something you have to test. If they are leaving your present site because they thought it was lousy, they are not going to click to another site you control.

If they are leaving a page because they have seen everything you have to offer, that means they probably would like more. Then, by all means, let them know they will find more good content at, "Our sister site," or "Our partner site," or some other similar phrase.

Another strategy would be to join other associate/affiliate programs (we'll talk about them shortly) and put the links on your top exit pages. That way when people leave your site you still have a chance to profit from them if they buy something at one of the sites you send them to.

You can use pop-up boxes as a great exit strategy. Despite the dire warnings from propeller heads around the world, pop-up boxes used judiciously still are very profitable in promoting e-zine sign-ups, affiliate programs, pick

your price promotions, and finance options. I use the program http://www
.amazingpopups.com/power.

Where do you send your buyers? Don't forget the confirmation page from
your shopping system. Heck, they already have their wallet out from buying
your products. This would be another great place to put affiliate links so you
can earn more commissions on whatever they buy from other sites.

I'll discuss these exit strategies more when I discuss the website sales process a little later.

WHAT YOU NEED TO KNOW

 Real people are visiting your website one at a time. They all must
find their way through your site to find the information they want.
Always try to think like a first-time visitor that never heard of you
when you are putting things on your website. Also try to think like
the least technically savvy person who is likely to visit your site.
Get others to help you figure out the most logical way to lead visitors from page to page. Use pop-up boxes and other exit strategies
to profit from those visitors who are leaving your site.

Link Trade Strategy

The next topic is the strategy that I love. It is called the *link trade strategy*
where your site and another site are *hyperlinked*. If you can click on a link
and go somewhere else, that is called a *hyperlink*. I suggest we all trade links.
Doing the actual trade now is quite different than it used to be.

In the old days, I would trade links with anybody that wasn't a porn site.
Now you have to be more careful about your linking so that it gives you the
most benefit.

One thing about links is that it's a much more stable, dependable, and reliable method of getting people to come to your website than depending totally on search engine traffic.

If any one of you and I trade links, unless we just close up our sites, that
link will be there forever. Therefore, it's a very stable thing. If I make a deal
with someone and we both trade links, great, we help each other out. I don't
have to be checking every day as I do with the search engines, and hoping
that, "Oh, I hope I did not lose a position today." It is there forever.

My philosophy about this is that I really hate the people that want to
guard everything they have. They think, "I created this information, and I'm
going to guard it the rest of my life and never create anything else." I'm not
like that. I want to link with you. But I must tell you, I'm not going to put
your link right up at the top where my picture is. I'll put your link on a links

page or even a hidden page on my site. If you learn what needs to be learned in this section, you pretty much won't care where I put the link because you know it will be benefiting you wherever I put it.

Link trading is mostly about getting higher search engine rankings. You must get that to be successful with this. Don't obsess about where the link is on someone else's site.

> **TIP:** The exception to this is that if the link page on the other person's site is buried in several subdirectories, then it's probably not worth trading links with that site because the search engines won't give a link buried that deeply much weight.

Example of a good link: http://www.antion.com/links.htm.

Example of a bad link: http://www.joeschmoe.com/others/colleagues/links .htm.

It's a bonus if you actually get some traffic from the other person's site. Again, I'm very open about this. I don't try to protect my traffic with a machine gun. I figure if I haven't sold the visitor on my great site and what I do, I would be happy to send them to my friend in Fort Washington, Paul Radde. I don't want to give Paul my business, but I don't mind giving him a shot at business that did not want me. For the same reason, I don't want to take Paul's business. I want a shot at the business that did not want him. A link trade strategy is designed to help both parties.

There are three major areas to address when linking:

1. Link popularity
2. Link reputation
3. Page importance

Here's some linking software: http://hop.clickbank.net/?powertips/link101.

Inbound Link Popularity

There's an extra benefit to linking that is becoming more and more important every day: the topic of link popularity.

This topic is really important. If you did a good enough job getting appropriate links coming into your site, you could probably do a terrible job of keyword placement and all the other things we've talked about to get high rankings and still do okay in the search engines.

Let's say someone in Massachusetts and I both do presentation skills. We both have the same keyword density and our sites are pretty much equal. My site is going to beat hers because I have more links coming "into" my site. The conventional wisdom is, that everything else being equal, if there's a lot of links coming into my site, the search engines think it is a good site. Therefore, I'm going to beat her out in the search results because I have more links coming "into" my site. I make every deal I possibly can to have people link to my site.

Remember the main goal with links at the beginning is not to get immediate traffic to your site through the link from the other site, although that would be a side benefit. The goal is to get so many links coming into your site that you get higher rankings in the search engines, which bring massive amounts of traffic to your site.

This is the biggest problem I have in my link trade strategy. It's hard to get people to understand the last paragraph. They have been scared by ill-informed webmasters and pseudo experts who told them it is bad to trade links. All of you out there reading this who want to be smarter than your competition, take heed and get a link strategy implemented on your site.

How This Has Changed

Definition of link popularity: Measure of the number and quality of the links coming into your site.

It used to be that search engines would just count up the links coming into your site. The more you had, the better. That has all changed now. Now it is important that the actual link text coming from the site linking to you has keywords in it that are meaningful to you (link reputation). This is called *anchor text*. It's also important to you how important the site that links to you is.

For instance, if you want to trade links with me, you must put the words that I want in the clickable text on your site. If you simply put http://www.antion.com, I won't trade with you. You must put something like Public Speaking Tips, which is the clickable part of the link. Yes, the link can still go to Public-Speaking.org, but the clickable part of the link must be a keyword that I designate.

To make this as easy as possible for those wanting to link to you, it would be a good idea to simply give them the entire code to make it easy for them. Here's an example:

```
<A HREF="http://www.Public-Speaking.org">Public Speaking Tips</A>
```

When they pasted this code in their website it would look like this:

Public Speaking Tips

Doing this will give you a much greater chance that people linking to you will do it in a fashion that is most beneficial to you.

How to Find Who Is Linked to Your Site

Use Alta Vista Search Engine, http://www.av.com. (This search engine will be disappearing soon.) Type in the search box link: antion.com (of course, you substitute your website for mine).

If you want to check an individual page add the complete page URL: link:antion.com/ezinesubscribe.htm.

If you don't want to see any of your own pages listed use this string: link:antion.com/ -url:antion.com (note there is a space between the forward slash [/] and the hyphen [-]).

If you want to have this done automatically and e-mailed to your regularly go to http://www.linkpopularity.com. It handles Alta Vista, Google, and HotBot.

You can also use the very handy tools at:

http://www.LinkPopularityCheck.com

http://www.MarketLeap.com/publinkpop

For HotBot (http://hotbot.lycos.com) there are two ways:

1. You can use the previously mentioned site: http://www.linkpopularity .com.
2. You can use this string in the search box: linkdomain:antion.com, or if you don't want links from your own domain to show up in the results,use this string: linkdomain:antion.com -domain:antion.com (there is a space between the .com and the hyphen [-]).

In HotBot, I show over 1,000 incoming links. In many of the others, I'm over 500. This is becoming more and more important for high rankings, so do whatever you can to get those links coming into your site. The bad part for me is that many of the links I had coming to my site did not have anchor text that were keywords, so the value of my links dropped considerably.

> **TIP:** For some unknown reason, the number of links you see coming into your site can vary considerably from day to day, minute to minute, and search engine to search engine.

> **TIP:** You can build link popularity for individual pages on your site that are important to you. You don't have to concentrate only on your home page.

Outbound Link Popularity

In the past, the number of links going out of your site didn't matter to the search engines. Now the search engines have gotten so sophisticated that many of them tally the outbound links that go to related sites that have similar keywords. So, if you have many links going to related sites, your site looks like a very valuable resource on the topic being searched, and it gets a boost in the search engine rankings.

On the other hand, if you have lots of links going to unrelated sites, it could hurt your rankings. So be careful who you link to:

Link Supertrick 1: Make sure every outbound link that is visible to the public is put in a "new window." You don't have to know how to do this yourself, but it is fairly easy. This means that when someone clicks on a link that takes them out of your site, a new browser window opens and your site is still running in the background. The visitor never actually leaves your site. This new window can be set to open slightly smaller than a regular window, which alerts the person that your site is still available in the background.

Link Supertrick 2: This is a really cool trick that takes advantage of outbound link popularity. As stated earlier, outbound links leading to other related sites give you a boost in the search engines, but who wants to give their visitors more and more chances to click out of their website? Nobody, so here's what you do. You make pages comprising of links to other sites that have the same keywords as you do. You put it up on your website, but you don't link it to the main site, so no one but the search engines know it's there.

Many people don't realize you can have hidden pages on your website. Since this page is hidden, no one will ever have a chance to click out of your site to go to any of these links, but the search engine will see them and think, "Wow! What a great resource site this is!" and give you boost in the rankings. Chalk one up for the webmaster.

TIP: Some search engines consider pages that have only links on them as spam. To avoid this issue, put some text on the page that relates to your topic and don't put too many links on one page. You don't want to be considered a "link farm," which will cause you trouble with search engines.

Link Reputation

A link coming into your site is more valuable if that link says something related to your site. This anchor text is actually clickable on someone else's site.

For instance, since I sell so much public speaking stuff, I want links on other people's site to have the term "public speaking" in the clickable part of the text. The link can go to http://www.antion.com, but I want the link "text" to actually say something like "public speaking tips" or something like that.

The reason many search engines give link reputation a greater importance is that it is generally harder to manipulate what other websites would say about you. It's harder because you are trying to control what is done on a different website.

This doesn't mean you can't play a better game than the next webmaster by linking your own sites together to your best advantage. You can also educate those linking to you in the strategies that will help you both out the most.

Page Importance

Since Google's "PageRank" is the standard by which most people gauge the importance of your page, we will use Google's terminology when we discuss the rating of the importance of a page.

You can determine the PageRank of any page on the Internet by downloading and installing a free tool from Google called the *Google Toolbar:* http://toolbar.google.com.

If you want to be a rocket scientist, understanding the entire way Page-Rank is calculated would be a good start. I don't want to be a rocket scientist. I just want to sell lots of stuff on the Internet so our discussion will be brief and easy.

PageRank is like a vote from all the other pages on the Internet. If they link to you that equals a vote for you. The more "votes" you have the better when it comes to the final determination of how important your page appears to the search engine and who shows up higher in search results.

When it comes to the value of an incoming link to you, one vote doesn't necessarily mean one vote. You can "stuff the ballot box" in your favor by getting pages with a higher PageRank to link to you. For instance, I just checked Yahoo and it has a PageRank of 10 out of 10. This is as high a score as you can get. I checked CNN also and found it to have a PageRank of 9 out of 10. A link from either of these sites to your site might be worth 20 or 30 links from sites that have no PageRank.

Here's what Google's site said about PageRank:

PageRank performs an objective measurement of the importance of web pages by solving an equation of more than 500 million variables and 2 billion terms. Instead of counting direct links, PageRank interprets a link from Page A to Page B as a vote for Page B by Page A. PageRank then assesses a page's importance by the number of votes it receives.

PageRank also considers the importance of each page that casts a vote, as votes from some pages are considered to have greater value, thus giving the linked page greater value. Important pages receive a higher PageRank and appear at the top of the search results. Google's technology uses the collective intelligence of the Web to determine a page's importance. There is no human involvement or manipulation of results, which is why users have come to trust Google as a source of objective information untainted by paid placement.

Bottom line: Put lots of effort into your link trade strategy because as the competition gets stiffer (there's a zillion web pages a day coming out) you want to be ahead of the game. So that's another reason why I suggest to everybody, let's correctly trade links. Figure out how to do it, or get your Webmaster to do it because it's going to help all of us. If you want some instructions to copy, feel free to go to http://www.antion.com/linktrade.htm and copy the text I've written for you. Put your description in, but it isn't necessary. If you want to leave mine in the space, it's fine with me!

Just copy the instructions, put in your description, and then use it and put a button on your website to say, "Want to trade links with us? Click here." Try to get more people to trade with you and it will make your site more valuable.

Now here's a way to get inbound links without having to put any more outbound links on your site.

Articles and Link Trades

I write articles and give them to people to put on their websites. I made about $11,000 from *Sales Doctors Magazine* alone. Somebody did not find my site directly, they found Sales Doctors site. They liked an article I had written for them, linked to my site, and hired me without a video or any other promotional materials. I never would have had a shot at this job had it not been for my article on Sales Doctors website.

We want to give people every opportunity to find us even if they don't find our website directly. Articles are a great strategy. Get your articles placed on other people's websites. It helps them by providing content. It helps you because you get the links that will pay off forever.

You're going to hear a lot about the value I put on article writing. Here are a couple tips. If you hate to write, but love to talk, you can get voice recognition software. Here are two programs that will take a load off your fingers:

1. Dragon Systems Naturally Speaking (http://www.dragonsys.com)
2. IBM ViaVoice (http://www-4.ibm.com/software/speech)

The next tip is to simply carry around a mini tape recorder and then get a college student to ghostwrite for you. Try the English or journalism department of your local university or community college.

Here's an e-book on using ghostwriters: http://hop.clickbank.net /?powertips/ggmine.

The way you get your articles placed is to look for sites that are in your field or complementary to your field. When you find a site that looks promising, you send them a personal e-mail. Here's how it will go: "I really liked your site. I was surfing the Internet, and I'm in a related field." Warning: Make sure they know you actually visited their site, or they might accuse you of spamming them.

You might say, "I especially liked the resource section you have and the article on so and so." I get this stuff all the time and it's spam. People send out a million of them, and they have never been to my site. So, if you make a personal letter (e-mail or regular mail), give them enough details so they know you visited their site. Tell them that you searched on the search engines for their types of sites. Send them a personal letter but don't send them the article right away. Let them respond and build a little relationship before sending them the article. Bam, you got a winner because they're never going to take it off. They're going to put it on there and archive it and your link is going to be there forever, and you did not even have to give one up a link in that case. Some of them might come back and say, "Well, we have articles. Maybe we can put them on your site." Then you have to decide if you want to deal.

The same strategy works with electronic magazines. People submit articles to me and in exchange they get a link back to their website, their e-mail address, or something, and that's their payment. Articles in other e-zines can bring you a lot of traffic and many potential customers, which is what you want. You suck them into your website and then get them to sign up for whatever you're selling.

One of the ways I use to draw people is to put articles on the site. I have not solicited articles from anyone else for my website. I have for the electronic magazine, but for the website, I have taken my *Wake 'em Up!* book, excerpted it all over the place, and made articles. I have special articles for meeting planners. I have all kinds of freebie things that are information oriented. That is what is getting many people to my website . . . all the free stuff. If they like my style, I build my credibility. If they like me, there's a very high chance they will eventually buy something, which is the reason I want them there. I want them to either buy or recommend me or a product. I want to get them to "opt-in" to my electronic magazine, which we will cover later.

So put your articles on the website. You're writing them for other sites anyway, or you're writing them for your own site. Writing articles is a fast way to make yourself an expert and get your name all the way around the world.

Here's a link for article writing help: http://www.soaringprofits.com /writing.htm.

Make It Easy on Them

You can buy a simple software program that will make you very attractive to people who want regular content from you to put on their site. Programs like

Master Syndicator allow you to have the website to which you are providing content put a simple piece of code on a page in their site. When you write an article and submit it to your control page, all the sites in the world that have the piece of code on their site will get the updated article instantly. What a way to multiply yourself. You can be a syndicated columnist on the Internet tomorrow if you want. Check it out at http://www.mastersyndicator.com.

Keeping Track of Link Trades

You can certainly do it by hand, but as in most things Internet-related someone has figured out a better way; http://willmaster.com/master/rlinks/index.shtml keeps track of all your link trade requests but also finds out who's cheating by taking your link off after you have put theirs on your site (linking software: http://hop.clickbank.net/?powertips/link101).

Link Considerations

Since everything you do on your website eats up a little or a lot of your time, it makes sense to evaluate the potential payback from your efforts. Here are some things to consider when working with links:

- ✓ Will the link be permanent? A permanent link will be far more valuable in the long run for both potential click throughs and link popularity evaluations. The exception would be a prominent short-term link to a high traffic site like CNN that could send tens of thousands of visitors to your site. Don't waste your time on free-for-all link deals. These are places where anyone can place a link. Search engines look unfavorably on them.
- ✓ A few links from really high traffic sites will most likely produce more for you than lots of links from low traffic sites.
- ✓ When granting an outbound link you will get more mileage out of the link if it goes to a specific related site. Outbound links to unrelated sites could hurt your overall ranking. But if it's an unrelated site that is giving you a reciprocal link, it is still very valuable to you. You will not be penalized because it is unrelated.
- ✓ A link to your site with related text located near the link will get more click throughs than a link by itself.
- ✓ A link buried among many others will not get many click throughs, but will still be valuable for link popularity reasons. Don't turn such a link down, but try to negotiate for a top or exclusive position in your category.
- ✓ Links in articles about the same topic get lots of attention and a good click-through rate.

A good link strategy can get you high search engine rankings. If anyone tells you that it's a bad idea to trade links, don't believe them. Just make sure you do it properly, or you will either be wasting your time or hurting your chance at high search engine rankings.

Is a Shopping Cart Necessary?

The answer is technically "no," a shopping cart is not necessary if you're willing to handle each order individually. But remember, your regular forms on your website generally do not calculate shipping fees or tax, and they don't take credit cards automatically, which will kill your sales.

At my site, they're buying all kinds of things. My store, The Speaker Shop (http://www.antion.com/speakershop.htm), takes seminar admission fees and sells books, tapes, CDs, and downloadable products all designed to help speakers. The system that I have installed allows you to put your credit card number in and buy the product. It will send the order to a credit card processing company, and in about 15 seconds, you'll have an authorization. It will e-mail a confirmation to whomever I want to ship the product without me touching a thing. This is also great for me when I'm on the road because I don't actually have to be here in my office to make money.

Previously, I had to type the credit card number into the system. If I was on the road, things were delayed, or I had to depend on an intern to do it right. The shopping cart will save you many of those hassles. Also, many of your digital product or e-book sales will come from the immediate gratification factor. If you make people wait even an hour or so, they will most likely not buy.

We'll get into how to select a shopping cart on page 123.

How Will I Ever Get This Stuff Done?

If you are going to invest in a website marketing strategy, you need to do at least part of all the work I have outlined so far to have a chance of the site showing up in a search.

I don't do all the work on these sites myself. I use a combination of methods. However, I'm a firm believer that you should learn how to at least update your site yourself so that you have a fast "speed to market." It took about a month and a half part time to become competent working on my website. I don't know some of the simplest things like how to put an icon on my desktop, but I honed in on the things that are necessary for me to know how to make money.

With some help, you can learn how to add pages to your site in about 10 minutes. I'm able to do most of this myself. If it is too complicated, I hire someone who trains me to do it or does it for me.

I recently hired an eleventh grader to run my entire computer system. He built a new computer to my specs and keeps everything running smoothly. I learn tons from him every time he comes over. I've got a ninth grader running part of the technical side of my new association: http://www.NetAim.Info. You can recruit a similar helper from any of the big computer stores, or just ask around at your local high school.

You can do this all yourself if you want to. The more you do yourself, the less it will cost you.

Even if you can afford to pay to have your website done for you, you should still learn how to update it yourself. There is too much delay if you have to depend on someone, and you'll miss opportunities.

Let's say you are a restaurant or a hair salon and you notice on Wednesday that the coming Friday is very short on reservations or appointments. You simply put up a special discount page on your website (that will take about two minutes). Send out a quick e-mail to your e-mail list of customers driving them to the web page (another two minutes) and watch the reservations and appointments pour in. You could never depend on a webmaster to react for you this quickly, which means you would not be able to fill up that slow Friday.

You don't have to know that much to do what I just described. However, it's up to you to manage your website operations. Otherwise, you can pay a fortune to a designer and nobody will come to your site. It's time to get over the excuses that you can't learn website stuff or "I don't have the time." Getting a little tutoring on this can most likely make you a fortune in less time than doing the things you have been doing.

Even though this isn't specifically about getting web pages done, the software at this link helps you organize your entire website business: http://www.promobuddy.com/cgi-bin/affiliates/clickthru.cgi?id=antion.

WHAT YOU NEED TO KNOW

 If you can get a grasp on the big picture of what is available to you on the Web and how you want to use it, you can get others to implement it for you. Being able to do simple things yourself knocks out lots of frustration, saves tons of money, and adds lightning speed to getting things done.

Getting People to Your Website

Let's talk about ways to get people to return to your website. That's a lot different than getting them there in the first place. Here are some ideas, although I don't do all of them. I could not possibly do all of these things. Different ideas will suit different people.

Discussion Boards

You've probably seen them. People can post questions, and other people visiting the site who are interested in the topic, service or marketing idea, can answer the questions or jump into the discussion.

There are moderated discussion boards and unmoderated ones. Unmoderated ones are a little more risky. They are risky because someone can get on there and start cursing, writing nasty things, or saying all kinds of crazy things. Unless deleted, it would be broadcast to all the people that stopped by. Therefore, that could be dangerous.

A moderated discussion board is controlled by you or the moderator. The questions come in to you and then you forward them to your members and filter out any ridiculous stuff. You could also change this slightly to be an "Ask the Expert" section of your site. You invite questions and then answer them as the expert.

The Internet has been notorious for offering free things, so you really have to give a lot to get the kind of money that I'm getting back. I'm always happy to answer simple questions for people, and I get e-mails by the zillions on many topics. I try to respond graciously and as fast as I can, so many of these people turn into customers or hire me.

Some web design programs like Front Page have their own instant discussion boards. You can set it up yourself right from the program. If you want an outside solution here are some possibilities:

http://www.multicity.com

http://www.vbulletin.com

http://www.GreatInternetMarketing.com/forums (This is the one I use.)

http://www.wowbb.com

http://www.thinkofit.com/webconf/forumsoft.htm

http://www.acromediainc.com/chatterbox.htm

Classified Ads

You can run classified ads. There are many free sites, and there is software that will submit them to these free sites. I'm not sure there is a big value to them because there are tons of them, and they're gone so fast. I don't know how many people see them, but that is a viable way to tell people about your site.

Some of the paid ones, like America Online, can be very good because America Online has over 30 million subscribers. CompuServe (now owned by AOL) also has many subscribers around the world. So if you have a product, you might try very inexpensive electronic classified ads to drive people to your website. I don't use any classified ads yet on other sites, but I do use them in my own publication *Great Speaking*.

I get people to visit my website with little ads in my electronic magazine and then I hit them with the strong advertising copy on the website. The little classified ad is not going to be able to sell too much, but when you get them to the website, you can put a lot more ad copy about yourself and your product. The whole idea is to get them to your website, and classified ads are one way of doing that.

Chat Rooms

You can have lively discussions going on right at your website while you're sleeping. Or you can announce your presence there at certain times and allow people to interact with you, ask questions, and generally get to know you and your expertise better.

A good idea to drive traffic to your site is to invite other website owners that do not have chat areas to use your site. They'll bring in new people that will be exposed to your site, and you can usually put ads around the chat area for them to see.

Simple chat rooms are not too difficult to install. Here are some possibilities:

http://www.tucows.com (search for chat rooms)

http://www.multicity.com (free chat and they even have instant translation chat for your global visitors)

http://www.freecenter.com/chat.html (includes a whole bunch of free chat room providers)

Streaming News

Another way to get visitors to return is to have news. There are places out there that will send news directly to your site so people can simply check your website for their news. There are many different industry news feeds. Many of these news feeds use Java Applets. Just make sure you don't junk up your important search engine pages too much with the code necessary to make these news feeds display. Some sites are:

http://www.7am.com

http://www.tickerland.com (Puts your news on other sites.)

http://www.anaconda.net

http://www.wunderground.com/about/faq/weathersticker.asp (weather)

http://www.weatherbyemail.com (weather)

What's New and Stuff

You can have a "what's new" portion of your website. A more valuable item is, "What's new in your industry?" You can have forms on your website so people can register for items or any events or "special sales" you might be holding. That gets them to come back. You might also include an ad for a new product or service on the registration form.

Once you get them there for any reason, you want to hit them again with something else to sell. It's very easy to put little links and little ads in among what people are already using from your site in order to keep your name and products in front of them all the time. For instance, when you register for the TeleSeminars at my site, I'll probably have ads for the next 10 seminars coming up. The idea is to have something else to sell them once you get them coming to your site.

Surveys and Polls

You can do surveys and polls as a means for getting people to come to your site. Then you can spit the survey results back to them because people like to know the final results as a benchmark.

You can also do live polling with this type of software. People like to come back and see the current results appearing on your site as more and more people respond to the poll.

Survey and Polling Resources

For polling try:

http://www.infopoll.com

http://www.7am.com/polling/index.htm

For surveys try:

http://www.perseus.com

http://www.zoomerang.com

http://www.surveymonkey.com

http://www.willmaster.com

Or type "survey software" or "polling software" into any major search engine, and you'll have lots of choices.

In the travel industry, the reservations link up various airlines, rental car companies, and hotels all over the world. One of the strategies the rental car companies use is having daily updates of your horoscope and the soap operas on their websites.

Free Horoscope Content

Here's a couple sites that have free horoscope content for your website:

http://www.luckyfortune.com/webmasters.html

http://free.horoscope.com

There are many ways to have recurring information to get people to return. These sites would not hit my target market, but for many of you they might. For example, if you had a sporting goods store, you could have football and basketball scores and all types of sporting news fed directly to your website. You don't even have to update the feeds once you put them on your site. They update themselves. Get a webmaster to find the feeds and put them on your site for you.

Contests and Sweepstakes

A contest requires that people compete in some fashion, and a sweepstakes is similar to drawing a winner out of a hat. Contests and sweepstakes are great, but you have to be careful. You can easily violate contest laws. There are sites on the Internet if you want to know all the ins and outs about this. Just type in "contest laws" and a bunch of sites will come up that will tell you what cautions to take. Make sure you get the proper legal advice if you do this. You need to be extra careful with sweepstakes and similar programs. As long as there is no money involved, you might be okay. For instance, I did the Valentine's Day "Tom Is Single" contest in my electronic magazine, and people are still talking about it.

In the contest, you had to count the number of times the phrase "Tom Is Single" was in the *Great Speaking* e-zine. The winners won a free copy of *Wake 'em Up Business Presentations,* which I was promoting and the losers won a date with me. It was hysterical. The contest was designed to push people to the website and then they won a book and one of my other products. I gave away five books, but no one accepted the date option. It cost me 10 bucks plus shipping to do a major promotion that people are still discussing. So these are all ways you can do this electronically with very low cost.

TIP: Don't accidentally run a lottery. When you have a prize involved as well as consideration (usually money) and winning is a matter of chance, you are running a lottery, which is pretty much illegal without the proper government authorization.

TIP: Give the grand prize to the winner. E-mail everyone else who participated that they were second place winners and can thus get a substantial discount on the purchase of the same prize. What a deal!

Here is a good article on contest law: http://www.howstuffworks.com /question541.htm.

Here's a great contest site: http://www.mlaw.org/wwl.

Be careful where you post your contest. If a large contest site gets hold of your offer, you may get thousands of entrants that try every single contest they can find. This is traffic, but it is not the kind of traffic you want.

Frequent Visitor/Buyer Plans

You could start a program just like the airlines and lots of other companies. Even Radio Shack has a Frequent Battery Buyer's Plan to encourage you to buy all your batteries at Radio Shack: They give you some free batteries after you buy so many.

Signature Files

The next topic is signature files, which are found at the end of your e-mails. I have a bunch of different ones. Check your particular e-mail program.

I use different signatures depending on to whom I'm responding. If I'm responding to a speaker I don't know, I'll send one with "free electronic magazine," and "buy my speaker video," and my name and other information. If I'm responding to a client, the signature will be different. Therefore, I have a bunch of different ones so that I can just click on the one I prefer, and it pops right in at the bottom.

You can't make it so massive that you say, "Hi, Joe," and then there is three feet worth of signature, but it is a legitimate way to have an advertisement on every e-mail you send.

Sample 1: This sig file is appended to e-mails going to people that I know are not on my e-zine list:

```
Get your FREE subscription to "GREAT SPEAKING"
Visit http://www.antion.com/ezinesubscribe.htm

New Speaker Video http://www.antion.com/speakervideo.htm
Tom Antion Communications http://www.antion.com
A Rare Mix of Business and Entertainment
Keynotes/Seminars and Advanced Presentation Skills
```

```
Voice 1-757-431-1366 Fax 1-757-431-2050
Box 9558, Virginia Beach, Virginia 23450
Trade Links with Us
http://www.antion.com/linktradeinstructions.htm
```

Sample 2: This sig file is appended to e-mails going to people who I know are on my e-zine list. The top of it promotes something that I haven't sold them yet:

```
New Speaker Video http://www.antion.com/speakervideo.htm
Tom Antion Communications http://www.antion.com
A Rare Mix of Business and Entertainment
Keynotes/Seminars and Advanced Presentation Skills
Voice 1-757-431-1366 Fax 1-757-431-2050
Box 9558, Virginia Beach, Virginia 23450
Trade Links with Us
http://www.antion.com/linktradeinstructions.htm
```

Sample 3: Here's an example of my sig file capability used to send routine correspondence without retyping everything. In this case, all I have to do is change the person's name and adjust the date. This saves me a tremendous amount of time and is another step in automating my business:

```
Dear Sally:

Your Butt Camp CD will ship Monday, July 31. You
will have plenty to do once you see all the
electronic marketing possibilities available to
you at no cost or very low cost.
   Because you bought the CD, if you want to see
the live seminar, you get $100 off the current
price at the time you register. You must call or
e-mail to get the discount. Here are the upcoming
dates:
```

Signature File Resources

http://www.marketingterms.com/dictionary/sig_file

http://www.vipgo.net/ab/network-marketing-mail.html

http://www.theallineed.com/webmasters/webmasters-039.htm

http://www.tech4speakers.com/marketing/yoursignature.htm

http://www.chris.com/ascii/index.html

Some people add ASCII artwork to their sig files if it matches their business purpose. Be careful and don't overdo this.

For a source of funny or profound sayings at the bottom of an e-mail: http://www.siglets.com.

Bookmarks

You should encourage visitors to your site to bookmark your page. Text could be placed on all your important pages reminding the visitor to do so. "Please bookmark this page now."

This is also known as adding your site to their "favorite" list. In both Internet Explorer and Netscape you can advise them to hold the control key down (Ctrl) and hit the "D" key. For Macintosh it's Cmd plus "D." In most cases, this will automatically bookmark your page in their favorite sites list.

You can also use a pop-up box to remind people to bookmark your site. For pop-ups, I use the software at http://www.amazingpopups.com/power.

Autoresponders

Another thing to use is called an autoresponder (infobot or e-mail on demand). Many of the places that host your website give them to you for free. I get 30 of them for free just from my hosting service. Here's what they do for you: If I told you to send an e-mail to mailto:sponsor@antion.com, you're going to get an e-mail back from my website giving you the details on advertising in *Great Speaking* e-zine. So this is an extremely valuable time and money saving tool. It only takes a few minutes to set up once you know how to do it.

These are the ways you can automate your promotions and keep them selling for you. You will not be sitting here in front of the computer all day long. Autoresponders are a great way to get the information out to your market.

If you have the shopping cart system http://www.KickStartCart.com, you have unlimited regular autoresponders and sequential autoresponders (advanced autoresponders that follow up with multiple e-mails).

It's a good idea to have a copy of the original e-mail sent to the autoresponder forwarded to you. Some people don't understand exactly what to expect from the autoresponder, and they put a message inside the body of the e-mail. If you don't at least take a peek at these e-mails, you may accidentally ignore a question from a prospective customer.

Autoresponders can handle many more e-mails than you could ever process manually. Also, you can send a 10-page e-mail just as fast and easily as sending a two-paragraph e-mail.

Don't forget to let people know that you won't sell or give away their e-mail address to other parties. It's okay for you to send them a follow-up e-mail, but people really don't want to be spammed because they took you up on your offer for information.

When writing the messages that will go out on your autoresponder, try to write them in such a way that you don't have to change them too often. If you do this, the autoresponder will work quietly behind the scenes with little or no attention.

The first place I would check for autoresponders is the place that hosts your website. Many give them to you, and though you don't even know about it, you may have them already. If not, just type in "autoresponder" in any search engine or see the links listed in the next section. They are often cheap, like a dollar a month, but most of the time they're just given away free. For example, the http://www.KickStartCart.com shopping system has them included for free.

How to Pick an Autoresponder

✓ They must be automatic. The person sending an e-mail to the autoresponder should not have to type anything specific into the subject or body of the e-mail for it to work. Many people would misspell whatever they were supposed to type, and the autoresponder would not work.
✓ You should be allowed an unlimited number of hits to the autoresponder.
✓ You should be able to make an unlimited number of changes to your return message, and you should be able to do this yourself any time, day or night.
✓ You should be able to capture the e-mail address of the person requesting permission.

TIP: This doesn't mean you have the right to put their name on your e-newsletter list.

Sequential Autoresponders

Inexpensive autoresponders are available that also send follow-up messages at intervals you specify. I just did a free seven-day minicourse on electronic marketing. The person would send an e-mail to mailto:MiniCourse@aweber.com and immediately get the first lesson and then another lesson each day for the next six days. I had 1,200 people sign up for this course in about five days, and they spent about $7,000 the first week after determining I knew what I was talking about when it comes to e-marketing. One month of this service was only $19.95, and it goes as low as $14.95 if you buy a whole year. You can check it out at http://www.aweber.com/?23558.

The way I do it now is totally integrated with my shopping system, and the autoresponders can be tied to a specific purchase, which is an extremely powerful sales and customer service technique. The way it works is that when customers buy products, they automatically subscribe themselves to follow-up e-mails. The e-mails can be used to give additional tips on how to use what they bought, or to sell them more products. Customers can unsubscribe themselves anytime if they don't feel your e-mails are of value.

Companies That Have Sequential Autoresponders

http://www.KickStartCart.com

http://www.aweber.com/?23558

http://www.getresponse.com

http://www.biz-e-bot.com

Electronic Magazines

An electronic magazine is a simple e-mail. It's called an e-zine or electronic magazine, or some people call them an electronic newsletter. I call mine a magazine because occasionally I'll drop in what's happening in the industry. Most of the time it's in a "how to" format: "how to be a great speaker," "how to market yourself," and so on. It also gives you some free speaker humor.

An electronic magazine is easy to create using the simplest word processor. It takes no graphic design. I'm able, if I'm in a hurry, to slam one together and send it out to over 90,000 people around the world, all in one day. Sometimes I use excerpts from my book, so I don't have to write new articles for each issue.

I've also used articles from big-name speakers, as well as some lesser known ones who happened to have good information, so that's why people stick with it. This is what I call *push marketing*. I suck them into the website, or get people to sign up after they see me speak. Once I get them signed up on this electronic magazine, I can market to them repeatedly for free. I put a sign-up button on every important page of my website, so just about wherever you go on the website, you can sign up for my electronic magazine.

It's very cost effective to do an e-zine. What you do is find your target market and your regular customers. It's a good way to keep them updated and it costs virtually nothing. You have to be careful not to spam people because some will get irate. I've had some people turn into total monsters because of an e-mail that slipped up and went to them by mistake. You need to be careful, but the benefits are just outrageous. In normal face-to-face sales, it is five, six, or seven contacts before you make a sale. On the Internet, it can be 20 to 30. E-zines let you make these contacts extremely inexpensively.

I always recommend the following site: http://www.e-zinez.com. If you read the entire site and follow all its links, it will give you everything you need to know, and it will even e-mail you a template.

There's nothing fancy in these e-zines. The only creative part is picking what kind of divider bar you want between sections. You either get a template from http://www.e-zinez.com, or you can take any one of my back issues at http://www.antion.com/ezinebackissues.htm. Just erase the template information and put in your material, and you can have your own e-zine today. I can tell you clearly, it's made me a fortune in the past six years. In the first week, it brought in $3,000 in consulting clients and a $2,000 barter deal on my next book cover. Just yesterday, I had a literary agent call me, and the e-zine was responsible for landing me my lucrative spokesperson contract with CBS Switchboard.com.

Many people ask me how I built my e-mail list? Was it primarily from the website, or did I do other things?

I got a jump start because I have been speaking for some time. Therefore, people see me with some frequency. Live appearances will get you quite a few subscribers if you make sure you mention it's available and collect business cards because that's what we call "opting in." They're saying, "Hey, I want to be on your list."

The best way to do this at a live event is by holding a drawing. You must tell the people that they will begin getting your e-zine unless they write "no e-mails" on their business card. If you are a good speaker and if you wait until at least halfway through your speech, you will have very few people refuse to receive your e-mails.

If you have a store, you can do some kind of fishbowl promotion where people put their business card in a fishbowl to win weekly or monthly prizes. Put a note on the fishbowl giving them the chance to write "no e-mails" if they don't want to hear from you.

We'll get into more of the e-zine stuff later. For now, I just wanted you to know that it is an excellent way to get people to return to your website.

Online Malls

I'm against them. I think they are a great idea for the organizers and a dumb idea for the merchants. The online mall people want you to think that it's like a real mall. Well, when you are in a real mall you can't snap your fingers and be in a different mall halfway around the world. In an online mall, your customer can click away in an instant. I wouldn't waste my time or money.

Search Engines

Most of the search engines are begging you to put a link to their site from yours. Some even give you the code to put the actual search box on your site.

I'm not a big fan of this, but you could have people coming to your site more often if they knew they could also do some searching while they are there.

Your Own Search Engine

I am in favor of providing your own search engine so people can search your site quickly. Indirectly this will make them want to return because they know they can find what they want quickly. Some of the web authoring programs will do this for you, or you can find free or paid programs to help you for example:

http://intra.whatuseek.com

http://www.searchbutton.com

http://www.searchtools.com

http://www.atomz.com

http://www.freefind.com

Other Cool Stuff

There are all kinds of useful and fun things you can put on your website to get people to return. I've provided links to quite a few of them earlier. You can put links to interactive maps, phonebooks, and all types of online conversion programs (metric, time, etc.). Just make sure you don't distract people too much from the business of buying your products. You could even use your e-zine and website to promote a big party in your chat room.

Viral Marketing

Viral marketing is a science in itself. It's a method where other people pass on your message to someone else who passes it on to someone else, who passes it on to someone else, and so on. Lots of people have gotten rich with viral marketing and even more have tried and failed.

Viral marketing can be as simple as giving out a free e-book about your topic that you allow other people to give away or sell, or it could be as complex and big as Hotmail that began as a small, free e-mail service that eventually sold for many, many millions of dollars.

Jimmy D. Brown is a super expert at viral marketing and has a great e-book on the subject. Check it out at: http://profitavenue.com/x.php?adminid=52&id =2592&pid=99.

Here are some other interesting sites where people have created things that are passed around in a viral fashion. Warning: Some are really offbeat, risqué, ridiculous, and downright disgusting:

http://www.viralmeister.com

http://www.viralbank.com

Checklist of Electronic Ways to Get People to My Website

- ✓ Discussion boards
- ✓ Ask the expert
- ✓ Electronic classified ads
- ✓ Chat rooms
- ✓ News
- ✓ What's new
- ✓ What's new in the industry
- ✓ Surveys
- ✓ Contests and sweepstakes
- ✓ Frequent visitor/buyer plans
- ✓ Horoscopes and other content
- ✓ Signature files
- ✓ Bookmarks
- ✓ Regular autoresponders
- ✓ Sequential autoresponders
- ✓ Electronic magazines
- ✓ Malls
- ✓ Search engines
- ✓ Your own search engine
- ✓ Other cool stuff
- ✓ Viral marketing

WHAT YOU NEED TO KNOW

There are a tremendous number of online tools that you can use to drive people to your website over and over, which hopefully turns them into loyalists who eventually buy from you. You could pick several items from the above list and devote a week each to implement the idea. Don't try to do everything at once. Your traffic will steadily increase if you are diligent in implementing and using these ideas.

Offline Marketing

We are going to discuss offline marketing of your website, which means all the things that really aren't electronic. They're going to sound like no-brainers, but I want you to go back and look through everything about your business and see if it is pushing people to your website.

Business Cards and Stationery

The first thing would be your business cards. Is your website listed? Is it readable? Does it have letters like the letter "L" that when printed in the lower case "l" looks like the number 1? Is the print large enough to be easily seen? Also check your stationery and make sure your website is mentioned there, too.

Voice Mail

What about your voice mail messages? If it's voice mail, then somebody is calling you that wants something. . . maybe information on your services. And they usually want it NOW because that's the way the world is. So if you don't mention your website, they're going to wait and get frustrated, or they're going to call your competitor. So go to your voice mail message and make sure your website is mentioned on it. Also, spell it out so it's very clear. I say, "antion.com, THAT'S A, N, T, I, O, N, DOT COM."

Something like that will make you money because it's out there advertising for you and letting the people get the information they need while you're busy speaking or simply sunbathing on the beach.

I also mention my website on virtually every phone call into my office. When I get done talking I say, "Don't forget, go to the website and check out our free stuff. I have lots of free articles for speakers, lots of speaker humor, and all kinds of good stuff on the website." Of course, when I get them to the website, they are going to be exposed to many things that they can buy from me.

Stickers and Labels

I do a lot with stickers and labels. They are an inexpensive way to promote your sites and jazz up your packaging. Everything that goes out of my office has a sticker on it with my website address. So whenever I am shipping a product, I have the website sticker on it. If I'm paying a bill, I send my bill with a sticker on it. I figure they get plenty of my money, so maybe somebody will trip on my website and decide to buy something.

My shipping label has my photo on it. I usually do a cute thing and put a little balloon and say, "Hi" to you personally. It has the website address on it, too.

Promote at Programs and on Handouts

If you use speaking or special events to promote your business, make sure your handout materials drive people to your website. These programs are used frequently by attorneys, CPAs, realtors, and even plumbers to prove their expertise and gain clients. Just about any kind of store can promote a special event. Toy stores could have a Frisbee expert give lessons, pet stores could give free dog training classes, and so on.

Signage

You could have magnetic signs if you have promotional vehicles. You could also have a custom-made license plate frame with your website on it:

http://www.autoplates.com

http://www.traffictalk.com

I've even thought about doing a billboard or bartering with the theaters to get a slide up while waiting to watch the movie. Wouldn't it be cool to have your name pop up? "Visit antion.com for free popcorn."

Print Ads and Packaging

Your print advertisements, products, and product packaging should all have your website referenced. When you look at my books and tapes, the website is on there. You want the website on your products because phone numbers change. However, if you have your own domain name, they can always find you anywhere you move in the world, so you don't have to worry about updating your phone numbers, and so on. If they can go to the website, they'll find you.

Advertising Specialties

Mouse pads, mugs, pens, monitor screen cleaners, and all kinds of things can be printed with your web address listed and given away. I'm not sure how well these items pay off. If I were to use this method, I'd want something that was designed to be near a computer, so when someone looked at it, they could immediately go to the web and visit my site. I get lots of my stuff at http://www.stamonline.com.

Free Publicity

You can get tons of website visitors by writing articles for trade publications and doing radio and TV interviews. Don't overlook this very powerful way to get people to visit your site. I coauthored a book on this very subject with

Joan Stewart (*The Publicity Hound.*) You can check it out at http://www
.antion.com/ebooks.htm. The title of the book is *How to Be a Kick Butt Publicity Hound* (Lanham, MD: Anchor, 2001).

Checklist of Offline Ways to Get People to Your Website

- ✓ Business cards and stationery
- ✓ Voice mail
- ✓ Mention website on every phone call
- ✓ Stickers and labels
- ✓ Promote at programs and on handouts
- ✓ Signage
- ✓ Print ads and packaging
- ✓ Advertising specialties
- ✓ Free publicity

WHAT YOU NEED TO KNOW

    Put your website address on traditional forms of promotion that
have nothing to do with the web.

Website Reference Materials

You're going to learn a ton from any reference you buy if you're a beginner.
One excellent book is *101 Ways to Promote Your Website* by Susan Sweeny
(Gulf Breeze, FL: Maximum Press, 2000). Others are *Marketing with
Newsletters* by Elaine Floyd (St. Louis, MO: Newsletter Resources, 1997)
and *Increase Your Web Traffic in a Weekend* by William Stanek (Rocklin, CA:
Prima, 1998). This one gets a little technical because it talks about the log
files and learning how to read them.

Here's a good starter book. It's a little bit old, but it is still worth reading:
Getting Hits by Don Sellers (Berkeley, CA: Peachpit Press, 1997). This is the
book that started me thinking, "Hey, I better get busy and promote this website,
or it's going to just sit there for another two years." One book that I already
mentioned is called *Web Pages That Suck* by Vincent Flanders and Michael
Willis (San Francisco: Sybex,1996). These guys are great at hype. The information is good, and it shows you many of the mistakes even big companies make.
For example, they show you many of the frame-constructed web pages that are
gorgeous, but they take 30 or 40 seconds to load and people just won't wait.

One of my favorites is called *The Non-Designers Web Book* by Robin
Williams . . . not the comedian . . . and John Tollett (Berkeley, CA: Peachpit
Press, 2000). It's a full-color book. It talks to you about the colors you can
best use on websites. It talks to you about when to use JPEG photos and GIFs

and lots of different details about your hyperlinks and where they should go. A tremendous book—I strongly recommend this one.

Two others are *Making More Money on the Internet* by Alfred and Emily Glossbrenner (New York: McGraw-Hill, 1996) and *How to Build a Successful International Website* by Mark Bishop (Albany, NY: Coriolis Group, 1998). You've probably never considered many of the details included in this reference. I think globally in my presentations, but I must learn to think globally on my website since I get product sales from India, Australia, New Zealand, Brazil, and about 35 other countries.

Oh, another one of my favorites is called *Poor Richard's Internet Marketing and Promotion* by Peter Kent and Tara Calishain (Lakewood, CO: Top Floor, 1999). It was such a surprise to me because it has a whole section on publicity and reaching the media.

Those are the resources I have handy, along with the Internet marketing course by Corey Rudl that I sell on my site: http://www.marketingtips.com /t.cgi/12273. In fact, this is the course where I started learning how to make large sums of money on the Internet. Those of you who know me, know I don't recommend anything that is not great.

Although I will discuss e-mail marketing in a different section, Corey's new e-mail marketing book is great, too: http://www.marketingtips.com /emailsecrets/t.cgi/12273.

Here are some web guys who are competent and have worked for me: jason@saeler.com and harold@haroldhingle.com.

Don't forget. Think globally. You don't have to be located anywhere near people who can help you in this business. We're all around the world. First, realize that none of these people are perfect, but the two guys I just mentioned do a very good job. The work they've done for me has meant a lot of money both earned and saved.

Janet Hall is a long time associate of mine, and she can tutor you on using Microsoft Front Page: janet@overhall.com.

A good site that teaches you how to make your website user friendly is http://www.useit.com.

White Paper: Tom Antion's One-Page Website Method

I have identified a method to create inexpensive websites that have an extremely high and ongoing return on investment. The method involves making one-page websites on tightly niched topics and selling digital products (e-books mostly) from these sites. You need little or no knowledge about the chosen topics.

> **TIP:** This method is absolutely *not* meant to replace my method for creating deep, content-rich sites to enhance your existing product

line. It is simply a credible way to get a regular profit coming in from the Internet.

Here is the exact method I use for creating one-page sites and some figures on my first three sites: http://www.Wedding-Toasts.org, http://www.Wedding-Speeches.org, and http://www.InstantEulogy.com.

The Wedding Toast e-book has taken in approximately $26,790 in 2003 and $31,544.55 in 2004. The Wedding Speech e-book took in $25,705 in 2003 and $28,213 in 2004, and Instant Eulogies took in $32,165.40 in 2003 and $43,247 in 2004. The $9.95 add-on product I developed for the Instant Eulogy e-book is called "101 Nice Things to Do After the Funeral." It took only eight hours work to create and took in $2,219 in 2004. These figures are what actually went through the shopping cart. Several more thousand dollars came in by fax and phone orders for all these products.

This amount of money came in with very little effort or attention paid to these projects.

In this section, I will cover the following steps:

- Topic selection
- E-book creation
- Site creation
- Dedicated hosting
- Pay-per-click search engines
- E-book delivery

Topic Selection

You can certainly pick topics that interest you, but that is not necessary for this idea to work. The important thing about the topic you select is that the numbers work out.

For the least risk and highest return you need to pick a topic that has a very high number of searches and a very low cost per click if you were to bid on the keyword or keyword phrase associated with the topic at a pay-per-click search engine.

If you are willing to bid high enough at the most popular pay-per-click search engine, Overture.com, you will show up at the top of Yahoo, Alta Vista (while it still lasts), Lycos, and many other popular search engines. This is generally called a *sponsored listing*.

It is important to stay in the top bids so that your listing shows up on all these other popular sites. Also, when you use pay-per-click search engines, you have little or no delay before traffic is reaching your site. Using the free submission area at regular search engines could take months to get your page indexed, if they ever get around to indexing it at all, and there is no guarantee of a high ranking.

To determine the popularity and cost per click for keywords I use an Internet tool called the keyword selector tool at the same http://www.Overture.com mentioned earlier.

I play with the tool until I can find words that have 20,000 and up searches and cost per click of less than 15 cents.

Skill and equipment needed to do this: nothing much but a computer, Internet connection, and a little time.

E-book Creation

Here's what I did on my http://www.Wedding-Toasts.org site. I put out a bid on http://www.Elance.com for two e-books. One for wedding toasts and one for wedding speeches. In the bid I also said I wanted two sales letters. In two days I had a contract with a writer from Ohio who had been in 12 weddings in the past two years. Total cost for two books and two sales letters. . . . Are you sitting down? . . . only $550.

My contract with the writer required the documents to be created in Microsoft Word because I knew I would want to put in my own material and tweak everything before converting it to the downloadable format I use. I spent about five hours adding material and formatting the toast book nicely for conversion to Adobe PDF for distribution. I spent another couple hours improving the sales letter. My college intern finished off the wedding speech book.

I won't bother putting the exact figures here because they will be obsolete tomorrow, but the toast book by itself brought in about $2,000 the first month with a profit, after considering the pay-per-click costs, of about $1,000 (i.e., the entire project was paid for, and made a profit, in the first month and actually self-financed the pay-per-click costs because they were only incurred as sales came in).

So far I've identified another 12 topics that we are developing, and soon I'll probably put several staff people on this full-time shooting for about $1,000 per month profit on each new project.

Skill and equipment needed for the previous section: You probably will want to get the Adobe Acrobat program to create PDF files so that you can make changes to the Microsoft Word document before you convert it. With a little help, you'll learn what you need to know about converting to PDF in about 20 minutes.

Site Creation

Knowing how to make a web page yourself cuts out virtually all the site creation costs. This simple skill is invaluable. If you have enough need, doing it yourself will save you a fortune. I had an intern that made me 200 websites in two weeks using the technique that follows. I could have easily done it myself, but my time is now better spent on other things.

TEMPLATES

If you visit http://www.Wedding-Toasts.org you will see a lovely wedding theme with the entire site shaped like a heart. This template cost me $15. I searched the web for "FrontPage Templates" and then searched the sites that came up for "Wedding Theme."

HEADER SITES

This little program makes the entire deal cheaper yet. I bought Armand Morin's header generator: http://www.ecovergenerator.com/x.cgi?adminid =814&id=22663&pid=2160. Figure 1.7 shows a sample. We used it to create beautiful headers for the top of each of the other 300 websites we are developing (Figure 1.7). We put the header at the top of the page. Then we put a box underneath it to hold the sales letter, and in less than five minutes a new money machine is born.

Skill and equipment needed for the previous section: You will need either someone to do this for you or the willingness to learn the basics of website creation. What is being proposed here is the lowest possible level of expertise.

Dedicated Hosting

My first one-page site is hosted on a high-speed server, which is overkill and costs about $24 per month. When you get several websites going, it's much more cost effective to get a "dedicated server," which means it only has your websites on it, and you pay a monthly fee. This does not mean you keep it in your basement. The machine is housed in a regular hosting company and maintained by them. They do the data backups, they provide the battery backup and generators to keep the thing running if the electricity goes out, and so on. It costs me $150 per month for up to 200 websites.

I'll probably never get all 200 sites on that server because I have made myself a personal rule: When the income from sites on that server exceeds $10,000 per month, I will get another dedicated server somewhere else. This is so that all the income does not stop in case of a catastrophic failure on the first server.

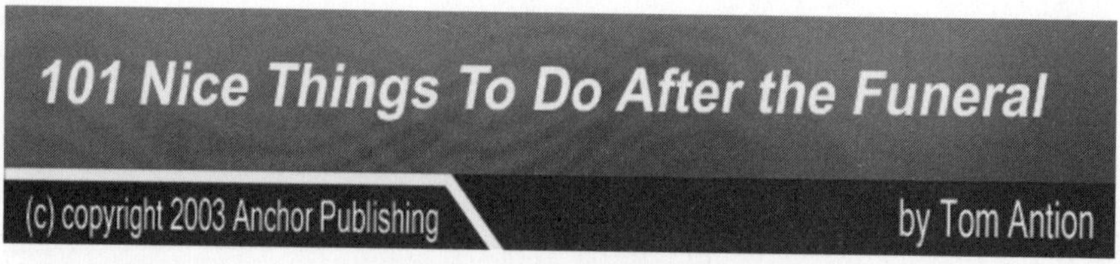

101 Nice Things To Do After the Funeral

(c) copyright 2003 Anchor Publishing   by Tom Antion

Figure 1.7   Example of a Header

Skill and equipment needed for the previous section: You will need the ability to follow directions. Do not get a server unless it has a no-brainer interface. Many companies expect that a person getting a dedicated server is a webmaster and technically capable of doing all the complex functions. Do not use this type of company unless you have such a person available to you! Make sure your host company includes training or get someone who knows what they are doing to run the server for you.

You could e-mail mailto:jason@saeler.com for a quote.

Pay-per-Click Search Engines

There are over 600 pay-per-click search engines, but at the time of this writing only two dominate: Overture and Google.

I suggest you don't waste your time on too many of the others because most ask for a deposit to be used against your clicks, but many of them are so small they will never deliver all the clicks. One exception you could test out is http://www.Business.com. They have a pay-per-click program that is run a little differently than either Google or Overture and they have quite a bit of traffic.

> **TIP:** Google does not allow pop-up boxes, so I make a separate sales page for them that doesn't have any pop-up boxes.

Another way to circumvent their "no pop-up boxes on a landing page rule" is to split your sales letter into two pages. The first page you drive them to from Google is the first part of your sales letter. You then entice them to the second page of your letter with some curiosity technique like "Click here to see the three biggest mistakes people make while giving wedding toasts." When they click on that link and go to the second page of your sales letter you can have a pop-up box on that second page.

E-Book Delivery

You can't forget this very important part of the deal. You must be able to deliver the e-book in real time. Much of the fascination with e-books is the "immediate gratification factor." You will lose most of your sales with this kind of thinking, and your costs to drive traffic will most likely exceed your sales, making this a losing proposition.

What I'm talking about here is selling electrons. The customer decides to buy your e-book from your good sales copy. He or she purchases it through your automated shopping system, downloads it, and the money automatically goes into your checking account. You have no printing, no shipping, and no postage.

If you are not already set up for e-commerce with digital delivery, you will have to make this happen. The nice thing about it though is that now you can run an infinite number of websites off of one e-commerce system. The more sites you add, the cheaper your costs are per site, and you can still run your entire store, if you have one, off the same system.

Skill and equipment needed for the previous section: minimal skill in learning how to add products to your website and shopping system. Make sure your shopping system includes training. http://www.KickStartCart.com gives you an extensive audio training orientation on how to set it up and also how to use the advanced sales strategies to sell more to the same number of visitors.

Break Even with This Method and You've Got a Winner

Some of my students have been discouraged because they didn't get a wildly successful winner on the first try using only pay-per-click methods. I disagree with them. If they can get the book to break even on pay-per-click search engines, they can then take further steps to make the book profitable.

Don't get lazy. Once you create this intellectual property you can explore many other ways to sell it and make it profitable.

These additional revenue ideas include:

Find affiliates to sell the e-book for you on their websites. You give them 50 percent of the money, but you only pay if they sell one, so your costs are fixed at 50 percent.

Join related affiliate programs and add affiliate links in your e-book. Then when someone clicks on one of the links in your book and buys a related product from someone else, you get a commission.

Consider printing your book or putting it on CD and selling it through regular bookstores and specialty stores.

One other thing you can do is use the book as a free bonus when you are trying to sell another product.

Consider giving the e-book away for free to create demand for your other products.

Good luck and contact me if you have questions about making one-page websites happen for you.

eBay

Another way to make money quickly is with eBay, the famous auction site. There are many auction sites, but eBay has the most action.

There are also plenty of resources to teach you how to do this. You can either sell your own products on the site, or yor can join their affiliate program, which is very generous and pays you for sending them auction bidders.

Here is a great DVD on learning how to sell on eBay: http://www.auction-secrets.com/ebaytricks?t2id=16270912.

Here is a collection of e-books on eBay selling: http://hop.clickbank .net/?powertips/vnotions.

Wow! We really covered quite a bit so far. I hope by now you are excited about all the things you can do to improve your website so you can beat your competition. We covered all the basics of domain names, website creation, web hosting, the importance and use of keywords, search engine and directory strategies, pay-per-click search engines, website optimization and graphics, link strategies, getting traffic, one-page websites, and plenty of references.

Now we're getting to my favorite part. In the next chapter, we are going to discuss all the powerful techniques that make your website sell.

The Website Sales Process

Things are different on the web. Now, we are going to get into the sales process. Before my Internet operation really took off, I paid $640 an hour for Corey Rudl, probably the most successful small business marketer on the Internet, to critique me. When I train small business owners, I don't hold their hands. If you want to be at the top, you have to identify your weaknesses and have a thick skin. You have to be willing to say, "Yes, I'm messing that up and if I want to be great, I have got to fix that particular part of my sales process." So yes, getting skewered by Corey hurt a little bit because I did have a good site. It was cranking money and doing well, but I wanted it to go higher. That's why I spent $640 an hour and why I listened and made the changes he suggested.

There are two types of things you can sell:

1. Small ticket ($20 or less) and
2. Big ticket. My definition of big ticket is anything more than $20, however, I'm not going to write as much ad copy for a $30 product as I am for a $300 product. So, we do have a range to deal with.

If your claim to fame is a $20 book or a $12 piggy bank, go ahead and put it anywhere on your website where you think it will sell.

The bulk of this chapter is going to concentrate on the overall sales process and psychology mostly for big ticket items, and those systems of products that cost way more than $20.

Case Study: Let's Fix Up Tom's Site

The first thing I had to fix was the extremely "busy looking" home page. Over two years, I kept adding stuff to the point where a visitor would be very confused. I was too close to it to see the problem. I had to get someone else to point that out to me. As a result, I took nine buttons off my home page.

When you go there now, it has a "home" button and then it says, "Need a Speaker" or "Be a Speaker." You make a choice. Which is it? It cuts out a lot of the confusion. I took all the banners off, too.

Actually, there is another choice that allows people to sign up for my electronic magazine. But the main choices are to either "Be a Speaker" or "Need a Speaker."

By reducing the choices to "Need a Speaker" or "Be a Speaker," I separated the two main types of clientele I have. The concept here is to make it simple for my clientele to go where they want. I also want to have different types of people follow different paths through my site. I don't want to burden the person wanting to hire a speaker with all the resources I have for people who want to be a great speaker. This would simply confuse them and waste their time, which would not reflect well on me.

Simple Navigation

Navigation on your site can be text links, buttons, or other graphics. You must keep your navigation simple and consistent.

If you are a bank, you might have navigation that allows the visitor to pick from, "New Accounts," Home Mortgages, and maybe "Certificates of Deposit." I don't know what a bank would have because I'm not a banker. That's where surveying your clientele comes in. Let your customers help you pick the areas that should be on your website.

A health club might have "New Members," "Personal Training," and "Equipment and Accessories." Just keep it simple so people don't feel confused because when they feel confused, they leave.

Color Scheme

Another important thing is the color scheme for your site. I fought changing it for years since it was so cool looking. My website matched my material sent to meeting planners. I had a red, black, and white theme. Corey said, "Man, you're just screaming off the computer screen that you're trying to sell something."

He said one of the main things you want to do is make people comfortable at your site. The colors that make people comfortable, are the colors they are used to seeing. Many people are new to this. They're scared to be on the computer in the first place. I reduced my color scheme to a gray and blue, which are used in many Microsoft programs. People are accustomed to seeing these colors, and they don't scream at you. And don't forget about using only web safe colors as mentioned in Chapter 1.

Naming Game

He said to rename some of the things I do. I used to have a product button that screamed, "I'm going to try to sell you something." I mean it was right in

Figure 2.1   Product Button

front of my face for two years. He said to change that to "speaking tools" (Figure 2.1) so that people would click on it and not feel threatened.

Selling Your Big Ticket Products

I took the word "products" out and put in the phrase "speaking tools." The main sales page for my flagship product is http://www.antion.com/speakervideo.htm. You can go there, see the picture of the product, read all the descriptions of the tapes, and decide if you want it or not.

He said most of the people who don't know me will leave the page the instant they see it's a product for sale. I found that to be true when I looked at the statistics. People were visiting the page, most likely scrolling quickly down to see the price and then immediately leaving. The big concept here is that on the web, people are accustomed to free stuff. You have to get them really excited and desperate for your product *before* they know it is for sale. The tip here is to not allow any inkling that you have a product for sale until at least three-fourths of the way down the page.

Advertorial

Unless you are selling commodity type products like cell phones where people are simply shopping for price, the key is to get people to your sales page, but to make sure they don't know it's a sales page until they have the chance to see all the benefits of the product. You make them think they are simply reading a bunch of tips or an article. This is called an *advertorial*. Give them tips and let them know what it is going to mean to them if they don't have these tips. You scare them a little bit and get them salivating for this information before you let them know that they can buy it.

I want you to see these two sales pages and look at the way the new page hides the fact that a product is for sale. Go to the first page, http://www.antion.com/speakervideo.htm, and you'll see that the instant you open the page, you know it's a product.

Now visit my new sales page, http://www.antion.com/public-speaking.htm, which is a major revamp selling the exact same product. See the difference? You already know there is a product at the end of the long copy, but try to think like a visitor who found this page in a search engine or clicked on a link from someone else's site to mine. They wouldn't have a clue that this was a product until they had already read the benefits of the product. This point is critical to your success selling big ticket products to people who don't know you.

Writing sales copy so that it doesn't look like sales copy is not easy. I structured my page to lead the reader through the benefits and scare them a little up until about three-fourths of the way down the page. Then I let them know it's a product, which they can buy.

If you look at that speaker video page, it is actually 17 pages long. The person teaching me and many top Internet marketers believe in long copy. Many people say, "Nobody is going to read that long copy." Well, the people who are interested in this service and this skill will read it and if you're going to sell a $1,300 product, the more you tell, the more you sell. So don't worry about long copy, but just don't let them know that it is a product until they are much deeper in and really want the product.

TIP: Long copy is great for sales but only if it's not boring.

Intriguing Subtitles

Another key point is that people scan pages before they read them on the net. The visitor scans the whole page first to see if the thing looks interesting enough to read. Your subtitles need to be intriguing.

Text Boxes

A very effective way to get someone to look at something is to have a table or a text box on your site or someone else's with just text and a text link in it. If you or someone else puts a testimonial in the text, you'll get a higher click-through rate. Someone is recommending that the visitor "click here" in a text fashion. It doesn't overwhelm the visitor like a gigantic graphic-oriented banner. That kind of banner simply tells them that you're trying to sell something.

Text boxes in your sales letter also work well because they set the comment apart from the regular sales copy and provide visual and intellectual interest.

Guarantees

We all love guarantees, right? We want to know that if we don't like a product we can return it. I put in a gigantic box with scrolled edges and a giant 100 percent money-back guarantee. I even signed it personally. Corey said, "Get that thing the heck off of there because it screams you're selling something."

His guarantee is just as good, but it is in the text at the bottom of the long page so people aren't hit in the face with it. If they see the guarantee, they know there is a product for sale when they scan. So they leave.

The web is not like a printed advertisement or brochure. In print that guarantee is important. However, on the web, you want a certain comfort level for the user. You don't want to scream you're selling something. Keep it low-key until it is time to close them. This is very important.

Guarantee Terminology

You want the prospective customer to feel like there is little or no risk in ordering from you. You also want them to feel like they can return the product without arguing with anyone. Even though you hide the guarantee to begin with, when the prospect is finally exposed to it, the wording must instill confidence.

Use terms like:

Satisfaction guaranteed

Fully guaranteed

Unconditional money-back guarantee

Ironclad guarantee

No risk trial

Guarantee Length

This is the topic that usually scares marketers to death. You should give a really long guarantee. This technique will help sell proportionately far more products than it will ever stimulate in returns (as long as your product isn't a piece of garbage). Quite simply, the stronger the guarantee, the more sales you'll make.

Long guarantees take the pressure off the purchaser. He or she feels like there is no hurry to evaluate the product immediately. The long guarantee gives customers plenty of time before the return rights are lost. This reduces their risk and apprehension about making the purchase in the first place. In most cases, after the purchase they never return the product even if they didn't like it all that much.

Long guarantees also build confidence. The message being sent to the prospective customer is that, "Our product is so good we could give you forever to return it and you wouldn't."

TIP: Return of customer shipping charges is not customarily included in your guarantee unless you included free shipping in the first place. If so, then customers would have to pay the return shipping charges if they don't want the product after receiving it.

One other note about long guarantees: You just might be violating your credit card merchant agreement by giving a long guarantee. Most merchant accounts limit your guarantee period to three or six months. Read your agreement to find out if your merchant account provider addresses this issue.

Know the Rules before You Break Them

I took the guarantee off my Wake 'em Up Professional Speaking System. My ad copy was so good that I was attracting tire kickers who would take my consulting time, look at the system, and then never lift a finger to become a speaker when they saw how much work it is. They would then return the product and ask for their money back. I got really sick of this and took off the guarantee. Yes, guarantees create more sales, but are they "good" sales?

Guess what happened when I took off the guarantee. . . . I sell just as many and the people buying are more serious. You might want to try this to see which method gets you the most good sales.

Credibility Builders

These are elements that you can add to your site so that people feel more comfortable and secure ordering from you. You should always have the attitude that most people visiting your site don't know you personally. They are probably skeptical.

Credibility builders can include:

Product logos

Better Business Bureau logos

Website awards

Warranty and guarantee information

Contact information

Credit card logos

Secure site alert

Return and refund policy

Shipping policy

It doesn't hurt if your site looks professional and is easy to navigate.

Bonuses

Bonuses are items offered as free extras if someone purchases your main product. In many cases, the customer can keep the bonus items even if he or she returns the main product, but that's not a rule unless you advertise it that way to prospective customers. One obvious value of bonus items is that they increase the perceived value of your offer.

Offering to let prospective customers keep bonuses even if they return the main product really makes them feel like they are in a good position. They feel they can shell out some money (only temporarily) just to get the free bonuses and then return the product. A certain percentage of your prospective customers will do this.

What you have to believe is that not all of the people who do this will actually return the product. They will either see it and like it, or never get around to repacking it to ship it back. Thus, there is a net gain for you. The important thing to remember is that more people will pull that wallet out to buy than would have had you not offered this incredibly good deal.

When you are offering downloadable products as the bonus, then when someone returns the main product, you won't even incur any costs other than a little administrative time.

A rule of thumb is that the bonus you include should be so valuable that you could sell it if you wanted to. In fact, many marketers use as bonuses products that they previously had for sale.

Multiple bonuses will generally get you more sales. Of course, if you use downloadable products you won't incur any more costs to include them.

Here are two more super tips on bonuses:

1. If you are selling to a corporate or organization market, a "personal" bonus will generally outsell a "corporate" oriented bonus. What this means is the person making the buying decision wants the Mont Blanc pen set that he or she will grab for free while paying for your main product with corporate or organization funds.
2. You can put testimonials on the bonuses to show how great they are.

Downloadable Products

Corey said to push electronic books (e-books) and downloadable products. It used to be that you could go to my website, put your credit card in, get a receipt back, and then I mailed you the book. Many people want instant gratification and want to download the e-book instantly. Now, you can go to my website, put your credit card in, get a receipt and download the e-book immediately. I don't have to print it or even go to the Post Office.

This is a really important thing for small business people who don't have unlimited budgets. The risk in selling or giving away informational products is incredibly low and the return on investment is incredibly high. Many times you can take the same file that is downloadable from your website and burn it on a CD and get two products for the price of one. We'll discuss this more later when we learn about e-books.

You can use these types of products to promote your other products or teach people how to use your product, which will reduce customer service calls.

Point-of-Purchase Upselling

The easiest person to sell is the person who already has his or her wallet out. That's what "upselling" or "bundling" is all about and this brief section could mean many thousands of dollars more in your pocket based on the same number of visitors you already have.

We sometimes call this section, "Do you want fries with that?" The gist of this technique is that you offer your customers something else to buy after they have chosen and committed to buying another product. This can mean an enormous amount of extra money to you!

Here's how it works. A customer sees one of your products and decides that she wants to buy it (this is the *point-of-purchase*). She clicks on your buy link. When she clicks on the link, your shopping cart system takes over and offers the customer another product or products. You have preprogrammed the cart to offer something that you think makes sense based on what the customer originally clicked on to purchase.

If you make good offers, it's almost certain some of your customers will go for the additional product(s) and you'll make another 10, 20, 30, or even 40 percent more total revenue.

The basic rule for making upsell or bundled offers is that it's much easier to get customers to go for the upsell if the additional product is (1) a special discounted deal and (2) a lower price than the original product they committed to buying.

Think of it like this. If a guy is buying a $400 suit, it's relatively easy to sell him a $25 shirt and $20 tie and an $8 pair of socks to go with it. Make it a two for one on the shirts and ties with the purchase of a suit and the upsell is almost a slam dunk.

On the other hand, if he came in for a $20 tie, it would take a very, very good salesperson to upsell him to a $400 suit.

Break the Rules for Big Money

You can upsell to a higher price product if it is a really good deal. One time I sold a $29.95 TeleSeminar and did an upsell for an 11 tape set for only $97, which was over $200 less than buying the tapes one at a time. Thirty-three percent of the people signing up for the TeleSeminar went for the $97 upsell. This made it a $3,800 promotion with only 60 people involved.

Back-End Sales (After-the-Sale Upselling)

Most marketing folks will tell you that this highly ignored area is the downfall of most people trying to sell their products and services. You must consider the lifetime value of customers when creating a marketing plan and product base. It's not the first sale that makes you a fortune, it's the continued purchases by customers over the time they can be expected to deal with you. That time length is expanded when selling on the Internet because physical proximity to your store is not important. If you had a local grocery store, you would lose customers if they relocated to another area. When selling on the Internet, your buyers could move overseas and still be loyal customers to you.

What this means to you is that you should be thinking two or three products ahead of your current product. It's almost like a chess game. To win you need to anticipate the moves of your opponent well into the future. In direct e-mail sales, you should be thinking about the products your clientele will need shortly after they buy your current product, and then what will they need next after they buy the second product. Repeating this pattern will get you the most sales.

Teasers for upcoming products can be inserted when you ship hard goods to your customers. Additional ad copy can be included in downloadable products. Follow-up autoresponders can be delivered by your shopping cart system.

Because the easiest people to sell to are the ones who have their wallet out or who have bought from you before, if you don't have anything to offer them, you are wasting this natural boost to your sales efforts. It costs you way more to get them to buy in the first place than to sell them a second, third, fourth, and fifth product. Don't let these easier sales opportunities go to waste by being a one-hit wonder when it comes to selling products.

Sales Exit Strategies

Smart Internet marketers make money coming and going . . . that is, when their visitors are coming and going. Obviously when visitors come to your site you want them to buy. Not so obviously to the new marketer is the fact that an enormous amount of money can be made from people leaving your site if you know what to do.

The beauty of many exit strategies is that people have already decided not to buy and by using these techniques you get them to change their mind.

Here are some exit strategies:

✓ *Sell-down technique:* I use this technique to offer a cheaper price when someone is leaving my sales page without purchasing. I actually call the pop-up box they get a "Pick Your Price" deal, but in actuality I have preselected three cheaper price points for them to pick from. "Almost" everyone picks the cheapest price, but some lovable souls choose from some of the higher priced options. The product they get is the same. This technique is best for digital download products like e-books because you don't really have any cost of goods sold.

You can see this technique in action at http://www.Wedding-Speeches.org. Leave the page without buying and you'll see an example of a pop-up box that consistently brings in orders.

✓ *Finance option:* This technique has meant several hundred thousand dollars to me. When people leave one of my sales letters without buying, a pop-up box is displayed that gives them a chance to finance their purchase. This technique is best suited for more expensive products you are willing to finance for the customer. To automate the entire deal including the additional payments the customer will make every month, you need a shopping cart with "recurring billing." http://www.KickStartCart.com has this.

I frequently test different selling methods for my big ticket products so I can't swear you'll see an example of the finance option when you visit and then leave the page listed next, but you might: http://www.Antion.com/public-speaking.htm.

✓ *Thank-you page selling:* A thank-you page is the page that pops up right after someone has purchased something from your shopping cart. What a great place to keep on selling! Remember, the person still has that old wallet out. You can have links on the thank-you page to your other sites or products. This is also a perfect place to put affiliate links to others who will send you a commission if your customer clicks through and buys something from them.

Good shopping cart systems let you make custom thank-you pages based on what the customer bought. This is especially great because you can customize the thank-you page links to offer your customer something complementary to what was just purchased. This is smart selling!

✓ *Coregistration:* Is a process of signing up e-zine subscribers for other publishers. The other publishers pay you for each subscriber who signs up through your site. (The opposite of this is how you can build your subscriber list fast by having other websites sign up subscribers for you. We'll see more about this in the e-zine section on "buying subscribers.")

Basically you use an exit pop-up that offers the other publisher's e-zine and you track the subscriptions using your shopping cart.

✓ *Confirmation page selling:* I don't know whether this is technically an exit strategy or not, but I don't care. It works.

When people fill out forms or sign up for your e-zine, a confirmation page usually appears that lets them know that the information they put in the form has been accepted. This is another great time to sell something.

When someone signs up for *Great Speaking* e-zine they get the confirmation page that says something like, "We've received your subscription. Your welcome letter and bonuses will be e-mailed to you shortly. In the meantime, read this special report on the business of professional speaking." This "special report" is my long advertorial type sales letter for my "Wake 'em Up Video Professional Speaking System."

The bottom line on all these exit strategies is to turn your visitors into as much money as you can. It costs you one way or the other to get visitors to your site, so you may as well get that money back and then some by selling to them coming and going.

Wholesale Memberships

One way to make sure your customers come back is to charge them a membership fee to get wholesale pricing on all your upcoming products. If customers feel they are the member of an exclusive club that gives them perks (discounts), they will be sure to come back. The membership fees give you revenues directly and pretty much guarantee sales to those customers who like you enough to sign up.

You can also make it a free membership if you don't think your clientele would go for a paid membership.

One of my students, Joan Stewart (http://www.PublicityHound.com), started a free membership sales entity called "The Kennel Club." She offers weekly discounts and specials to members of the club and has added many thousands of dollars to her bottom line by doing so.

The reason I like this idea so much is that it reminds me of first grade when the teacher would ask, "Who would like to be my special assistant today?" Of course, all the kids would be waving their hands to get picked.

When you get your website visitors and e-zine subscribers to sign up for your membership discount club, you have people basically waving their hands in the air like first graders saying, "Sell to me teacher! Sell to me!"

Paid Membership Sites

If you have a strong enough following of clients or information not easily found elsewhere, you can start a paid membership site. Your members would allow you to charge their credit cards regularly to keep their membership in force. This can be very lucrative if you can recruit lots of members.

You'll have to decide the level of security you want to have on your member area. It can go from no security where you just have hidden pages that the general public doesn't know about to full-blown automated password generation and retrieval.

This e-book gives you all the details: http://hop.clickbank.net/?powertips /paidsite.

Survey Your Market

If you really want to reduce your risk and virtually guarantee sales, survey the people in your target market and give away some big prizes. You need to test your actual market and see what "they" think. That's always more important than what "you" think.

Your actual constituents will be the best ones to tell you what they like or don't like about your website, e-zine, products, seminars, and so on. I want to give away lots of stuff to get people to answer my survey. The survey results will give me the information I need to make sure my next product is really on target and will pay me back many times over for what I gave away.

I might even pay people in my target market to go through my sales process, read my sales letter, and tell me what turned them on about it. You also want them to tell you what they "didn't" like about it. Be sure to get the real feedback from your actual constituency.

I listed these links in the last chapter, too, but they warrant another mention because of the critical information they can provide you that will mean increased sales at a very low risk.

For survey software try:

http://www.perseus.com

http://www.zoomerang.com

http://www.surveymonkey.com

Or type "survey software" or "polling software" in any major search engine and you'll have many choices.

Super Survey Your Market

I learned this technique from a great marketer named Bill Harris and it produced over $19,000 in additional sales the first month.

There are three steps to this technique: (1) an exit survey, (2) a customized autoresponder series, and (3) a direct mail piece.

The Exit Survey

A techie guy helped me create a survey form that I put in an unblockable pop-up box. I gave him the questions to include in the survey. Here's an idea of what was included:

Wait! Tom will give you an hour-long CD on Professional Speaking for FREE just for taking a few seconds to give your honest answers to the questions below:

Question 1: Are you interested in using the "Wake 'em Up Video Professional Speaking System" to learn professional level speaking techniques? Yes _____ No _____

Question 2: What is your main goal with regard to public speaking?
—It's a hobby.
—I just want to do better at my presentations at work.
—I want to promote my business.
—I want to get paid to speak locally.
—I want to get paid to speak in my own country.
—I want to get paid to speak internationally.
—I want to do my own public seminars.
—I want to speak on cruise ships.

Question 3: What brought you to our website?
—Banner
—Search engine
—Post card
—Magazine ad
—E-zine article or ad
—Friend's recommendation
—Other

Question 4: If your used a search engine, which one did you use?

Question 5: If you used a search engine what subject or keywords were you using when you found our site?

Question 6: If you did not finish reading the detailed description of our speaking program, what kept you from finishing it?

Question 7: Are you planning on acquiring the "Wake 'em Up Professional Speaking System" along with the consulting that goes with it? Yes _____ No _____ Maybe _____

Question 8: What is the main thing holding you back?
—I need more information.
—I'm concerned about stage fright.
—Cost.
—I'm skeptical.

Thank you for your help. To receive your FREE CD or audiocassette and FREE special report, please list your name and address below. (Then put places for the person to put in name, address, cassette, or CD, e-mail, etc.)

When the person submits the form, the entire results are e-mailed to me and some of the results are sent to the company below.

Customized Autoresponder

This is where the really powerful and cool part kicks in. Questions 2, and 8 have several choices that are normally put in a drop-down box. The person filling out the survey must pick from one of these choices, that is, they can't write in their own answer. I picked the choices from my experience in the field of public speaking and after having spoken to thousands of people interested in speaking.

The survey form was created so that the selection they make from questions 2 and 8 are transmitted to a company called http://www.DataBack.com. This is a very advanced autoresponder company.

I provided DataBack with prewritten responses to the selections made by the person filling out the survey.

Example: The answer to question 2 is "I want to get paid to speak locally."

DataBack plugs in the following paragraph to the text-based e-mail autoresponder message sent to the person filling out the survey:

```
Dear Joe:

I noticed you said that your main goal with speaking
was to get paid to speak locally. I know lots of
speakers who do this.
      That's really the beauty of the speaking business.
You can structure it to suit your own needs and
preferences. I've got a friend in Florida who, the last
time I checked, charges about $6,000.00 per speech, but
he won't travel. He wants to sleep in his own bed every
night and be with his wife and kids.
      In most areas of the country, there are numerous
opportunities to speak at events that are within
```

driving distance, or a short flight from where you live.

I won't kid you though. Unless you live in a fairly populated area, you'll always make more money if you are willing to stay overnight at least one night at your speaking engagement. This opens up half the United States if you happen to live here.

The "Wake 'em Up Video Professional Speaking System" you were looking at yesterday teaches you how to market your speaking services anywhere you want. If you want to stay local, you aim the specialized techniques I show you to your local market. If you want to expand to a larger market or travel, you can always refer back to the system and adjust the techniques later.

Then DataBack takes the response from question 8 and plugs in an appropriate response that I have prewritten. Let's say the person filling out the survey was concerned with cost. Here's the response that would get plugged in:

I also noticed you said the cost of the system was a problem for you. I can tell you that I'm very cost conscious, too, so I understand your concern.

Let's take a look at what you are trying to do here and see if spending for a training system like the "Wake 'em Up Video Professional Speaking System" makes sense.

If you are doing this as a hobby, I can really understand your concern. With no plans of charging to speak, the actual dollar amount invested won't get paid back.

What I'd like you to think about is the amount of money you spend on other hobbies like, golf, cars, boating, and so on. You'll find that no amount of money spent on those things can compare with learning a skill that means you can stand up anywhere and touch people emotionally and move them to action. Hey, you don't even have to pay a greens fee or anything to stand up and speak. AND on many occasions, with this skill you'll probably be the hit of the party.

If you are looking for a new profession, or you are trying to get promoted at work, or you want new clients for your business, you already know that you have to spend money to make money.

How do you think you'd feel cashing that first check for $3,000, $4,000, or $5,000 for a one-hour speech?

How much is a raise at your job worth to you? $5,000 a year, $10,000 a year, or more? Will you get the raise on your good looks, or because you are a dynamic individual who has the communication skills to move the troops to action?

How much is just one new client worth to your business $1,000, $10,000, or $100,000? What if you landed just one more every time you spoke? What if you landed three or four?

How much would a master's degree or a PhD cost you in both time and money? And as you probably know, there are tons of broke and out of work MBAs and PhDs.

The "Wake 'em Up Video Professional Speaking System" has the potential to break you in at $1,500 to $2,500 per speech even if you don't have much experience. If you've got some business experience, or a life story that's really inspirational and you are naturally dynamic you might break in at $4,000, $5,000, or even more.

The cost of your training is a drop in the bucket compared to the amounts of money and time you'd spend on getting credentials that set you up to make way less money than even a mediocre professional speaker.

Don't let a small amount of money stand in the way of your dreams.

Can you see the power of this? The person filling out the survey (my hot prospect) is getting a totally customized response to the survey he or she filled out.

DataBack holds up the e-mail until about 3:00 A.M. before it releases it to the person who filled out the survey. If the e-mail came back totally customized within a minute after the person submitted the form, it wouldn't be believable that I had returned a custom response that quickly, that is, they would know it was automated and not personal.

When people get this the next day, they swear that I sat down, read their survey, and responded personally. This is a powerful sales tool.

Direct Mail Piece

In this case, I promised the person who filled out the survey an hour-long CD or audiotape that must be sent in the mail. You could offer a download-able report if you wanted to, but I don't think it would be as effective over-all. Here's why.

It is not a totally digital world yet, or maybe it never will be. There are many people who, although they use the Internet, are not comfortable sitting in front of their computers for long periods of time. . . . Especially not to read your long sales letter.

The same people who hate sitting in front of their computers could still be totally interested in your products and services but would prefer curling up in their easy chairs to read about your stuff or even reading it before going to bed. If you stay totally digital, you will miss the sales from that type of person.

This isn't a book about direct-mail selling, but I will give you a briefing on what I send in my follow-up direct-mail envelope:

CD or audiotape

Sales letter

Lift letter (This is an endorsement letter from someone else—the bigger their name the better.)

Nice looking order form

Deadline slip

Return address envelope

Results: The first month I used this technique it brought in about $19,000 in sales with about $2,000 in costs. And the best thing is, when you think about it, all the people who bought had already decided not to buy and were leaving my site.

Online Customized Sales Letters

The next wave of customized sales tools is the customized sales letter. In this case, customers would fill out some information like their name, level of ex-perience with your product, and so on. This information would be plugged into the next page they see, which is your sales letter.

For instance: The information collected tells me "Sally" is the "Mother of the Bride" and she has "never planned a wedding reception before" and her daughter's name is "Peggy."

My sales letter, which would pop up right after Sally filled out the form, would read:

```
Sally, even though you have never planned a wedding
reception before, your daughter Peggy will think you
are an angel from heaven when you show her the tips you
learned in *Successful Wedding Receptions*.
```

Until someone comes out with a program to easily make this happen, you'll have to get a programmer to help you with this technique. This idea came from my friend and teacher John Reese who has used it very successfully.

John has a really powerful Traffic Generating course that has my highest endorsement. You can find it at http://www.MarketingSecrets.com/powertips.

Testimonials

Don't forget that people want to know that you've done good work in the past and they want confirmation that your products have helped other people. Testimonials are good to sprinkle in to your sales text. I like to spread them around because they are too easy to skip over if you put them all in one place.

Audio and video testimonials are easier than ever to put on your website because of advances in technology. They also carry much more weight and create a ton of impact compared to simple written testimonials. Visit http://www.KickStartSound.htm for a samples of really simple-to-implement web audio and video. Also visit http://www.GreatInternetMarketing.com /mentorprogram.htm for samples of audio testimonials.

Try to get and use testimonials that are results based, which means they aren't just a pat on the back.

Here's an example of a weak testimonial:

Tom, we loved your program. You were so funny. Thanks for a great day.

Sally from Tulsa

Here's an example of a good testimonial that is results based:

Tom, we used your "sell down" technique and in the first month increased our web income by 30 percent. I can't wait to implement all the other techniques you taught us.

Sally Carraba, Director of Sales, Big Company, Inc.

Here's one for a lawnmower company:

I couldn't believe it. After I hit that rock with my mower blade I thought you'd have my mower for six weeks. I was shocked when you called me the next day telling me I could pick it up. Your service was unbelievably fast and courteous.

Bob Blades, homeowner

Here's one for a drycleaner:

> Thanks so much for getting the stain out of my favorite dress. Three other cleaners told me it couldn't be done, but you did it. You now have a very loyal new customer.
>
> Joyce Juice

Feedback

One of the most important aspects of large sales on the Internet is to encourage a dialog with your visitors. Give them easy ways to make comments or ask questions. This can mean e-mail addresses for your different departments (if you are a one person show, they can all be forwarded to you), 800 numbers, fax numbers, or simply chatting or instant messaging. These are all ways that can make it easy for your customers or potential customers to interact with your organization.

A speedy response is important. If you let customer inquiries go for several days, that's worse than not having a feedback mechanism at all.

Potential customers are turned into paying customers much more often when you or your staff show willingness to spend time with them to satisfy their questions. Existing customers are more loyal because they see that you don't disappear as soon as you get their money. I have also reduced the number of returns of my products to a miniscule percentage by spending time with people on the phone or via e-mail.

> **TIP:** I know for certain that a few people planned to buy my products, copy them, and then return them for a refund, but they were too embarrassed to go through with it since I was so nice and attentive to them!

Statistics

Earlier, we talked briefly about statistics. Now I want to show you how knowledge about your website visitors can mean money in your bank account. One of the programs I use is called Click Tracks. You can visit http://www.clicktracks.com/entrypoint.php?a=46673 and get a free trial.

For a fun and visual statistics site, check out: http://www.visitorville .com/?id=234.

Click Here Trick

Here is a cool trick: if you determine people are leaving on a certain page, put a "click here" button on that page leading to anywhere you want (preferably a very popular part of your site). Don't say where the link goes. People can't help but click on it. It is unbelievable. You can only pull that trick once, but if you have a page that you can't figure out why people are leaving, give them another chance to see something they like by putting a "click here" button on it. Some people put a "don't click here" button that is even more compelling to click on. It's just a goofy trick, but it certainly costs nothing to try if you're losing people on a certain page.

Statistics are critically important to your success in this field. You must know what is happening with your website. Most people who read this book are going to be depressed when they see the statistics on their site. There is a high probability that no one is visiting . . . it may be a beautiful site, but nobody is coming to see it.

The only value for a small businessperson to have a site like that is so you can refer people to it instead of sending them materials in the mail. This will save some money. Nevertheless, it will never get you any new business since new people won't find it unless it comes up high in the search engine.

Some website hosting services give you statistics programs for free. Some of them are not very comprehensive, but they are better than nothing. The really good program like Click Tracks http://www.clicktracks.com/entry-point.php?a=46673 is almost a $500 program. Spending the $500 on the program is money well spent. You'd blow more than that on just one small mistake in navigating your site. Or, you could waste the money on more design work to make your site prettier.

Making Money with Statistics

When you know who and why someone is coming to your site, you can create specific things to sell them. The marketing tip here is that you shouldn't only try to sell what you think people want, find out what they want and create it to sell to them.

Here's an example: I noticed from my statistics program that over 900 people per month were coming to my site for dog humor. . . . DOG HUMOR! The reason is that I have a giant selection of humor categorized on my site. When someone needs speech humor on a particular topic, they can find it at my site. Apparently, many dog lovers have linked to this page after finding it in the search engines.

How does this make me money? I'm creating a downloadable dog humor e-book. When someone visits the dog humor page, they will get a sample of the book and a link that says, "For the largest selection of dog humor on the planet click here." I'll charge around $10 for the e-book. Even if I only sell 10 a month, that's $100 going directly into my checking account with no work whatsoever. If I can sell 50 of them a month, I'll be throwing parties and dancing in the street!

Statistics Programs

Here is a selection of statistics programs. I haven't reviewed all of them, but it is important to get some kind of good statistics about the performance of your website. Check these programs out and see which ones you like best. Then start learning about your site. Also, remember that many of the free services will ask you to put a banner or some other kind of advertising on your site:

http://www.clicktracks.com/entrypoint.php?a=46673 (considered by many to be the best and most understandable)

http://business.realtracker.com

http://v2.superstats.com

http://www.stats4you.com

http://www.webstat.com

http://www.extremetracking.com

http://www.webtrends.com

Coupons and Rebates

I'm not much of a coupon kind of guy. In fact, on many occasions I have come close to going berserk in the checkout line of my local grocery store. When I see that thick stack of coupons coming out of the purse of the person ahead of me, life starts going down hill fast. But it is true that many people like coupons and they are an effective sales tool along with rebates. You can put printable coupons right on your site, and also offer cash rebates on your products.

http://www.KickStartCart.com has a coupon module that generates coupon and discount links that are automatically deducted when someone visits the website and buys something through those links. The discount is automatically taken care of by the special links.

Advertising Copy

Commonly known as copywriting, this topic is probably the most important part of the entire sales process. You can do everything else perfectly in these first two chapters and still fail miserably if you mess up this part. The words that make people want to pull out their credit cards are not easy to write. Just like any other skill, special techniques are involved.

You must learn the elements of good copy to really maximize your sales potential. This is so important that I suggest you take a separate course in it. For a more detailed discussion on this, I have a two-hour recording called "Copywriting 901: The Fast Track to Writing Words That Sell" (http://www.antion.com/cds.htm). You will use the skills you learn over and over again throughout your entire career and in most areas of your business. The following section introduces some tips to get you started.

Copy Tips

Headlines

The headline is the most critical part of copywriting. If your headline doesn't entice the reader into looking further, then your offer will never be seen. When you send an e-mail, the subject line is the headline. It is designed to get readers to stop what they are doing and open the e-mail or at least not delete it out of hand.

I don't actually write headlines anymore. I re-write headlines that are known to work. I got an e-book called *Copywriting Combo* that included 2001 headlines at http://www.ProfessionalSpeaker.com/catalog.htm. I printed it out and keep it near my desk all the time. Whenever I need a headline, I simply refer to the book and pick out all the ones I might be able to use for a particular product.

Subheads

As a person scans down a web page, he quickly scans the subheadings along the way. If the subheadings aren't quickly understandable and enticing, then it is doubtful that the person will decide to go back and read the entire page.

Guess where I get the subheadings. . . . I use all the headlines that didn't make it as the main headline as subheadings.

Teasers

I use teasers at the top of my e-zine before the masthead. I say things like, "Outrageous free marketing tip (see below)." This pulls people into the publication and encourages them to look through it as they search for the outrageous free tip.

Guarantees

We covered guarantees and guarantee terminology on pages 89–91, but actual practice in writing them should not be ignored.

Scare Tactics

This copywriting technique tells readers what will happen if they don't take action. Example: "You're a seasoned speaker. You've got experience on the platform born from years and years of hard knocks. Wouldn't it be a shame if the young bucks beat you out for speaking engagements simply because you don't know how to use the Internet effectively?"

Urgency Techniques

People are so busy, it is likely they will forget about you and your offer if you don't get them to act immediately. Example: "Purchase before midnight tonight and get four extra bonuses worth $900."

Billing Statements

Include advertising copy in both your printed and electronic billing statements. Sell at every opportunity.

Reason Why

An extremely powerful copywriting technique is the "reason why" or "because" technique. You are surrounded by this technique every single day of the year and everywhere you go. You'd have to be a monk on a mountaintop to elude its reach.

Have you ever seen or heard an auto dealer say, "Boss says we're overstocked and we'll all get fired if we don't move these cars out by Sunday midnight." The reason why? We're overstocked.

Have you ever seen an ad for an oriental rug company that's going out of business? The bankruptcy court says they must liquidate. The reason why? The bankruptcy court says so. (Of course, the bankruptcy goes on for at least three years.)

Yes, I know these appear to be hokey examples, but I'm certain you have heard of these kinds of promotions and hundreds of others.

Why do you get bombarded with the "reason why" technique? Because it works.

Let's look at how you can use this same very powerful technique in a professional fashion:

> "We're having a giant customer appreciation sale to thank all our loyal customers for their support this year." The reason why? Thanks for being a customer.

"We're only producing 100 of our leadership courses as a content test so we're offering it to the first 100 clients at 50 percent of the regular price of $149.95." The reason why? We're doing a content test.

Our new improved washing machines are coming in and we're liquidating last year's model at an incredible 75 percent off. The reason why? The new machines are coming in.

Returns Are Good

Here's one last tip I'll throw in: If you're not getting returns, then there is something wrong with your ad copy. What this means is if everyone is perfectly happy with your product, you are probably underselling it. Although I do believe in underpromising and overproducing, it's not that great of an idea for product sales.

Am I suggesting overselling your products and services? Absolutely not! Never claim something that you cannot produce. However, let's look at money that you are leaving on the table if your advertising copy is poor.

Let's say 100 people bought a widget using your present ad copy. The copy is very simple and just tells about the product. Let's also say everyone that bought your widget was very happy with it because it is an excellent widget. Not one of them returned it.

Now let's say that you write good advertising copy that pushes the benefits of the product and touches the emotions of the readers, painting rosy pictures of the product in their minds. In this case, 150 people bought your widget and 3 people returned your widget. The 147 people that bought the widget were really happy because it's a good widget and the 3 people who returned the widget told you that it was the worst widget they ever saw. Hmmmmm. Let's see who wins here.

Because of good advertising copy, you sold 47 more widgets to people who were harder to sell to than the first 100 people. Those 47 people who took an extra nudge to buy are happy with the product and the 3 people who returned their widgets could be just goof ball rip-offs, or misread your ad copy, or who knows what their problem is? They could be chronic whiners or people who are never satisfied with any product. It's very likely that they didn't need your widget in the first place, but your ad copy was so good that it convinced them they did.

If you aren't getting any returns, you need to keep improving your ad copy to push the most number of people to buy. If your returns percentage is very high there are two things that could be wrong. You are clearly overselling the capabilities of the product or the product truly is a piece of junk and I can't help you with that.

Copywriting Courses

Copywriting combo and 2001 Headlines: Find it at http://www.Professional-Speaker.com/catalog.htm. Look halfway down the page. 2001 Headlines will be delivered immediately in PDF format and you will get a training course mailed to you in a big binder.

You might also want to check out this new long copy sales generator. It reduced the time it takes me to rough out a sales letter from two weeks to two hours. It also trains you in copywriting as you go. Find it at http://www.marketingtips.com/salesletters/t.cgi/12273.

Some courses to look at include:

Here's a course by super copywriter Jeff Paul: http://hop.clickbank.net/?powertips/killercopy.

Hypnotic Copywriting and Marketing Resources by "Mr. Fire" Joe Vitale: http://hop.clickbank.net/hop.cgi?powertips/outrageous.

Copywriting Resources by Lorrie Morgan-Ferraro: http://www.kickstart-cart.com/app/aftrack.asp?afid=168423.

Testing

It's scary to think where I might be if I had paid attention to testing during the time I have been marketing on the Internet. When I first started, e-magazines were not overdone like they are today, spam wasn't the kind of problem it is today, and it was relatively simple to make some money if you knew what you were doing.

I made mistakes all the time and I was still very, very profitable overall, but I really didn't know which advertisements were making me money and which were siphoning off profit.

After meeting a wonderful guy and top Internet marketer, John Reese, I'm changing my tune about the way I approach my Internet sales. John has politely reminded me for over a year that I should become a fanatic at testing. He taught me that top Internet marketing wasn't about coming up with the next gazillion dollar idea. . . . It's about putting an offer out to the marketplace and counting how many people respond to the offer. John says, "Marketing is simply a math problem. One hundred people see ad number 1 and 10 people buy from that ad. The same number of people see ad number 2 and 18 people buy from that ad. Ad number 2 wins. End of story. Thanks for playing."

John goes on to say that it's not really the end of the story. Now that you have an ad where 18 people out of 100 buy, you change some element of the ad and count how many people buy after that change. If more buy, the new ad wins. If less buy, go back to the old ad and try another change. You are constantly trying to increase your number of sales by changing elements of the ad and testing to see which one gets more sales.

All my friends who sell a ton on the Internet have stories of how one small change in a promotion or ad gave them a much higher response.

I always go through this process that is called *split testing* to run one ad against another until I can't get a higher response rate. When I can't beat the highest pulling ad, that ends up being the final ad.

http://www.KickStartCart.com integrated shopping system makes split testing easier than ever. All you have to do is have the cart generate a special link that sends one person to ad A and the next person is shown ad B. The next person is shown ad A and so forth. The cart rotates ads A and B automatically and tracks how many people bought from each ad. You will have an exact answer at the end of the day (or whatever period you are tracking) of which ad made more sales.

This method is so unbelievably powerful and good for your bottom line that I beg you to start right from the beginning testing everything you do.

Here are some elements of your ad you can test:

- Headlines
- Subheadings
- Preheadlines
- Color of your headline
- Color of your background
- Guarantee
- Price
- Offer
- Testimonials (written, audio, and video)
- Bonuses, and so on.

TIP: Don't test more than one element at a time or you won't know which element caused the increase or decrease in sales.

Testing Other Stuff

Besides testing one ad against another you need to test different places to put your ads and different mediums. You could try banner ads, which are much less expensive than they used to be. You could try online classified ads, and you could test advertising on different kinds of websites that are complimentary to your offerings, and so on.

Don't forget to test offline places to advertise like newspapers, magazines, card decks, and whatever else may make sense for what you sell.

Customer Service

Customer service has to be as good, or better, than it needs to be in face-to-face sales. There is very little personal contact when making sales on the Web, which breeds an inherent mistrust that you must strive to overcome if you want to maximize sales.

Here's how I do it on the Web:

✓ *Respond quickly:* I answer all customer inquiries as fast and as thoroughly as possible. Most of these inquiries come to me by e-mail, many by phone, and a few by fax. It's hard to be perfect at this when you have a busy operation, but it really impresses people, so do whatever you can to respond quickly.

TIP: Use your sig file capability to make responses for routine questions, or keep them in a file so you can cut and paste them. This saves tons of time.

✓ *Get a good cell phone plan:* You should have heard my customers responding to me when I called them personally from Thailand! From what I can remember, everyone ordered something.

✓ *Don't leave them wondering:* When someone orders a product, the shopping cart automatically lets them know the order went through. This is extremely important because you don't want people who are apprehensive about ordering on the Internet to be worried about whether their order went through or not. You also don't want them hitting the submit button repeatedly causing multiple orders.

TIP: This might warrant a note next to the submit button saying, "Only hit the button once and you will receive confirmation in less than one minute."

✓ *Give shipping date and begin dialog:* As soon as I get the notices of orders via e-mail, I e-mail customers back personally thanking them and giving them a shipping date. I also take this opportunity to begin a dialog with the customers who buy the bigger ticket products. I ask them where they heard about the product and what made them decide to invest. I don't do this every time for the smaller products because it's just too time consuming, but if I'm sitting around the office at the computer anyway, I do try to send a personal note. I can't tell you how many people who initially bought a $20 product ended up buying a $700 product and a $1,600 consulting package and then went on to attend a live seminar!

✓ *Shipping notice:* When the big-ticket product ships, I send another e-mail telling them that their product is on the way and when to expect it.

✓ *Follow-up note:* About 10 days later, I do another e-mail to the big-ticket buyers checking to see if the product arrived, if they have any questions, and check to make absolutely sure they are satisfied with the product. This is impossible to keep up with personally when you are busy, so I use autoresponders so that I never miss thanking a customer.

✓ *Tell the customer where to go:* Boy would I like to do that some times. What I mean here is to direct them to FAQ pages or listings of contacts in your organization so they can e-mail the right person on the first try.

You will find that it is much easier to give consistently good service when you automate your systems and let technology do the work for you. Yes, I know sometimes the systems are a pain to set up, but in the long run they make you infinitely more productive. A good reference is *Make Your Mouse Roar: The High Performance Guide to Automating Everything* by Bill Bruck (Merrifield, VA: Round Earth, 2000, http://www.bruck.com).

Live Customer Service

If you are in a situation where you have full-time staff, you can have instant live customer feedback and help available right from your website. You'll see when visitors are on your site and you can even initiate the interaction. Many of the systems are free and can be turned on and off so you can go to the bathroom or on vacation:

http://www.humanclick.com

http://www.sessio.com

http://www.LiveHelper.com

Build Trust

The entire process is designed to build trust. I'm taking people that may be apprehensive about ordering something on the Internet and responding quickly to their need for information and letting them know that I am accessible. Then when they order, the shopping cart is letting them know immediately that everything is okay. I also e-mail them several times letting them know I didn't disappear after getting their money. I even e-mail them yet again to let them know I am interested in their success with the product.

Is this time consuming? Absolutely, even though much of it is automated or now handled by one of my assistants. Frankly, I'd much rather be spending time on the phone with a customer building trust than wasting my time cold calling.

Does this pay off? Sure it does. Many of my customers buy anything I produce partly because of my service, and partly because of the good information they know they'll get. Oh, and by the way, even when you do all the things I've outlined to build up this trust, you can ruin it all by selling one shabby product. So, make sure there is plenty of value in everything you do.

While we are talking about trust, don't forget to put things on your website that indicate you are a reputable firm. When appropriate, you could use the phrase "Licensed, bonded, and insured," or put in the Verisign Banner showing a secure site, or post the Better Business Bureau Seal or Privacy Seal if you are a member. Check out http://www.bbbonline.org for details.

Here's a couple more places you can be rated and possibly apply for their seal of approval:

http://veribiz.com

http://www.Internettradebureau.com

http://www.e-safecertified.com

http://www.truste.com

http://epubliceye.com

http://www.privacyalliance.org/resources/ppguidelines.shtml (more privacy stuff)

Frequently Asked Questions (FAQ)

Another way to build trust and give customer service at the same time is to give as much information as you can about the product. You can do this with a FAQ page. This helps customers make informed decisions, and also builds credibility in your organization.

A side benefit is that it can also be another sales page. The questions asked can give you a chance to plug your product or service again. Here's an example from my page http://www.antion.com/faq.htm. You can visit this page for more examples of selling while answering questions.

```
How can we get extra value by engaging you?
   Many groups that hire me to do a keynote presentation
also have me do a breakout or spouse session at the
same event. This gets you a big discount on the second
presentation and saves you travel and expenses. I will
also help you design exciting convention openings and
closings, even if you are on a bargain basement budget!
```

Here's another way to give great service. The site http://www.peoplesupport.com keeps a smart database for you and responds to questions. The customer types in a question in plain English and your database responds with the answer. The more the system is used, the smarter it gets.

Tell Them What to Do

Good service also includes giving explicit directions for ordering. No matter how easy you make the ordering process, someone out there will screw it up.
Use phrases like:

Click here to . . .

Just fill out our easy and secure online form.

For questions call us at . . .

Read our FAQ page for more info.

WHAT YOU NEED TO KNOW

 The sales process is different on the web. You hide your big-ticket products. You hide your guarantee. You have to learn how to write advertising copy to get people to buy. Once you do sell something, your customer service must be better than it would be for an in-person sale. One page websites can produce a quick and consistent cash flow when you identify the right digital product to sell.

Associate/Affiliate Programs

Associate (or affiliate) programs allow you to make money by recommending other people's products. You get a commission if someone buys something.

These programs also allow you to have an army of commissioned salespeople selling your stuff around the world and you don't pay them anything unless they sell something.

There are basically two ways to make money with associate/affiliate programs:

1. You put other people's links on your site, or in your e-zine. When someone clicks from your site or e-zine to the other site and buys something, you get a commission. You can even tell people about the link or put the link in printed material. When they visit the link and

buy something, you still get a commission. It costs nothing to participate in such a program.

2. You purchase tracking software and have other people putting your links on their sites. When someone clicks from their site to yours and purchases something, you owe them a commission that the software tracks for you. This software goes from free to many thousand dollars. If you have the http://www.KickStartCart.com integrated shopping cart system, it includes top-notch affiliate software.

This software will assist you in finding affiliates to sell your products and services: http://hop.clickbank.net/?powertips/affinder.

The most well-known associate program is run by the big online bookseller Amazon.com. You put a link on your site and then you make money when people click through to buy things. If you go looking around websites, you'll see a lot of people who are selling books for Amazon.com by putting a banner on their website.

I could put a banner on my website and if you bought a book by clicking through that link to Amazon, I'd get a commission on it. Amazon is getting a whole bunch of people selling books for them. But I don't recommend using Amazon's or any of the many lesser known programs because they give you such a small commission. You're getting somebody to click out of your site for maybe a buck or a buck and a half and the affiliate won't even pay you until your commission reaches a certain level. It could be six months later. I'm against them. So hold out for the ones that pay good money.

I am an associate for Corey Rudl's marketing course. This is the course that started me on my way to becoming a multimillionaire so obviously I can endorse it readily. I get $75 a shot from him, so it's worth it to me to have someone click through. An average individual person who comes to my site is not worth $75.

If you buy the course, make sure you contact me before you buy any of the software Corey recommends. I can tell you from experience that most people in our market won't be able to figure out much of what he sells to a more sophisticated audience. The ideas in the course, however, are excellent. Here's the link: http://www.marketingtips.com/t.cgi/12273.

I also have my own software so that I can recruit associates to sell my new speaker video and all my other products. If people want to put my links on their site, there's a sophisticated tracking program to monitor when someone clicks through from your site, and to notify me of such an occurrence. For example, at the end of the month you'll get a check from me for almost $200 for each Wake 'em Up Professional Speaking System you sell.

If you would like to sign up to sell my products and services visit: http://www.kickstartcart.com/app/afsignup.asp?MerchantID=16070.

When you sign up you'll get a complete sales course in how to maximize your commissions from me.

Affiliate Fraud Tip 1

If you have your own associate program, you may want to consider paying your affiliates using the online payment program http://www.PayPal.com. Although I don't advocate this service for collecting money for your main product line, it does give you some protection if you have affiliates who may counterfeit your checks and try to wipe out your main checking account.

Some merchants who run affiliate programs keep a separate checking account with just enough money in it to pay affiliates so that if people counterfeit your checks, they can't get away with too much money.

Counterfeiting checks is not common in the United States, but if you have affiliates in many countries foreign to yours, you must watch closely for potential fraud.

Affiliate Fraud Tip 2

Scenario: You get an oddball order for a large amount of money. The e-mail address is from a free service like Yahoo. The credit card is accepted. You see on your order form that an affiliate from a foreign country sent you the order. Most likely it's a fraudulent order.

Here's what probably happened: Either two criminal buddies paired up, or one person did the entire scam and pretended to be both the affiliate and the customer.

They steal a credit card, which at the time is good because the theft is still undetected. One member of the criminal duo buys your stuff through the affiliate link of his partner. They hope you will send a legitimate affiliate check to the affiliate who will cash the check and/or counterfeit it like the fraud tip above.

Eventually the credit card will be reported as stolen and the credit card company will charge back the sale to the customer's credit card. You'll never be able to recover the money from the fake affiliate and your entire checking account could be compromised, plus you're out the cost of the product.

Here's the fix: Don't ship the product. Don't send the affiliate check and call the fraud division of the credit card company immediately. Also remove the bad affiliate from your database.

At all costs try to avoid getting associate software from one company and a shopping cart from another company. And heaven forbid you try to install associate program software yourself unless you are extremely technically savvy.

When I first started, I had a shopping cart from my web host and an associate program from another vendor. When things didn't work each company blamed the other and I was left holding the bag. It took six months to get things going and it never did fully work right. Don't get caught in this kind of mess!

Using http://www.KickStartCart.com I never have any trouble. If any issues arise, I have only one company to call and it can't pass the buck to anyone else.

Setting it up to sell your own products is when the complications arise. It is complicated from my end to sell my products, but from your end to sign up as my affiliate and sell them it's simple. I'm doing all the work so it's easy for you.

Just because it's simple to sign up as an affiliate doesn't mean it's no work. You've got to do a good job getting traffic to your site and endorsing my links or you won't make much money in commissions.

You have to put forth some effort to make a lot of money, but you could make a couple thousand dollars a month just off joining my affiliate program if you hustled just a little bit.

It takes a little bit of effort to get it going, but everything I have done in electronic marketing took some effort to get going. However, it brings in money like crazy while I'm sitting here and not on an airplane. So the benefits are there if you're willing to be consistent and work with it.

The Mistakes I Made

When I started my associate program I was sure I was going to be rich instantly. I thought, "I have a big list of speakers. They will all sign up and sell my stuff and I'll be rich in no time." HA!!! The mistake in my thinking was that I didn't know at the time that most websites suck and don't get much traffic. This is a numbers game. If you aren't getting traffic, no one will click through to my site and neither one of us will get any sales.

The lesson learned here is that you shouldn't fool around signing up people that have no traffic to their site. One high traffic site could make you many thousands of dollars per month. Do whatever you can to make deals with high traffic sites and you'll have much quicker success with associate programs.

Here are some of the criteria to consider when picking associate program software for your site:

Real-time tracking for associates: This means your associates can check how many people they have sent to you and how many sales they got any time day or night by going to a web page and putting in their pass code.

Order confirmation for associates: When an order is placed, associates gets an e-mail telling them about it. This is motivating for your associates.

Fair payment for associates: Your software should track the sales accurately.

Automatic check writing capability: Writing commission checks by hand can be very time consuming. Automatic checkwriting allows the software to output to your accounting program so you can print the checks for your associates.

Associate newsletter capability: This function allows you to broadcast an e-mail to all or part of your associates.

Web-based administration center: You must think globally. This function allows you to work with your associate tracking system wherever you have web access. You are not forced to be at your home computer.

Associate search capability: Associates are forever forgetting their pass codes and other simple administrative things. This allows you to find them quickly in your database to help them out.

Link Cloaking

Sometimes you can protect your commission when you have a savvy audience by cloaking your links so they don't look like affiliate links.

If I see a link that someone asks me to click on that looks something like http://www.ImGettingACommission.com/t.cgi/joeblow I know that I can simply type in the first part up to the .com and cut Joe out of his commission. The person running the affiliate program won't know the order came from Joe.

There are also ways that really Internet savvy people can rob you of your commissions. So what do you do? Get a tool that cloaks or hides your real affiliate link, for example:

http://hop.clickbank.net/?powertips/cloaklinks (affiliate link cloaker)

http://www.associateprograms.com (good resource to see lots of other associate/affiliate programs and how they run)

Here's an e-book on making money without even having a website: http://hop.clickbank.net/?powertips/webnotreqd.

See the e-book by the famous Michael Campbell (one of my advisors) *Clickin It Rich* (http://hop.clickbank.net/?powertips/dmcorp).

Here's a piece of software that helps you keep track of all the affiliate relationships you have: http://hop.clickbank.net/?powertips/newprairie.

Here's a magazine dedicated to all aspects of affiliate marketing: http://www.revenuetoday.com/?powertips.

Affiliate Networks

There are companies that manage affiliate programs for many other vendors. All you have to do is sign up with them once and you have access to thousands of affiliate programs.

ClickBank (http://www.ClickBank.com) is a great place to go to find digital products to sell. When you visit their store, the digital products are ranked by popularity so you'll pretty much know which ones are selling best.

You can also sell through Clickbank, but the book you're reading right now will teach you how to use much higher grade software and techniques to sell more of your products and services.

Here's an e-book that will tell you how to use ClickBank: http://hop.clickbank.net/?powertips/alkhtcsh.

Commission Junction (http://www.cj.com) is another very popular affiliate management company. They manage the affiliate programs for some super big companies like eBay.

Link Share (http://www.linkshare.com) is another place where, just like the affiliate management companies earlier, you only have to sign up once and you have access to many products and services to sell.

Here are some places to find affiliate stuff to sell:

http://www.affiliatesdirectory.com

http://www.associateprograms.com

http://www.refer-it.com

This site specializes in programs that pay a recurring commission: http://www.lifetimecommissions.com.

WHAT YOU NEED TO KNOW

Associate programs are one of the ways you can literally make a fortune. You can have other people all over the Internet selling your products on a commission basis. This requires and investment in time and money to get your program set up. You can also make money by selling other people's products. This requires no, or very little, investment. You can be exposed to thousands of affiliate programs by signing up with an affiliate network.

We've reached the end of another power packed chapter on the theory of selling lots more of your products and services on the Internet. We covered ad copywriting, selling big ticket products via advertorials, customer service, exit strategies, simple navigation, guarantees, building credibility, membership clubs, statistics, coupons and rebates, and affiliate programs.

In the next chapter, we work on the actual mechanics of making all this happen on your website and how you can use powerful yet inexpensive small business software to virtually automate your business.

3

Mechanics of
Website Sales

In Chapter 1, you learned how to build a web site that gets traffic. In Chapter 2, you learned how to make that traffic want to buy your products. Now you have to make it easy for your customers to do so. There are many options for how to build your payment and fulfillment process, and new ones are invented every day. I'll try to cut through the hype for you and give you some fairly simple choices.

When I first started selling on the Internet, all I had was a form that I made myself using Microsoft Front Page. I had individual pages describing the products that also included the picture of the product. Clicking "order now" took you to the form where you checked off the product you wanted, how many you wanted, and put in all your contact information and credit card number. The form e-mailed me the information that I processed manually and then I shipped the product.

This worked well for me, but it had significant drawbacks. First of all, the site was not "secure." I'm sure I lost some sales because of this. Back in those days, there was lots of talk about your credit card getting stolen when shopping on the Internet. This undoubtedly influenced some customers. They could have simply printed out the form, filled it in by hand, and faxed it to me, but that's too much hassle for most people.

The next big drawback was that customers didn't really have an exact total of tax and shipping without getting their own calculator out and figuring it out themselves. I probably didn't lose too many sales over this, but it was more work here in the office. We had to process the credit cards manually, too. All of this time adds up when you have a busy office.

I eventually moved to a totally automated system that was a bear to set up. I would never do that again.

Don't Build Your Store from Scratch

Building your store from scratch is the most complicated way to go because five different entities (or six if you have an associate program) have to interact

121

to make the transaction work. Once you are done building this system, the fees are usually more because programming is not cheap and you better be prepared for some frustration and delays making it all work. Before better methods came along, this is the way I built the Speaker Shop, the shopping area on my website.

I was already a Visa/MasterCard/AMEX merchant, so at least I didn't have to fight with that from the start. The first thing I had to do was find out from my bank what credit card processing company they used and what Internet "real-time" credit card facility would be compatible with the processing company.

Real-time credit card processing is the method by which customers put their credit card information into your website and within about 15 seconds the money is heading toward your bank account with a confirmation of the order going to both you and the customer.

Here are the six elements that must work together:

1. Your bank
2. Your bank's credit card processing company
3. The real-time credit card company
4. Your shopping cart
5. Your web host
6. Your associate program, if you have one

Whew! It was already getting complicated. I found out that the credit card processing company was compatible with a real-time company called Cybercash (http://www.cybercash.com). Fortunately, Cybercash is one of the biggest and best known real-time credit card companies. Unfortunately, they filed for bankruptcy March 2001, but they were eventually bought out by Verisign.

Although you could do it much quicker now, it took me several months to get the basic shopping cart and credit card system working, and a full six months to get the associate program working with the rest of the system. This downtime equated to a tremendous loss of revenue. You do not have to do this now and if you do, you will probably regret it.

If you are technically oriented (which I'm not) and thick-skinned (which I am), you could tackle this yourself. I don't really recommend it though. It was just too tough and my system was so complicated that it was stifling some of my business plans.

Turnkey Stores

Going to the other end of the spectrum, you could be up and running tomorrow with a store from Yahoo (http://smallbusiness.yahoo.com/merchant) or some other major vendor. These stores aren't really totally turnkey. You have to put your products in and learn how to use their interface (which isn't that tough). There are also plenty of custom programmers out there who would be happy to give your store a custom look if you think you need it . . . for a fee.

For a Yahoo store (now called "small business merchant solution"), you'll pay from $40 per month up to $300 per month plus a percentage of your sales.

You still have to have a merchant account, or Yahoo has a partner that will charge you additional fees and set-up charges.

I am definitely not in favor of this method because they dummy things down so much and you have no advanced features like good shopping systems do. You also pay a premium price for something that's not all that good when compared to professional systems that actually sell for you.

A list of some places to build stores follows. Remember, let the buyer beware and in this case the buyer is you. Check out the store thoroughly and get references from others who are using the same store. I'm definitely not endorsing any particular store builders; in fact, I'm not in favor of them at all. This is a sample of what is out there:

http://www.shopfactory.com (available in 35 languages)

http://www.onlineorders.net

http://www.uburst.com/uShop (available in 11 languages)

http://www.uburst.com/uStorekeeper

http://www.pdgsoft.com

Shopping Carts

Picking a shopping cart system is a very serious decision that you will likely have to live with for some time. Many systems are frustrating to install and once installed are incomprehensible and extremely difficult to use, which means lost sales for you.

You really want to automate every part of the system so it's less work for you and extremely easy for your customer. Today's smart shopping system technology can make this happen at a price that any small business can afford.

In addition, smart shopping systems will dramatically increase sales because they manage the entire shopping process including upselling the customer, making special offers, handling special sales and discounts, and completely managing your extremely valuable database of prospects and actual customers.

There are thousands of simple shopping carts on the market either for free or for a low price. Basically, they just take the order like the cashier at a grocery store. They do nothing to help you sell in the first place.

Custom Carts

Webmasters may try to sell you a custom shopping cart, which can cost anywhere from a few hundred dollars to tens of thousands of dollars. They tell you that what you want to do with your site will require lots of expensive programming and custom adaptations. Well, there are very few small business people (and I've coached hundreds) who need something so sophisticated that it would cost thousands of dollars. Keep your wallet in your pocket when you get around these people.

You may already have a ton of money invested in your shopping system and you may not have the sales you think you should. It might be time to consider scraping the old system in favor of a new, less expensive system that has sales tools built in. Sticking with an antiquated system just because you have lots of money invested makes no sense and it will continue to hurt your sales in the future . . . what's that saying about pound foolish and penny wise?

What Is a Shopping Cart?

A *shopping cart* is actually a piece of software. The metaphor is—you guessed it—shopping. You push your cart through the cyberstore. When you see something you want to buy, you put it in your cart by clicking on it. Then when you are ready to leave, you check out of the store. This is where the shopping cart totals up your purchases and adds the tax and shipping for you.

You then fill in your name, address, phone number, and shipping information along with your credit card and expiration date. Once you hit the final submit button, all the mechanisms kick into gear to send that money hurtling toward your checking account . . . minus the credit card company percentage, of course.

Real-Time Credit Card Processing

The credit card processing is not actually done by the shopping cart. Many people don't realize this. You still have to have a credit card merchant account to process credit cards. If you don't have the real-time processing capability, your shopping cart will simply e-mail you notice of the sale. You log in to your cart to get the credit card number for manual processing later.

When you do have *real-time credit card processing* capability (which you must if you want to totally automate your system), the customer puts her credit card in your shopping cart and about 15 to 20 seconds later gets a notification that the sale went through. Sometime later that day, the money is deposited in your bank account.

The credit card number is encrypted as it flies through cyberspace. This is a process called Pretty Good Privacy or PGP. I think I'd rather have Darn

Good Privacy, or Invincible Privacy, but PGP is all we have at our level and it has shown to be Darn Good Enough.

After the transaction is complete, in sometimes as little as five seconds, you either get an e-mail regarding shipping the product, or the customer gets a link to download the product directly. And that's all there is to it. I've simplified it considerably, but believe me, you don't want to know all the details. You just want it to work!

Again I want to emphasize: Your shopping cart system is separate from your merchant account and from your real-time processing mechanism. The shopping cart must connect to the credit card system, but it is a separate system. If you need a merchant account, I will tell you later how to get one in about 10 minutes for $199.

How to Pick a Shopping Cart System

Here are some criteria that are important when it comes to picking a shopping cart:

✓ *Calculate shipping and tax:* This is one of the reasons why you have a shopping cart. It's a basic function, but some do it better than others. Make sure you have several options on how to calculate basic shipping charges. Don't forget, some customers will want fast shipping like FedEx. Can the cart handle this?

✓ *Soft and hard goods:* This is extremely important for anyone who wants to sell informational products. A hard good is a physical product that has to be shipped to the customer. A soft good is a downloadable product or software type of product. You want the shopping cart to be able to handle both types of products in the same transaction so the customer doesn't have to go through the ordering process twice if ordering one of your widgets and a downloadable e-book at the same time. Also, when the cart is delivering a downloadable product, it should generate a web page for the download that disappears automatically after a short time so that the customer can't give the link to all his or her friends.

✓ *Customizable "return to shopping" pages:* Sophisticated shopping carts allow you to customize the "Return to Shopping" button so it takes the customer to a related product of your choice. This one feature can dramatically influence whether the customer simply checks out because it's too difficult to find related items, or purchases something else because you made it easy.

✓ *Offer management:* Most lower end shopping carts don't have the capability to offer discounts for multiple purchases, or to offer "one free when you buy three" or similar special offers. Having this capability can really increase the average amount that customers spend when they shop with you.

✓ *Receipt and confirmation e-mails:* The shopping cart should be able to send an e-mail confirmation automatically to the customer and also generate a receipt for you to put in the package if you are shipping a product.

✓ *Multiple order and drop ship e-mail capability:* The shopping cart should be able to e-mail suppliers who ship directly to your customer (drop ship). The e-mail sent to the supplier would not have the customer's credit card info.

✓ *Web-based administration page:* If your shopping cart has a web-based manager's administration page, then you can work on your shopping cart, that is, add products, change prices, and so on, anywhere in the world. You are not stuck at your home base to make these changes.

✓ *Encryption:* This is the PGP stuff I talked about earlier. Just make sure you have it.

✓ *Back end-output to your accounting software:* This is a very handy feature that allows you to export the sales data directly from your shopping cart to popular accounting packages like Quickbooks, Quicken, and Peachtree.

✓ *Associate program compatible:* An associate program means that someone else (your associate/affiliate) can put a link to your products on their website. When someone clicks on the link and visits your website, associate program software tracks the person to your website. If they buy something, you pay your associate a commission for sending them.

This basic premise made Amazon.com a billion dollar company. Now millions of small businesses are taking advantage of the same concept. It's like having an army of commissioned salespeople working for you and you don't pay anyone a nickel unless they sell something.

If you plan on having other people sell your products by means of an associate program, try to get a compatible or integrated system right from the start. Otherwise, it could be difficult or impossible to add one later. A really good system will have an associate program built in so everything is compatible.

✓ *Upsell modules:* Good shopping cart systems will have the capability of suggesting related products to shoppera based on what they have already bought. This is what I call the "Do you want fries with that?" method of selling. I mentioned earlier how much money just one upsell promotion can earn.

I'm sure you can see this is real power and something you absolutely want in the shopping cart system that helps you run your business—and you can have it at your fingertips at a fraction of the cost of custom programmed systems.

✓ *Database handling:* Customer data coming into a shopping system should never have to be retyped, and it should be able to be manipulated to increase sales. High-end systems will have this built-in.

Before I had a modern shopping system, we would have to print out the orders and have them typed into an ACT database program by an administrative person (complete with all the mistakes, typos, and hourly fees, I might add).

If I wanted to e-mail these customers, I would have to be a genius to export the data from ACT in comma delimited format and then also be a genius to import the data into an e-mail program so that I could send out the e-mail a half hour later—if I was lucky.

Now, at the touch of a few keys, I can instantly e-mail everyone who buys a particular product and even put their name in it (this is called mail merge) with no administrative help whatsoever. This is a massive cost savings and errors have been reduced by 90 percent.

✓ *Broadcast capability:* Most shopping carts require you to export your data to another unrelated system where you have to massage the data in order to send e-mails back to the customer. You generally have to be a database expert to do the manipulations. Good shopping carts have integrated mailing capabilities that can allow customers to be sorted and broadcast to immediately. You should be able to e-mail to all customers or only to ones who bought certain items. You should also be able to broadcast an e-mail to your affiliates right from the system.

TIP: Don't make every contact with a customer a sales pitch. They will most likely ask to be removed from your mailings. Alternate a helpful hint based on what they bought and a product offering.

✓ *E-mail list management:* If you are starting an electronic newsletter/ magazine, a good shopping cart system can manage all the subscribers for you automatically. It will automate the process and give you a form for your website that lets people subscribe and unsubscribe themselves, which is a tremendous time and money saver.

✓ *Mail merge capability:* E-mails that are personalized normally get a much higher response than generic ones. Most of the time you must do sophisticated export and formatting manipulations on your database and send the results to a separate and expensive mail merge program. Good shopping cart systems integrate the database with an included mail merge program so that reaching your customers in a personalized fashion means only pushing a few buttons.

✓ *Coupons and discounts:* Only the finest high-end shopping carts are able to do percentage and fixed amount discounts when selling your products. These coupons and discounts can mean a tremendous boost in sales. Having this option can mean a big difference in gross and net income.

✓ *Multiple website capability:* Most shopping carts are only good for one website. You are required to buy a completely separate system for each website you want to develop. This can be enormously expensive, time consuming, and frustrating. Shopping cart systems that can handle products from multiple websites save tons of money and development time. A side benefit is that completely different product lines can be sold with the customers from one website never even knowing about the products sold on the other website unless you want them to.

✓ *Integrated autoresponders:* Sequential autoresponders are one of the most powerful sales tools on the Internet today. They send follow-up e-mails to customers and prospects to keep your sales messages going out automatically. You usually have to contract with a separate company and somehow get the shopping cart and autoresponder company to work together. Only the most advanced carts would have this function integrated.

Even when integrated in very high-end shopping systems you have the problem of an autoresponder sequence being delivered to sell a product that the customer has already purchased. This makes you look foolish and irritates the customer. The most advanced systems would have autoresponders available for each product and a special feature called "unsubscribe on purchase." This automatically takes customers off the autoresponder when they purchase the item. It can also then put them into a different autoresponder to continue to try to sell some other product.

Autoresponders can be used to train the customer in the use of your product and/or suggest other products that would likely be of interest. The best part is that after they are set up, the entire process goes on autopilot totally unattended, which saves you time and money. A recent survey on ZDNet found that 98 percent of customers would repurchase from a company if they were asked. Autoresponders make sure they get asked when you are too busy to do it yourself.

Another big benefit of autoresponders is that they tend to decrease returns especially on big-ticket products. Buyer's remorse can really increase your return rate. A simple automated series of follow-up e-mails will let customers know you aren't going to disappear now that you have their money. It can also reassure them that they made a wise decision in purchasing your product.

✓ *Ad tracking:* Again this is one of the most powerful cost-saving and money-saving tools available to people selling products and services on the Internet. Integrated ad tracking allows you to tell which of your on-line links or banners is paying off.

Old style nonintegrated systems only tell how many people clicked on the link or ad. The most advanced integrated systems not only tell how many people clicked, but also tell how many of those people bought.

You might think an ad is great because it got many click throughs, so you keep buying the ad over and over. You might also think that another ad is not worth it because it has only half as many click throughs, so you cancel it. Integrated ad tracking could tell you that the ad that is getting all the click throughs is producing only a tiny number of sales and that the ad that got less click throughs is producing a very high percentage of sales. Without this information, you would keep the bad ad and cancel the good one, . . . which is not a great way to make money.

✓ *Conversion ratio:* This term is the number of website visitors as compared to the number of buyers. To figure it out, simply divide the total number of visitors to your site by the total number of people who bought something. So if 100 people visited your site (or sales page) and one person bought, you would have a conversion ratio of 100:1. If you can use your shopping system to raise that figure of people that buy to only 2 people out of 100 then you have doubled your sales without even increasing your traffic and the technology did all the work. Simple shopping carts do not have the capability to do this for you, but shopping systems do.

✓ *Ad rotation (split testing):* This is a tremendous feature found only in the most expensive high-end custom programmed systems. It will really make you a ton of money and keep you from losing a ton of money (which you will do if you continue to run ads that aren't selling). This feature allows you to have several advertising pages running at once. The shopping system alternates the ads automatically for you. When you combine this feature with the ad tracking and conversion ratio features, you will get instant feedback on which ad is making you the most money.

✓ *Order form sell through:* This feature helps you overcome the biggest problem Internet marketers face—people quitting the sale just as they get to the order form page. A good shopping cart lets you put customized text right on the order form page that recaps all the good reasons the customer should complete the sale. Of course, this sell-through information is customized depending on what the customer ordered. This is an awesome feature to have and it will get more people to complete the sale.

✓ *Recurring billing:* This is another awesome feature you must have to make big money and to get residual income (income that comes in automatically every month). This feature allows you to offer packages that are billed to your customer every month. You could do a "Tape of the Month" promotion, or a monthly coaching package, or just about anything you can think of that you sell on a regular basis.

This feature is also useful for offering finance options on your more expensive products. I use this for my Wake 'em Up Video Professional Speaking System (http://www.antion.com/speakervideo.htm). If someone doesn't buy it and pay the full price, she gets a chance to buy it and make payments. The shopping cart handles all the billing. I make a lot of extra money this way.

✓ *Sales reports:* A good shopping cart system will give you sales reports in a number of different ways so you can choose the one that gives you the information you want. You should be able to switch between reports instantly and have many to choose from. Some common reports are:

—*Sales by date:* This, of course, tells you how much you sold on a certain day.

—*Sales by item:* This tells you how much of a particular product you sold and you should be able to put in a date range. For example, you sold 22 widgets for $418.00 in the five-day period from November 20 to 25.

—*Sales by client:* This report is a listing of your clients and how much money they spent. This is handy for identifying big spenders and rewarding them or giving them special thanks and/or incentives.

—*Sales by card type:* This report breaks out the amounts of money that come in from different credit cards. This is handy for reconciling your credit card fees each month.

—*Sales by ad campaign:* This report tells you exactly how one of your promotions performed.

—*Sales by affiliate:* This report tells you how well each one of your affiliates is selling for you.

If the shopping cart you are considering doesn't have these kinds of reports, I'd be very reluctant to use it. You will never know how well you are doing or if your promotions are working.

✓ *Tell a friend:* A good shopping cart system would make that easy for you to do by giving you simple links that automate the entire process for you. You could have a "Tell a Friend" form on your websites within minutes.

✓ *Questionnaires:* It's imperative that you know what your customers are thinking and asking them is the simplest way to find out . . . well, it's simple if you can get a questionnaire form on your website or in your e-zine without three months of trouble figuring out how to do it. A good shopping cart system will make it easy for you to survey your customers. The hardest part really is just figuring out what are the main questions you want to ask.

✓ *Pop-up boxes:* In certain technical and educational markets, pop-up boxes are annoying and frowned upon. In most other markets, used judiciously, they can tremendously increase sales by recommending other offers if shoppers decided not to purchase the offer on the page they are looking at. Sophisticated shopping systems have wizards that lead you through simple pop-up box creation questions with no programming required on your part.

✓ *Help with off-line shopping:* Make sure the shopping cart gives the customer an option to print out the order form so the customer can fax or mail it to you. You should also post your 800 number for customers who want to call in an order. Do whatever it takes to make it easy for them to order.

It will be extremely difficult to get everything on this list in an inexpensive shopping cart. Go through the list anyway when you are considering a shopping cart system. Pick the cart that has as many features as possible that are important to you. If it only has say five out of six, that's pretty good and you can usually pay a custom programmer to add the sixth feature.

Secure Servers

There is still quite a bit of concern about security on the Internet. Even if there were no real threat of people having their credit cards lifted while purchasing on the Internet, they are still worried about it and many are reluctant to order unless they are on a "secure server."

To add to their worry, both Netscape and Internet Explorer browsers have a security information box that pops up when someone tries to submit information to an unsecured site.

How do customers know for sure they are on a secure server? If they are using Internet Explorer as their browser, they will see a yellow padlock in the middle of the bottom bar of their browser. When they are on a secure server, this padlock will be locked. In Netscape, there is a padlock in the lower lefthand corner. Again, it will show itself as locked when on a secure server.

Whichever browser you use will most likely show the URL in the address box near the top of the screen beginning with "https:" instead of "http:" The "s" indicates Secure Server.

You can get a guide to securing your website as well as a logo you can display that tells your customer your site is a safe place to order from http://www.verisign.com. This isn't free. The charges are in the $400 to $500 range. You would have to hold a gun to my head to get me to pay that much money for this service. If for some reason you think you need this, get your webmaster or your Web Host to help you. It's one of those things that's important, but just like with your car engine, you don't have to be able to explain internal combustion to be able to drive to the grocery store.

If you have a secure server, make sure you brag about it. Tell your customers that they can easily order at your "secure" online store. Post this at prominent areas of your shopping cart.

Checklist for Evaluating a Shopping Cart System

Remember, most pieces of software are simply shopping carts and not complete and integrated sales systems. Whenever considering any shopping cart or shopping cart system ask questions in the following list. Most have either yes or no answers. If you start getting answers like, "Well, if you wanted it to do that, we could custom program it for you," or "Yes, it will do that if you buy another module from a third-party vendor," or "I think we could get it to do that, but we've never had anyone ask before," then you may be on pretty shaky ground by going with the system or shopping cart in question.

Here is your checklist:

✓ Will it calculate shipping and tax?
✓ Does it handle specialized shipping like FedEx and UPS?
✓ Will it deliver soft and hard goods in the same transaction?
✓ Does it offer customizable "Return to Shopping" pages without needing custom programming?
✓ Does it allow you to make special offers?
✓ Does it deliver receipt and confirmation e-mails?
✓ Does it allow multiple order and drop ship e-mails?
✓ Does it have a Web-based administration page?
✓ Does it use encryption technology?
✓ Does it deliver easy output to your accounting software?
✓ Does it have its own associate program or is it easily compatible with other major brands of associate software?
✓ Does it have integrated upsell modules?
✓ Does it have an integrated sales and prospect database?
✓ Does it have broadcast e-mail capability?
✓ Does it have mail merge capability?
✓ Will it deliver your e-zines/e-newsletters and automate the subscription process?
✓ Can it handle coupons and other discounts?
✓ Can it work for multiple websites with no extra fees?
✓ Does it have unlimited and fully integrated autoresponders?
✓ Does it have ad tracking tied into actual sales?
✓ Will it rotate ads for you and tell you which one makes the most money?
✓ Can the order form page be customized?
✓ Will it do automatic recurring billing?
✓ Does it give you a variety of sales reports?
✓ Does it have a "Tell a Friend" module?
✓ Will it allow you to easily make questionnaires and surveys?
✓ Does it have a pop-up box builder?

Table 3.1 Cost to Build the Old Style Shopping System Piece by Piece (Rough Estimates)

BASIC SHOPPING CART	FREE TO $7,000
Downloadable module to deliver ebooks, programs, and so on	$500 to $1500 (custom programming)
Customizable "return to shopping" pages	$500 to $1,500 (custom programming)
Offer management module	$500 to $1,500 (custom programming)
Upsell module	$500 to $1,500 (custom programming)
Database	$500 to $3,500 (custom programming)
Broadcast e-mail	$500 to $1,500 (custom programming)
Mail merge	$500 to $1,500 (custom programming)
E-mail newsletter list management	$240 to $3,600 per year
Coupon and discount module	$1500 to $3,500 (custom programming)
Multiple website capability	Most systems won't allow this. You must purchase a cart or additional license for each website.
Associate program	$500 to $2,500 (custom programming)
Sequential autoresponder	$300.00 per year each
Basic ad tracking	$60.00 per year per ad
Conversion ratio module	$1000 to $5,000 (custom programming)
Ad rotator	Generally not available in a shopping system $500 to $2,500 (custom programming)
Customizable order form	$500 to $2,500 (custom programming)
Recurring billing module	$500 to $2,500 (custom programming)
Sales reports module	$500 to $2,500 (custom programming)
Tell a friend module	Generally not available in a shopping system $150 to $500 (custom programming)
Questionnaire module	Generally not available in a shopping system $150 to $750 (custom programming)
Pop-up boxes	Generally not available in a shopping system $50 to $250 each (custom programming)

✓ Does it have a printable off line order form?

✓ Can you recommend the cart to others and get recurring income from doing so?

To build a bare bones system that includes all of these features you would pay about $9,450 and get one sequential autoresponder, one ad tracker, one pop-up box, and a really cheap associate program. It's most likely that you can only use the shopping cart on one website.

For a good quality usable system with 10 sequential autoresponders, 10 ad tracks, ad rotation, recurring billing, quality sales reports, "Tell a Friend" module, questionnaire/survey module, e-mail list management, order form sell through, three pop-up boxes, and a good associate program that you can still only use on one website at the high end, you could pay nearly $49,700 . . . and I have heard quotes this high from people who probably don't have the skill to put together an extremely complicated system like this.

If you doubt any of these figures, call a reputable programming firm and go down the list step by step (Table 3.1 on page 133). Reputable means they actually have professionals with the skills to build these features and make them work. It does not mean a smart high school or college kid who will quote you a pie-in-the-sky price and then never be able to make it all work, if he finishes it at all.

I must also warn you about technical people saying things like, "You don't really need sequential autoresponders." Remember they are techies who don't think like marketers and never made a dime on the Internet.

My Recommendation

I have resisted giving my recommendation because there was really nothing on the market that satisfied those requirements. Now, that has all changed. I can confidently recommend a system that has all the features listed in the checklist.

The name of the new system is Kick Start Cart and you can check it out for free for 30 days (http://www.KickStartCart.com).

The Kick Start Cart Integrated Shopping System Includes:

- *Hosting on its server:* This means no expensive and time consuming installation on your server. Kick Start Cart's technicians maintain the entire system and you never have to worry if it has problems. They fix it immediately and for free and they know what they're doing.
- *Free upgrades:* This company is aggressively upgrading the system and adding new features constantly. The company is not only technically able, it is run by people who think like marketers so they are always developing new ways for the system to help you make more money.

- *Ease of use:* You can literally have your Kick Start System working in about an hour with no technical experience whatsoever and they have a video tutorial and complete manual online to help you really maximize the sales features of your system.
- *Multiple websites:* Run sales from as many websites as you want through the Kick Start System. This alone could save you many thousands of dollars per year. The other neat thing about this is that you could be selling bibles on one site and lingerie on another site. Website visitors from one site would never even know about the other site unless you wanted them to.
- *Autoresponders:* This is one of my favorite features. The Kick Start System has unlimited autoresponders. This means that each product can have it's own set of follow-up e-mails. What a powerful tool. When someone buys a particular product the autoresponder follows up with additional offers based on what the customer already purchased.
- *Discount and coupon capability:* What an extremely advanced feature and it's included in the Kick Start System. You can offer coupon banners and other percentage discounts to certain groups of people and the system handles all the details. This used to be a big nightmare for me because I had to take discounted orders by phone, fax, or e-mail. My old shopping cart couldn't do it.
- *Offer management:* Want to encourage people to purchase multiple units of your products? The Kick Start System will handle just about any deal you can make up. Offer one free for every three purchased, or buy 10 and get a discount. This is yet another advanced feature usually only found in extremely high-end shopping carts.
- *Integrated upsell:* You can't be there 24 hours a day 7 days a week to suggestively sell your shoppers additional products and services, but the Kick Start System can.
- *Soft and hard goods:* Information is the highest profit product you can sell. All you are really selling is electrons. It's all pure profit! The Kick Start Shopping System makes it easy for your customer to buy an e-book or computer program and have it instantly. We live in a society that wants instant gratification. Without your ability to deliver the products instantly you will definitely lose sales.
- *Customizable "return to shopping" button:* Send your customers directly where they can find additional products that specifically interest them. This one feature will make you lots more money.
- *Database:* All top marketers know the value of their databases. Many businesses end up selling their business and getting paid only on the value of their customer list. Who cares about computers and furniture when you can get $100 to $1,000 per customer? (A conservative example for a really tiny business: 3,000 customers valued at $400 each means you sell out for $1,200,000. *Note:* This is not all that hard to do.)

Your database of customers is also very easy to sell to when you have a new product or offer. They have already bought before and are much more likely to buy again from you. The Kick Start Integrated Database keeps track of prospects and customers and totally eliminates retyping, labor costs, and database mistakes. Having a good database is literally a license to print money.

- *Broadcast e-mail:* How would you like to reach your customers with no advertising costs, no printing, no stuffing envelopes, and no postage? That's what responsible permission based e-mail marketing allows you to do. When it's integrated into your shopping system, you have nothing more than a few keystrokes to reach all your customers at once, or only the ones who bought blue widgets.

- *Mail merge:* Broadcast e-mail is great, but e-mail merge is the greatest! This feature of the Kick Start System lets you personalize each e-mail that goes out. This gets you a much higher response. Think about it. Don't you pay more attention to an e-mail that has your name on it than one that says "Dear Friend"?

- *E-mail list management:* You can run an e-zine or e-mail newsletter and be up and running in no time at all. I have made a fortune on my e-zine because I can send good information (and offers, of course) to my sub- scribers who then buy my products and services. You need this function.

- *Ad tracking, conversion, and rotation:* Only the high-end expensive systems can do that and it's still a hassle. When ad tracking is built right into your shopping system, you can immediately maximize the value of your paid ads because your conversion module tells how much money actually came from the ad and the rotation module tells you which ad was the best. You can also do tons of testing on your own site to find out which ads pull in the most number of sales and which parts of your website attract the most buying customers.

- *Order form sell through and much more:* Kick Start Cart has many cus- tomizable areas that help you sell. Having this capability separates the ho hum Internet merchants from the ones that really make the cash register ring.

- *Recurring billing:* You want to do whatever you can to get money com- ing in regularly and automatically from your customers. Kick Start Cart's recurring billing module gives you total flexibility to give fi- nance options to close big-ticket sales and to regularly charge your cus- tomer's credit card and send the money right to your bank account.

- *Sales reports:* Kick Start Cart gives you seven different sales report options. You'll always know just how well you're doing with this kind of reporting.

- *Tell a friend:* This is called *viral marketing* and no shopping system makes it easier for you to have your customers singing your praises than Kick Start Cart.

- *Questionnaires:* You have to know what they're thinking. Kick Start Cart will have your customers pouring strategic information into your head in no time. You'll use this info to sell targeted products back to your customers who have just told you what they want.
- *Pop-up wizard:* I've never seen this included before in a shopping system. I used to pay high school kids to search out scripts for basic pop-up windows, now in a few seconds I can generate simple pop-ups that, when used judiciously, massively increase sales and visitor subscriptions to my e-zine.
- *Affiliate/associate program:* Want thousands of websites all over the world selling your products and services for you? That's what an affiliate program is all about. Other websites link to yours and you only pay them if someone clicks from their site and buys something from you.

If you really want to sell your products and services on the Internet, the Kick Start System will make it happen immediately.

In fact, you can be putting your products into the system five minutes after you sign up.

Merchant Accounts

To make money at this Internet game, you have to have some way to take credit cards. You must have a way to capture a sale immediately when you create the impulse to buy in your customer. You don't even want your prospects to have to get up from their computer. Anything that distracts them could translate into a lost sale.

One of the most important ways to grab the sale now is to have your own Visa/MasterCard/AMEX merchant account tied to your shopping system.

I almost forgot that I promised to tell you how to get a merchant account in about 10 minutes. Go about halfway down the page at http://www.KickStartCart.com, and they have one that's relatively inexpensive and compatible with Kick Start Cart.

You'll run into all kinds of deals where people will want to lease you card swiping equipment . . . unless you have a brick-and-mortar store, you will never see a credit card. All the sales are either via Internet or telephone. Sometimes a fax will come in. You simply don't need a card machine.

Get firm numbers on up-front fees, monthly fees, credit card percentages, and per transaction costs. While you're at it, find out exactly what a transaction is? Does calling for an "authorization only" constitute a transaction? Does doing a return equal a transaction? All these fees add up, but you'll consider them chump change when you start doing lots of business.

The big three that you need are Visa, MasterCard, and AMEX.

One of the places I've heard you can get merchant accounts is at the big warehouse store, Costco. I don't know the details, but apparently if you shop there, they have a program to get you a merchant account. It's certainly worth checking out. Just make sure their "online gateway" is compatible with http://www.KickStartCart.com. You should always choose your shopping system first because it will be the most important part of your system when it comes to selling more and automating your business. You then find a merchant account that's compatible. Don't do it the other way around just to save a nickel or two on your merchant account. If you do, you'll pay for it dearly when the free shopping cart they give you is a piece of junk.

You must sign up with American Express directly. You can do it online at http://www.americanexpress.com/homepage/merchant.shtml.

Assistance on securing merchant accounts: http://www.KickStartCart .com (scroll halfway down the page) and http://www.acceptcreditcards.com.

Third-Party Accounts

If you don't want all the hassle of becoming a merchant, or if your credit makes you a little worried to even try, third-party companies will come to your rescue. Here are some companies that will take your charge payments for you and send you a check. I have not used any of these companies. I've heard that it's a useful service for many people doing transactions on the web. You might suffer just a little prestige-wise, but it's a quick sign-up with most of these companies and there is very little hassle in getting started. Some are for informational (downloadable) products only. Check these companies out:

http://www.paypal.com

http://www.digibuy.com

http://www.ibill.com

http://www.ccslide.com

http://www.netbanx.com (mostly U.K. businesses)

http://www.ifulfill.com (also does fulfillment and customer service, which is likely to cost quite a bit)

Other Ways to Collect Money

Although you always have to balance time and hassle when considering other options, here are some other ways you can receive funds from people.

Online Checks

This is something I haven't bothered with yet either, but it is very easy if you are using the http://www.KickStartCart.com shopping system, which is already set up for it. When customers want to pay by e-check, they see a representation of a check on the check-out page of the cart. They just fill in their bank numbers and submit the order.

There are two methods you can use. (1) Print and pay where you actually print the check on your printer and submit it like you would a regular check and (2) using a service that handles the transaction online like http://www.onlinecheck.com.

You have to make sure your bank will accept print and pay checks and you might have to get special paper to print them on. Check it out thoroughly with both your shopping cart vendor and bank before proceeding. You also have to be sure there are funds to cover the check. Some online services will guarantee the checks for an extra fee.

Debit Cards

You won't notice much difference if someone uses a debit card instead of a credit card. You must make sure your merchant account provider allows their use. I get quite a few of them now.

Payment via E-Mail

There are safe ways to do this and a not-so-safe way to do this. The not-so-safe way is for someone to e-mail you his credit card number and expiration date. This is totally unsecure and the number could be intercepted anywhere along the path between you and the buyer. Discourage this because if the number is intercepted and used fraudulently, the buyer will think you had something to do with it.

The next best option when someone really needs to get you their credit card number is to have them split the number in half and send one half in one e-mail and the other half in another e-mail. The expiration date can also go along in a separate e-mail.

The most secure option is to have the buyer use his own online banking service that allows payment to someone else's e-mail service or to use something like PayPal that does the same thing. One advantage of this option is the buyer can stay relatively anonymous and neither one of you see the other person's account numbers.

800/900/Fax

We take lots of orders on our own 800 number. We do a brisk business, but it's not a high volume business. It's a high profit business so we simply handle the calls in-house.

If you have a high volume business, you may want to get an answering/fulfillment service that takes the orders for you. The only problem is the cost per order can be very high.

There are also companies that will set you up a 900 pay-per-call line. I've never done business this way, but it is an option.

I still get some orders via fax and it's probably a good idea to continue to make that available.

Big Ticket Transactions

If you are worried about getting the money on really large sales, you can use an online escrow service to handle the deal. This works just as well if your potential customers are as worried about you as you are about them. Customers may be very apprehensive about sending a large sum of money to you and you really can't blame them. This is where you jump in to save the sale by recommending an escrow service.

The escrow service protects both buyers and sellers in a transaction. Sellers want to be sure to get their money, and buyers want to be sure they get the merchandise as it was described. Escrow services act as a disinterested third party to help this happen. The escrow service gets a small percentage of the deal for its efforts.

Here's an article about online escrow:

http://www.nclnet.org/shoppingonline/escrowtips.htm

Articles on escrow fraud include:

http://www.auctionbytes.com/cab/abn/y02/m10/i25/s01
http://www.bankrate.com/brm/news/advice/scams/20040517b1.asp

Escrow companies:

http://dir.yahoo.com/Business_and_Economy/Shopping_and_Services
/Financial_Services/Online_Escrow_Services
http://www.escrow.com

Bad Credit Cards

If the credit card is no good at all, or over the limit, then the sale is never processed. I get e-mail notice of the attempted transaction and sometimes I attempt to save the sale if I see the expiration date is way off of normal or if I see missing credit card numbers.

Cardholders may have an expired card or may be over their credit limit. If customers really want the product, they can always mail in a check or money order, as long as you put your contact information on the site where they can see it.

If the card is bad because the person ordering just stole it five minutes ago, then your system will process it as normal and you will ship the product and won't know that the card was bad until it's too late. You will receive a chargeback from the credit card company weeks or even months later. The chargeback means the money is taken out of your account and you might get a decent explanation, but in most cases you won't get a tremendous amount of detail. You're pretty much stuck.

I have had almost zero trouble with this in the many years I have been in business, and it's likely that you won't either unless you are in a high-risk business selling Rolex watches online or something like that. The chances of you having any significant trouble with fraud is very small. Here are some things to watch out for though that will help you catch any intended fraud:

- ✓ Don't fill the order unless you get the complete contact information for the customer, including phone numbers.
- ✓ If you start having trouble with fraudulent orders, consider not accepting orders that use free web-based e-mail services, or mail forwarding services as their address. It's virtually impossible to trace them back to a real person.
- ✓ If you have any reason to suspect that an order is fraudulent, simply call the customer and check with him on the phone.

Verification Methods

One way to add another safeguard to your process is to use real-time address verification. This means the customer's billing address must match the one on file with her credit card. Many merchant accounts have this as an option you can turn on and off.

Another way is to require the additional verification numbers usually on the back of the credit card (AMEX is on the front). Your merchant account most likely has this as an additional option that you can use if you want to.

Again, it is doubtful that you will have major trouble with fraudulent orders. Watch out for it, but don't lose sleep over a couple that might slip through the cracks.

For more information on fraud prevention visit: http://www.antifraud .com/tips.htm. Companies with advanced fraud screening include:

http://www.worldpay.com

http://www.verisign.com

http://www.cybersource.com

http://www.fairisaac.com

Firewalls

With more and more small and home-based businesses getting high-speed, full-time Internet connections, like cable modem and DSL, there is an increased need for firewall software and/or hardware.

A firewall can be many things, some of which are much too technical for me to even begin to understand. What you need to know is that without one you are at risk of someone breaking into your computer. You were at risk before you got full-time Internet access, but if you are connected to the Internet full time like you are when you have a cable modem or a DSL line, you are at a much greater risk of someone accessing your computer from a remote location.

Basically, a firewall limits the access to your computer from the Internet. This has nothing to do with your website. That's your web host's responsibility: to protect your site (which is another reason to make sure you have a reputable firm hosting your website). We're talking about someone accessing the computer that's sitting on your desktop right now.

I was amazed at the number of alerts I got when I first installed my firewall. Each alert meant that someone or some automated robot was trying to access my computer.

Begin by immediately downloading and installing some free firewall software. You could visit http://www.firewall.com for many choices and more technical articles about firewalls.

I got my free firewall at http://www.zonelabs.com. It provides a good beginners level of protection. http://store.mcafee.com has a popular firewall for about $40. So does http://www.networkice.com. It has one called Black Ice Defender. As your business grows, you probably will want to graduate to more sophisticated software and hardware solutions. Just know that you must do something and you must do it now.

Virus Protection

First of all, what is a virus? A virus is a computer program that is written by someone either wanting to be cute, or more maliciously, wanting to do real damage. It can be distributed either online or via computer disks. In many cases, the virus replicates itself on its way to delivering its dastardly deed.

That deed could be something as simple as making a pop-up box say, "Bill Gates is a jerk," or something more insidious like erasing your entire hard drive or worse.

Viruses can't damage hardware. You don't have to worry about your screen blowing up or your hard drive being physically damaged. Viruses only damage software and data files, which are usually much more valuable to you than hardware anyway.

What do you have to do to protect yourself from viruses?

- *Backup:* If you backup your files regularly, viruses will have little chance of doing great damage to you and your business. Good backups allow you to simply rid yourself of the virus and restore your files to the way they were before you got the virus.
- *Antivirus software:* McAfee (http://www.mcafee.com) and Symantec (http://www.symantec.com) are favorites that make virus software. Have your computer advisor, or someone familiar with each program, suggest which one might be best for you. And don't think these are the only programs available. I just like to stick with well-known and well-supported programs. Keep in mind that you need to continually update these programs weekly, or even more often. It does little good to have these programs if they are even a month old because new viruses are being identified all the time. Also, having them and using them regularly still won't guarantee you won't get a virus. You could get a new one before the virus companies realize it exists. So, virus software is not a substitute for backups.
- *Beware of downloads:* Only download material from sites that you feel are trustworthy. This is a judgment call in some cases. You can generally trust large, well-known companies.
- *Beware of attachments:* Don't open e-mail attachments unless they are scanned and found free of viruses. Just don't do it. Also, train your employees on this issue. Pay special attention to attachments that are typically known to carry viruses like .exe, .vbs, .bat, .pif, and .scr files.
- *Scan floppy disks:* A friend might give you a floppy disk with program or data files. Be sure to run it through your virus program before you attempt to use it. Your friend may not even know a virus is on the disk.
- *Scan everything else:* Even programs downloaded from the Internet can carry viruses.
- *Isolate infected computers:* If you have several computers in your home or office, remove them from your network and do whatever it takes to quarantine or remove the virus. You don't want to let one bad apple spoil the bunch.
- *Do your windows update:* Windows computers are attacked all the time. Microsoft sends you "Windows Updates" designed to make your computer run better and safer and you should use them. Sometimes

you'll have to do a quick update every day. To set your computer to receive the updates in Windows XP click "Start," then click "help and support" then click "Windows Update."

If you faithfully do these things, you should have very little trouble with viruses. Oh, and one more thing: Don't be a big dummy and forward virus warnings. Virtually all of them are hoaxes.

Or even worse, some of these hoaxes give false instructions for fixing the virus, which makes people who use the instructions destroy their own computer software.

If you have any doubts about the authenticity of a hoax, visit one of these sites:

http://www.vmyths.com

http://www.hoaxkill.com

http://vil.mcafee.com/hoax.asp

The International Computer Security Association (http://www.trusecure .com)has in-depth and up-to-the-minute information on viruses and other computer security issues.

Sources for computer insurance:

http://www.safeware.com

http://www.insureandgo.com/computer-insurance.html

http://www.insurancewide.com/computer_insurance.html

Articles on computer insurance:

http://insurance.yahoo.com/hr/pc.in.html

http://www.insweb.com/learningcenter/articles/rent-computer.htm

Passwords

Your online security, and that of your customers, is of utmost importance. The judicious use of passwords can increase the security level of all your operations. Hackers can easily crack simple passwords, so you don't want to make it easy on them.

Here are some tips for picking and handling passwords:

✓ Use between six and nine characters.
✓ Use a combination of letters and numbers.

✓ Use a mixture of upper and lower case letters.

✓ Use different passwords at different sites. (Using the same password for everything is really risky.)

✓ Don't use words that are in the dictionary. (Hackers can run a program that compares your password to every word in the dictionary until it finds a match.)

✓ Don't tape your password list up so the world can see it.

✓ Change passwords every four to six weeks. Change it immediately if you feel your password has been compromised, or if you had to give it to someone to do some special work on your site.

If you want to get out of all the hassle of generating and remembering passwords check out these programs: PassMan (http://www.ijen.net/passman.htm) or http://www.winguides.com/security/password.php.

Web Confidential for Mac and Palm: http://www.web-confidential.com.

Spyware

Spyware covertly records information from your computer and transmits it to someone else. In many cases, you unknowingly download and install the spyware yourself when you download and install shareware and freeware programs. In fact, you actually agree to install the spyware when you quickly click the "I Agree" button on the software agreement. They have buried the notice of the spyware in a bunch of hard-to-read legalese.

This spyware can send relatively mild information to advertisers to tell them your buying habits or it can do more ominous things like record and transmit your passwords, user IDs, customer information, e-mail addresses, and just about anything it can get its software hands on.

To check to see if any spyware is on your computer, you can use a program like Ad Aware. You can download it for free at http://www.DownLoad.com Type in "Ad Aware" in their search box.

Internet Scams

To best serve your customers, you should know about Internet scams to help protect them from falling prey to financial Internet predators.

Phishing ("Brand Spoofing")

You receive an e-mail that appears to be from a legitimate organization. The e-mail requests that you click on a link and update your credit card, password, user ID, address, social security number, and other information. The link takes you to a fake site designed to look like the legitimate site. If you put the information in, it is used for identity theft.

If your customers order from you just about the time they fall prey to a "phishing" expedition, they might blame you for somehow breaching their security even though they did it themselves.

It's to your advantage to remind customers from time to time that you will never ask for personal information via e-mail.

The term *phishing* comes from the term "fishing" where someone throws out "bait"(spam/fraudulent e-mail) with hopes of catching something.

Here's a website dedicated to stopping this foul practice: http://www.antiphishing.org.

There are many other scams you should be aware of. Just keep in mind the golden rule. If it sounds to good to be true, . . . it is.

Here's another website you should visit once in a while: http://www.scambusters.com.

Also, want to keep yourself from looking stupid to your customers? Don't forward any dire warnings of new viruses and notices that the post office is going to charge a nickel for every e-mail sent, or some little girl needs a kidney.

Check things out first at:

http://hoaxbusters.ciac.org

http://www.UrbanLegends.com

Uninterruptible Power Supply

Commonly known as UPS, an uninterruptible power supply protects your computer and data from electrical outages and flickers (Figure 3.1). If you are working on an important document and the electricity goes out or even falters briefly, you will lose the information you put in since the last time you saved it (it's a good idea to save every few minutes just for this reason).

Basically this device is a battery that takes over instantly if the electricity goes out. If you want just enough protection to shut your computer down normally when you lose power, a small UPS will do. If you want it to be able to run for a while, then you have to get a bigger UPS. Since it's a battery, the longer you want it to last, the bigger and heavier it must be.

Surge Suppression

Another thing you want to protect your computer from is electrical surges. These can come from both the power source and through the phone line

**Figure 3.1   A Combined Surge Suppressor and
Uninterruptible Power Supply**

attached to your computer. Many UPS units include surge suppression for both your power input and your phone line input.

If you are on a tight budget, you can simply purchase a surge suppression power strip. These strips normally only handle the electrical input to your computer. To handle the phone input, simply unplug the phone line from your computer when you are not using it. You will be at risk only while your phone line is connected.

Other UPS Resources

http://www.apcc.com/solutions/home

http://www.jetcafe.org/~npc/doc/ups-faq.html

http://www.compinfo-center.com/pchard/ups.htm

http://www.pcguide.com/ref/power/ext/ups/types.htm

http://www.sysopt.com/userreviews/products/ups.html

Other Security References

http://www.alw.nih.gov/Security/security-faqs.html (lots of links to security articles) http://www.softdd.com/lock-protect/index.htm (free lock and protect—software to prevent anyone from running specified programs on your computer while you are away)

Other Helpful Equipment

Scanner

A scanner is used to take a hard copy of a photo or graphic and digitize it so it can be used by your computer. Remember, as we saw in the graphics optimization section, that 72 dpi is all we need so just about any cheap scanner will do. Mine cost only $49.95. It's plenty good enough. All scanners come with some simple software that will take care of most web tasks.

If you're planning on handling your website yourself, you'll run into all kinds of situations where you want to throw a photograph or line drawing up on a web page real quick. The scanner makes this happen.

You may also have old articles that aren't on disc that you want to get into your computer, but you don't want to retype them. Your scanner coupled with Optical Character Resolution (OCR) software does the trick.

> **TIP:** You'll still have some proofreading to do because OCR is rarely perfect. Textbridge Pro OCR software gets high rankings for accuracy and ease of use (http://www.scansoft.com/products).

Digital Camera

This has saved me a fortune. I used to use a really top-end professional product photographer for all my products and it would cost hundreds and hundreds of dollars for each shot. I'm not complaining about his work. It was just overkill for the normal needs on the net.

I'm laughing as I write this because on some of my products you will see what looks like a nice blue background in a photographer's studio. It is really an old T-shirt I found in the laundry room in my basement. I snapped a few pics with the digital camera and five minutes later it was in the shopping cart on my website and for sale to a worldwide market.

WHAT YOU NEED TO KNOW

 You have to have a very secure method to allow people to order from your website. You have to be able to process credit card transactions if you want to make real money and you must have a really powerful shopping cart system like http://www.KickStartCart.com. You have to protect your computers from damage and you may need to provide promotional graphics and photos to help sell your products.

Shipping Hard Goods

When you finally jump through all the hoops and get somebody to buy something, it is up to you to give the product the best chance of arriving in good condition and within a reasonable period of time.

Free Shipping Materials

Almost all of my U.S. sales go out via priority mail. There are several reasons for this. The first is that they provide different-size shipping boxes for me free of charge and they'll even deliver them to my house for free. In addition to the boxes, they give me free packing tape (Figure 3.2). This is a tremendous savings. Visit their postal store at http://www.usps.com.

For inside packing, I simply use crumpled up newspaper. It's really cheap or free and it's a form of recycling so it's good for the environment.

Use plenty of paper. Really stuff it in there to keep your items from flopping around and getting damaged. You don't want to get returned products because you simply didn't pack them properly.

**Figure 3.2 Priority Mail Boxes Come in Many Sizes and
Shapes . . . and They're FREE!**

I use the shake test on every package we send out. If you can hear rattling around inside the package, then you haven't packed it tightly enough.

Another thing I like about priority mail is that the boxes are colorful. It adds to the perceived value of the product when it arrives at its destination. The shipping time is not guaranteed, but there's a high probability that you will get the package in the hands of the buyer in a reasonable amount of time.

In my operation, the customer pays the shipping, so most of the time I get off totally free when I use priority mail.

Other Shipping Materials

Some smaller products go out in a bubble bag, which is a handy item to have around. It's lightweight and padded (Figure 3.3). I use the self-seal bubble bags so we don't have to staple or tape the package shut and the customer doesn't risk cutting himself on a sharp staple when he opens the package.

You might also save the popcorn-type shipping material you get when something is delivered to you. You can also buy it in large garbage bag quantities from office supply/pack and ship stores.

You should have a packing tape dispenser or two handy. We keep one full of priority mail tape (which is free). We also keep several around with clear

Figure 3.3   Padded Bags Used to Mail Smaller Items

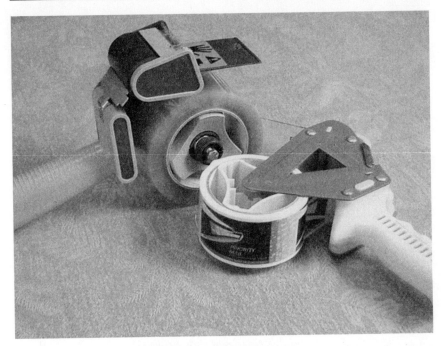

Figure 3.4   Tape Dispensers

packing tape in them. We use clear as opposed to brown tape because many times we want to tape over the address label to protect it from rain or moisture (Figure 3.4).

We also keep a razor blade knife around along with magic markers, cellophane tape, and packing slip pouches. Packing slip pouches stick to the outside of a package and hold the piece of paper that describes the contents of the package (Figure 3.5 on p. 152).

Federal Express (FedEx)

When I absolutely have to have something somewhere, I use FedEx. They have only let me down twice in 20 years. Again the packaging is free as in priority mail, but the big difference is the precise handling of the packages. I don't trust anyone else with my most important packages. In my opinion, no other overnight service can hold a candle to them.

You can sign up for a FedEx account and they will give you a starter kit of supplies and deliver it right to your door (http://www.fedex.com). I haven't bothered with it, but you can run your entire FedEx account online (as you can with many of the other carriers).

Figure 3.5   Packing Slip Pouches

International Shipping

I can't use my priority mail boxes for shipping outside the United States so I keep a small supply of regular cardboard boxes for those shipments. Also, I'm not above reusing boxes from packages I've received. When I buy boxes, I usually get them from http://www.uline.com.

You can get a supply of customs forms from your local post office. It is much easier to fill them out before you leave for the post office.

I won't go into too much detail about International shipping here because rules and regulations change quickly. As you start doing more business on the Internet, you will naturally learn the ins and outs of shipping out of your own country.

Here's a link that will come in handy when you do lots of shipping in and to the United States: http://zipinfo.com/search/zipcode.htm.

Running Your Business from Afar

You'll find it very handy to reach your home or office computer when traveling. When you start doing lots of business, things will come up when you are on the road that need handled. You could have a backup with you of all your critical files, but in real life it's very difficult to anticipate every single thing you might need.

I use a service called "Go to My PC" (http://www.qksrv.net/click-1464114 -3215923). This allows me to contact my home computer securely from anywhere in the world I can get Internet access. I've used it without a hitch from Australia, New Zealand, Canada, and Asia.

There are other programs that will do this, but you have to be a total propeller head to use them. This one is pretty easy. I highly recommend it.

Keyboard Analyzers (Bad)

You must be especially careful when traveling and using Internet Cafes and Kiosks. I know it's tempting to check all your sales, bank accounts, and shopping cart reports, but you never know if someone has installed a keyboard analyzer on those machines. This records all the keystrokes on the computer you are working on. The crook then retrieves all the things you typed in and has immediate access to your passwords and private information.

Keyboard Analyzers (Good)

I once had a guy working for me and I caught him operating his own porn sites while he was supposed to be doing my work. I had another girl who was supposed to be doing some writing and she was actually snoring when I walked in on her.

I work too hard to have slugs like that taking advantage of me. Now I have my own keyboard analyzer. I use http://www.SpectorSoft.com products.

This software sends me an encrypted e-mail every thirty minutes and gives me a complete report of every single thing done on one of my business computers. If an employee tells me we have been working on writing a manual for the last couple hours, I have the evidence right in my inbox, . . . and I could be on the road 3,000 miles away.

I prefer to use this software as a deterrent rather than to catch someone, so I tell people when they get hired not to do anything on my work computer that isn't work related.

You might want to check with your lawyer, but pretty much the consensus is that things done on your computer, on your Internet connection, in your business belong to you.

WHAT YOU NEED TO KNOW

 If you are shipping from the United States, you can get free boxes and shipping supplies from the Post Office. You must pack your products tightly so they do not suffer damage in transit. You should get a free account in advance from FedEx so you are ready when someone needs something in a hurry. You should have the ability to contact your home computer when you are traveling. You must be careful when using public computers and you can monitor your own business computers with the use of keyboard analyzers.

4

How to Create and Distribute a Kickbutt Electronic Magazine

This chapter deals with prong two of our three-prong attack on electronic marketing. If you do what you learn here, you will have a profitable entity virtually right from the start because the cost of this attack is low or even nonexistent.

You probably have the equipment right now to create an electronic magazine (e-zine). You may want to purchase additional software to make the process easier, but it's certainly not necessary. My e-zine, *Great Speaking*, which has been online for more than six years, has made money right from the first week.

An e-zine is an extremely cheap investment for your business, and learning how to do the magazine and the website together is the best investment I've made in my entire business life.

What is the difference between an e-zine and a newsletter? They're used simultaneously, but many organizations have electronic newsletters just for informational or customer service purposes. They don't care about the money. They just want to get the message out without printing a newsletter. IBM might have one for their employees. I call mine an e-zine because it has mostly "how to" information with some news articles of happenings in the industry and some humor, and *e-zine* sounds cooler. There's not a big difference in the terms, but the term *e-magazine* (e-zine) also denotes a commercial venture that includes advertisements along with business items.

Can Spam Act

You have to comply with certain rules when you send e-mail. This act doesn't affect legitimate e-mail marketers much, so it's nothing you have to get yourself crazy over. The act took effect January 1, 2004, and outlines guidelines and requirements for commercial e-mail.

I don't want to waste a lot of time on this because legitimate e-mailers do most of the right things anyway. Here's the bottom line from my point of view on what you should do and not do to be in compliance:

- Legitimately obtain your e-mail addresses and get permission to e-mail to each person. You'll see how to do that here.
- Make sure a real and legitimate e-mail address is in the "From" and "Reply to" areas of the e-mail. We want to be contacted about our products and services because we aren't ashamed of them.
- Make sure the person getting the e-mail can unsubscribe easily and that your unsubscribe mechanism works. Use a legitimate broadcast e-mail program such as http://www.KickStartCart.com for an automatic unsubscribe mechanism.
- Put a physical mailing address in each of your e-mails. It's easy to add.
- Make sure your subject line accurately reflects the contents of your e-mail. Not doing this ruins your reputation.
- Sternly warn any affiliates that they must use only permission-based e-mails or you will cut them off immediately. If you catch anyone out of compliance, remove him or her right away and document the circumstances.

I'm not a lawyer, so definitely consult one if you have any questions about whether your e-mail is in compliance with the Can Spam Act.

Netiquette

As you get more deeply into the field of electronic marketing, you will obviously be dealing with more and more e-mail. It's probably a good time to do a quick review of the unofficial rules of Internet etiquette or *netiquette*.

When communicating online, you can easily misinterpret someone's meaning. It's also easy to have what you write misinterpreted by the person receiving your e-mail. There are no corresponding body language and voice inflections that help to convey your meaning. Even in the fast-paced society in which we reside, you should take your time before hitting the send button or damage could be done.

In addition to how you word your message, a few tips will make your e-mails welcome in the recipient's inbox:

✓ Be careful how much you write and how often. People are busy. Some prefer brief notes once in a while, and some are happy to read longer messages and are willing to read them more often. The best thing to do is ask and act accordingly.

✓ If you send out jokes to your friends, check once in a while to see if they still want to receive them. Also, make sure you don't send offensive, political, or off-color jokes to people you don't know very well.

✓ Do not type in all capital letters, which is considered to be shouting and very rude. You can, however, use all capital letters sparingly for emphasis.

✓ Do not use misleading subject lines or send e-mail marked "urgent" just to get someone to open your message. If you have misled the receiver, he or she probably won't open another one of your messages.

✓ Use emoticons (emotional icons) and abbreviations to add extra meaning to what you have written. LOL means "Laughing out loud," and :) means you are smiling as you write or just kidding. Some of the more well-known emoticons and abbreviations follow:

```
<g>        Grin
<G>        Big grin
<GRIN>     Big grin
:)         Smile (Turn your head sideways to look at
           these.)
:-)        Smile with nose
:(         Frown
:-(        Frown with nose
;)         Winking
ROFL       Rolling on the floor, laughing
ROFLMAO    Rolling on the floor laughing my ass off
IMHO       In my humble opinion
IOHO       In our humble opinion
IMO        In my opinion
BTW        By the way
@—>—>——    A long-stemmed rose
```

For more emoticons, see http://www.cknow.com/ckinfo/emoticons.htm.

✓ When you distribute a message to a list of people, don't send the e-mail with everyone's e-mail address showing unless you want others to know who is getting copies. Learn to use your e-mail blind carbon copy (Bcc) capability.

✓ When replying to an e-mail, don't simply say, "Yes, that's right." The person who sent you the original e-mail may not remember to what you are agreeing. Copy only a small part of the e-mail you received into your reply.

TIP: Don't copy the entire e-mail into your reply unless every word of it is necessary.

✓ In personal correspondence, don't post a personal e-mail that you have received to a group without permission. However, if you send me something ridiculous, as the publisher of *Great Speaking* e-zine, I may publish it as a letter to the editor.

✓ Keep in mind you may be corresponding with someone from a different culture. Humor doesn't translate well and you could easily offend.

✓ Be forgiving of other people's mistakes and politely teach them what they did wrong.

Netiquette resources:

http://www.onlinenetiquette.com

http://www.albion.com/netiquette

http://builder.cnet.com/Business/Rules (lots of website etiquette)

WHAT YOU NEED TO KNOW

 Some things on the Internet can make you look foolish, which hurts your professional reputation, and some things can make people downright mad and get you in trouble. It will be worth your time to review the preceding section so you don't hurt your reputation.

E-Zine Types

There are two types of e-zines. The first is web-based. For example, http://www.presentations.com has a printed presentations magazine and a website, which is their online version of the magazine.

The second type of e-zine is an e-mail-based e-zine, which is better because it can be done with no fancy formatting and no graphics. It's simple to create; plain text is delivered to people via e-mail. You can have both web-based and e-mail-based if you'd like, but it's not necessary to have both. Having both takes quite a bit more work, and if you don't know how to do the website yourself, you must depend on someone else and there may be a significant time delay. However, the web-based e-zine will look nicer than the text-based one.

In most cases, a web-based version is counterproductive. In many areas of the world, it is much easier and more cost effective to download e-mail and read it offline. In addition, people check their e-mail regularly but do not remember to visit your website regularly to view the new issue of your magazine. E-mail allows you to put your message right in front of your recipients as soon as you have it ready.

Use the Nike advice, and "just do it." I'm an example of making a decision and just doing it. I did not know how to do teleseminars. One day, I did one and made a fortune on it. If you just do some of these things, you can make a lot of money. The technology will greatly expand your potential.

If you want to see some of my work, I have back issues on my website at http://www.antion.com/ezinebackissues.htm. I suggest that you read them as part of your strategy that we talk about later. You can see how different elements have changed in my e-zine over the years.

HTML or Not?

Someone in my Butt Camps always wants to argue with me about whether they should do their e-zine in plain text or HTML (so it will come out all nicely formatted and looking like a web page). You just have to realize that a certain percentage of your audience will be lost because they won't be able to read your carefully formatted document. This is not that big of a problem now, but there are other significant problems with sending HTML e-mail.

These kinds of decisions all depend on your market. If you have a tightly targeted corporate market, entirely in the United States, you probably can use an HTML format because most have more sophisticated e-mail programs. The problem is recipients might be able to read it, but are not "allowed" to read it or even get it at all. Many corporations discourage the receipt of HTML e-mail because it just eats up resources for no good reason.

Some of the newer list management companies are able to detect whether the recipient is able to read HTML e-mails and will deliver a plain text version automatically. Some publishers simply ask their subscribers whether they want plain text or HTML.

HTML will create more work for you, too. It's expected to look nice, which demands more work on your part.

Some estimates say that as much as 40 percent of HTML e-mail does not get to its recipient looking like it was intended to look. This means if you aren't a real pro e-mailer, you probably don't know all the tricks necessary to make your HTML e-mail look good when it gets to your subscriber.

New software is being developed that allows template-based HTML e-newsletters to be easily created and delivered. The delivery mechanism recognizes e-mail readers who are not capable of reading HTML and delivers them a plain text version. The software also recognizes AOL addresses and delivers them a special version of the e-mail. To look into these systems, which are constantly improving, visit http://www.imakenews.com (very expensive) and http://www.constantcontact.com. These fancy programs are not a save-all. They still limit your design and are time consuming to use.

Also, porn filters tend to target HTML e-mail, which could further limit its delivery.

The biggest and most telling reason not to use HTML e-mail is that many of my colleagues, as well as me, who pull in over $1 million a year won't use HTML e-mail. . . . Think about it.

Your final decision should be made by testing in your market. I suggest you start with plain text and ask your market before you attempt HTML e-mail.

Pros and Cons of HTML E-Zines and Newsletters

Pros

✓ You can include graphics and pictures.

✓ Your response rate could be higher.

✓ You have more options when it comes to the types of links you include.

✓ You can track how many people actually open your e-zine/newsletter by noting how many times a certain graphic was served.

✓ You can track what time the e-mail was viewed.

✓ You can track actual ad click throughs more easily.

✓ You can provide a more seamless experience between the newsletter and your website since they can look nearly identical.

✓ Because many recipients of HTML newsletters are online when they read their newsletters, you can put the entire article on your website and only put teaser copy about the article in your newsletter. This will increase visits to your website.

Cons

✓ You will clearly lose readers who either cannot read HTML, don't want HTML because of the larger file size, or aren't allowed to receive HTML e-mails because of corporate restrictions.

✓ It's much more work for you to prepare HTML e-mails and make them look good.

✓ HTML file sizes are usually bigger than an equivalent text-based newsletter, so some people will resist subscribing because they must pay for download time and file transfer amounts.

✓ If you have lots of subscribers on AOL, you will probably have lots of trouble because their e-mail program now comes with the HTML capability turned off, and many AOL users wouldn't even know how to turn it on if they wanted to.

✓ HTML newsletters are normally meant to be read while someone is connected to the Internet. In many cases, the images are not included in the e-mail, but served from the website to keep the file size of the e-mail low. If someone tries to download your e-mail and read it offline, it could look really bad because the graphics will be missing.

✓ HTML newsletters are more difficult to forward and frequently get corrupted in the process. This means you'll lose recommendations because the person receiving the forward either can't read it, or it looks so terrible they don't want to read it.

✓ HTML e-mail is targeted by porn filters, and you'll get a negative point (explained later) just because it's an HTML e-zine.

For many more helpful articles on e-zine formatting in both HTML and plain text, visit http://ezine-tips.com/articles.

WHAT YOU NEED TO KNOW

 You have to make an initial decision on whether you want to do a plain text or a fancier HTML (looks like a web page) e-zine.

Reasons to Publish an E-Zine

Helps Make You the Expert

The first thing a good e-zine does is help to establish you as an expert. I was considered an expert in advanced presentation skills for some time. I had books, tapes, and videos, and I was coaching people all over the place. What the e-zine does is tell more people I'm an expert, and it does so for almost no cost. It really spreads the word with only a little bit of time invested.

Fees Rise

My consulting rates started out at $75 per hour. When my book came out, they jumped to $150 per hour. Since my magazine has been out, I jumped to $250 per hour because my time and efforts are multiplied so much. Now they are $1,000 per hour. My time is better spent with the magazine because it brings in so much more money than working with just one person. Therefore, if just one person talks to me, I have to get more money out of it. The magazine helps build your expertise and eventually makes you the expert and makes you the most sought-after person to call.

Increases Sales

Another way you make money is to sell a lot more of your products and services. My own all-time personal record happened December 28 of last year. I sold over $50,000 worth of product in three days just from the e-zine tied to the website. One of my students used the exact same promotion and took in more than $20,000 a week later. Another one of my e-mails sold over $20,000 promoting four free teleseminars, which in turn made offers for products and services. It's not millions overnight, but that's a lot of money coming in for sitting here in this chair.

Fills Up Seminars

You have an instant way to fill up your seminars. When you build an e-mail list, it can be a very valuable part of your business and there's no time delay.

I sent out my e-mail for one teleseminar two days in advance. I almost filled it on my first e-mailing. I did the same seminar two other times, and they both sold out with only two days' notice. You can test things immediately for virtually no cost. It not only makes you money but also saves you money and time.

Barter

Another way you make or, in this case, save money is to barter for things. In the first week, the $3,000 I made was in cash and $2,000 came in bartered services. I'm getting a professionally designed book cover for my next book, and all I'm trading is classified ads in my magazine, which costs me nothing. It's a tremendous barter tool, and I'm starting to see how magazine and big list people think. The e-mail list is very valuable, and it does not cost me money to get the services I need. Therefore, it's a tremendous tool for barter. I've traded for a cool poster of me. I've even traded for some professional copywriting.

Ad Revenue

You can also make money through ad revenue. In fact, for some people the only reason they do newsletters is to sell ads in them. Once you get your subscriber count up enough, maybe 3,000 or so, you can start selling ads. You can even have fewer subscribers if it's a highly targeted professional list. You can get ad revenue, and there are companies that will broker it for you. They do all the work and take part of the money as a commission.

Ad Placement

Should you put the ads together or intersperse them with the copy? All the savvy publishers put the ads either right in the article; that is, they split the article with the ad or put the ads between the articles. There are two major reasons for this:

1. If ads are all bunched together, the reader can instantly skip over them and get to the articles. They could still skip over them placed between the articles, but psychologically if they are reading an article their mind has slowed down to comprehend the article, and the ad has a better chance of being seen and acted on when the reader is in the slow mode.
2. Many people print out e-zines to file or read while they are traveling or offline. If the ads are bunched together, the page they are on can be thrown away and never seen—not a good deal for you or your advertisers.

Focus Group

Having your own e-mail list is like having an instantly available focus group to test ads and other promotions. You can reward the group with download-able informational products that cost you nothing. The same kind of testing in person would cost thousands of dollars.

Paid Subscriptions

If your content is good enough, you can do a paid e-zine. A really good book on how to do this is *Paperless Newsletter* written by super gurus Monique Harris and Terry Dean, available at http://www.paperlessnewsletter.com.

Gets You Published Quickly

The last thing isn't really a direct moneymaker, but it allows you to be pub-lished fast. This entire set of Internet resources, websites, and e-zines allows you to be a published person a lot faster. You can write articles and distribute them through your own newsletter. Other people will distribute them for you on their websites and in their e-zines. This sends people back to your website to sign up for your electronic magazine.

How do you create this terrific marketing tool? Well, the first question you have to ask is, "What is your purpose in doing it?" Do you want to use it to give service and user tips to your customers? That one might not have ads in it. Do you want to be considered an expert? You might have a different slant on your e-zine if you wanted that. Do you want to sell products? Some people simply want ad revenue. That's the only reason they do a newsletter, and it can be very lucrative if you get your list numbers up high.

Some companies pull in $20,000 a week on classified ads. That's also a possibility. Then you have to decide, do you want to make it free or paid? A gentleman talking with me recently wanted to do a free version and then an advanced or a gold club or something for pay. I have never done that, but get-ting paid for your newsletter is certainly a possibility. It happens all the time in regular printed newsletters. The great thing is that it does not cost any-thing to test it. It's a wonderful way to test out your concepts whether you want to do it as a free or paid publication.

I do a free publication because I want to get many people "opting in." The more people I can contact, the more chances I have to sell consulting ser-vices on a business-to-business basis, videos, and every other product I have. I also get referrals for speaking engagements for which I pay a commission, so I want to reach as many people as I can. Since I'm not worried about tar-geting a certain demographic for the ad revenue, the more the merrier to me. The e-zine does have a common theme, though. People on the list are interested in speaking in some fashion. They want to either improve for their work or be paid to speak. The more targeted the list, the better. The people who can't make any money with these lists are the ones who try to sell everything to everyone.

If you have a department store, you certainly can still use the concept of an e-zine. Your subscribers will not be interested in just one thing. You'll have to keep it more general and pop around with the topics more to have the best chance of keeping subscribers. You'll also have to use it frequently to announce special "subscriber only" sales. That tends to keep people on the list because they don't want to miss the sales.

Now let's jump to the other end of the spectrum. Let's say you sell a very sophisticated piece of industrial machinery in a highly competitive field. You use an e-zine to give weekly user tips to the engineers who run the machinery and to announce monthly free teleconferences to answer user questions. You can even use your e-zine and teleconferences as support bonuses to help your sales team make the sale in the first place.

What if you just have a simple mom-and-pop ice cream store? You can announce weekly specials, and you could even have a birthday club that sends e-mails automatically counting down to Junior's birthday. Don't forget you could have an ice cream cake-making class right at your store and fill up the store with participants with no radio or newspaper ads. You simply send e-mails to the customers on your list. Here's a bonus tip. Give them a free coupon for an ice cream cone if they bring a friend who has never been to the store.

What You Need to Know

 Publishing an e-zine has tremendous benefits, and I don't want you to resist like I did and waste any more time. I would have 50,000 more subscribers and be earning double what I am now had I moved on this when I became aware of it.

Frequency

You also have to determine the frequency of your e-zine. My e-zine happens to be roughly twice a month with special inserts.

Don't bury people in e-mails from you. This is what causes them to unsubscribe. You have to test the waters with your target market to see how many times they are willing to hear from you without asking to be removed from your list.

Decide on Length

Then you have to decide how short or long your e-zine is going to be. Long will be okay if it has good content that people need. Many of e-zine issues aren't read immediately, but people tell me that they save them. Many print them out, put them in a folder, and then look at them when they are on planes or whenever they normally read their periodicals.

Keep in mind that the content is what keeps them on the list. Use whatever length it takes to put out good stuff, but if you are going to err, err on the side of shorter. It does take work to get the articles done, but I show you later how to lessen that load, too.

You have to ask yourself, "How much time am I willing to devote to this thing?" That will also help determine how short or long it is. The one thing you need to watch is its length. If it gets too long, AOL will turn your e-mail into an attachment, which is very bad. It's a lot of trouble for people to download material. It doesn't come through right, and they don't want to do it. Experiment with the length and send it to friends who have AOL or send it to yourself if you have AOL. If it comes through okay without turning into an attachment, then it will be okay for all AOL members. And don't forget to do this test *before* you send out your e-zine to your list.

A nice thing about creating this e-zine, since it is all text, is that you don't have to buy any fancy programs. In fact, every computer out there will do simple text in Windows, which is what I am using. I do mine in a text-based word processor called Textpad (http://www.textpad.com). I like to have the advanced editing functions that Microsoft Notepad doesn't have.

There are some cautions you need to take. I found out if I used WordPerfect or Microsoft Word and sent it out, the apostrophes were turning into some weird Greek character. So I *never* suggest doing your text-based e-zine in an advanced word processor program like Word or WordPerfect. You will be sorry if you do.

Templates

I keep my newsletter on a template, so all the recurring things that are in each issue are saved in a file. When the next issue comes up, I get that file out, save it as Volume XXX, Issue #YYY, and start working. That cuts out tons of work. So once you do the first one, then the next issues involve only filling in the articles and ads, which is fast to do.

Make sure you visit this website: http://www.e-zinez.com. This is where I learned a lot about this subject, and it's a good place for you to start. Read every page of that site, and follow all the links you find there. It will take you a couple of days, but you will get a complete education that will mean many dollars in your pocket. If you play your cards right like I have, it could literally mean a small fortune coming your way every month. In addition, the site has a simple template all ready to go: http://www.e-zinez.com /handbook/template.html. You could just take their template, erase their main headings, put yours in, e-mail it to yourself, and have a newsletter tonight. It's very simple to do.

Link Tips and Tricks

Another cool thing to include when creating a newsletter is *links,* also known as *hyperlinks.* When someone receives your e-mail newsletter, the link you put in may or may not be clickable. Many e-mail programs will recognize the link, so all the reader has to do is click on it. Some people (AOL included) will have to cut and paste the link into their browser window and hit go, or press enter to go to the link. Maybe AOL will fix this one of these days.

Here's how to format the link so that most e-mail readers will recognize it and turn it into a link. For example, with:

http://www.antion.com

you must put the "http://" at the beginning, and you must put a space at the end of the link for it to work. Don't hit the enter key. Make sure you use the space bar to add a space at the end. If you use that format, you will have the greatest chance that someone will simply be able to click on your link instead of being forced to cut and paste it.

If you're going to put an e-mail address in your e-zine, this is the format:

mailto:tom@antion.com

You must use the "mailto:" format and don't put any spaces in the entire string. Again, you must put a space at the end to help the recipient's e-mail reader recognize the fact that it is a link. In this case, when the e-mail link is clicked on, it fires up recipients' default e-mail program, and the e-mail address you want them to go to is already in the "To:" line of the e-mail. All they have to do is type their message and hit "Send."

Advanced Link Tricks

When you really want to get fancy, you can make an e-mail link automatically include the subject line, too. Sometimes this is called a *forced link.* It presently works about 95 percent of the time. This feature is important if the filters on your list management company require a certain subject line. It also makes things easier for your clientele, which is always a good thing. Here's how you do it:

Following the main e-mail address, put a question mark, then the word *subject*, then an equal sign (=), and finally the information you want included in the subject line. You can't have any spaces in the entire string. Anywhere you want a space in the actual subject put %20. I don't know why and I don't want to. I just know it's a handy thing to know. Here's an example:

```
<mailto:tom@antion.com?subject=SUBSCRIBE%20GREAT%20SPEAKING>
```

Here's another trick: On long, clickable links like the preceding one, you should put < > symbols around the entire link. If you don't and the link is so long that the recipient's e-mail reader wraps it to the next line, it is very likely it won't work. The < > symbols help to keep it working, but it's not 100 percent effective. Again, I don't know why it works and I don't care. If you know you have very short links that are on the left side of the page, then you don't have to worry about the symbols. The symbols do, however, make a link requiring punctuation at the end look a little nicer. For example: <mailto:tom@antion.com>.

When you don't use these formatting techniques, you are making it harder for people to do business with you. You want them to be able to click links and quickly go to your website to buy and/or e-mail you.

Now it really gets crazy.

When doing this forced link, the first forced item begins with a question mark (?) symbol. Second, third, and fourth forces each begin with an ampersand (&) symbol. The forced item itself is the header line name (or "body" to automatically fill in body text), followed by an equals sign (=) and then the content.

So, if you want the "To:" address to be tom@antion.com with a carbon copy being sent to janet@overhall.com, using "Send speaking info" as the subject and body copy of "I want to be a professional speaker," your link would be:

```
mailto:tom@antion.com?cc=janet@overhall.com&subject=Send%20
speaking%20info&body=I%20want%20to%20be%20a%20professional
%20speaker
```

I told you this would get crazy! Notice that the blank spaces in the subject and body are replaced with the "%20" code. For some reason, anything that is not a number or a letter must have a special code. To complicate things more, question marks, ampersands, percent signs, and equal signs all have specific meanings, so if you want to make them display when using these tricks, you have to give them a code.

The code is a percent sign followed by something else. I think it's called a hexadecimal equivalent. If you want to display a space, you insert the "%20" code. If you want to display a quotation mark, you insert "%22" and so on. Here are some common codes:

```
space     = %20
"         = %22
%         = %25
&         = %26
;         = %3B
=         = %3D
?         = %3F
new line = %13%10 (You must insert both of these codes.
This works only in the body area.)
```

Special Note about AOL

AOL is always a concern because its proprietary system can be troublesome. We do need to address AOL, though, because it has close to 30 million subscribers whom we sure don't want to miss. The reputation of AOL is that many of the people using its system are not very Internet savvy; that is, they are newbies. In some instances, you may want to give extra instructions for these people.

For instance, some AOL people would see the mailto:tom@antion.com and try to cut and paste the entire thing into their e-mail program. They don't know they only needed to cut and paste the e-mail address. So, they dutifully put the entire thing including "mailto:" in the "To:" area of their e-mail program and try to send the e-mail. The "mailto:" is designed only to make an automatic system recognize the fact that this link is an e-mail. You can't send an e-mail with the "mailto:" term in the address.

If you have quite a few AOL members on your list, you might have to put a note next to the link that says something like this: "AOL users, just copy the e-mail address—not the 'mailto' into the 'to' line of your e-mail program."

Or, you can include an extra HTML markup that will allow AOL users to click your links. This is done as follows:

```
<A HREF="http://www.yourwebsite.com/"> AOL users, click here</A>
```

Remember, if you do this, you will sacrifice some of the nice looks of your document because you'll have to put every link in twice just to satisfy AOL folks.

WHAT YOU NEED TO KNOW

Don't freak out with what you just saw. You will learn the link tricks as you need them. Some of them you may never need. Just make sure you can format a basic website link and e-mail address link in your e-zine. You'll also have to do a little testing of your market to see how often to send your e-mails.

Formatting

You can add some formatting elements to your e-zine to make it easier to read and to emphasize key points. You can also make up graphic elements that make it more interesting visually.

Dividers

Following are ASCII divider bars. What does ASCII mean? Who cares? It just has something to do with plain text (remember, we don't want to become techies; we just want to make money). Heavier weight bars will get more attention and make more of a separation than the next example, which is a simple thin line.

_____

¤⁰º`º⁰Ħ∅,,,∅Ħ⁰º`º Ħ⁰∅,,,∅Ħ⁰º`º⁰Ħ∅,,,∅Ħ⁰º`º⁰Ħ∅,,,Ħ∅⁰º`º⁰Ħ∅,,,∅

:~*~:...:~*~:...:~*~:...:~*~:...:~*~:...:~*~:...:~*~:...:~*~:.

.:**:_.:**:_.:**:_.:**:_.:**:_.:**:_.:**:_.:**:.

.^..^.*.^.*.^.*.^.*.^.*.^.*.^.*.^.*.^.*.^.*.

@@@@@@@@@88888888%%%%%::%::::::::::::.:...:.. . . .

###

===

<><><><><><><><><><><><><><><><><><><><><><><><><><><>

Don't use the next two examples as divider bars. They are likely to make your e-mail look like spam to a spam filter.

$$

!!

Experiment to come up with your own custom divider bars.

All Caps

Although using all capital letters is considered offensive by most Internet users (it indicates that you are shouting), it can be used effectively to add emphasis in your e-zine.

Keep all caps to the absolute minimum or eliminate them altogether if you can because excessive caps also set off spam filters.

Quotation Marks

Because you can't italicize something in a plain text document, you could simply use quotation marks to add emphasis. Of course, you will use them for actual quotations, too.

White Space

Not leaving enough white space (blank lines) between paragraphs and sections of your e-zine is a major mistake. I get e-zines all the time that might have good content, but because they appear so hard to read, I usually end up deleting them.

Blank Spaces

I'm not talking about blank lines, but rather blank spaces between the left margin of your e-zine and the beginning of your text. It's not a good idea to try to use tabs in an e-zine. You just never know how the recipient's e-mail reader will interpret them. You can indent text by using your space bar before typing the text. Trying to indent several lines of text could be an exercise in frustration. Even if you get them to line up on your system, you can't be sure they will also be lined up for your subscriber.

Bullets

I use these plain text characters whenever I want to make a bullet:

=> (the "equal symbol" and the "greater than" symbol typed next to each other)

Most of the time I don't even attempt to indent the second line of text. If I do, I use the same number of indent spaces for each line that is underneath a bullet.

Weird Line Wrapping

Sometimes I get things that have a long line, then one word on the next line, and then another long line. Here's a sample from *Great Speaking* e-zine:

```
WORDS THAT SELL by Tom Antion

The title of this article is the same as a famous book
by Richard Bayan that is used by marketing
professionals
around the world. As I was looking through it the
other
day I realized that the same kinds of words could
be used in presentations to get the same kinds of
effects.
```

In the preceding sample, the e-zine was sent with the words wrapping naturally at whatever the sender's margins were set. The same text with line breaks (hard returns) inserted at the end of each line follows:

```
WORDS THAT SELL by Tom Antion

The title of this article is the same as a
famous book by Richard Bayan that is used by
marketing professionals around the world. As I was
looking through it the other day I realized that
the same kinds of words could be used in
presentations to get the same kinds of effects.
```

In the old days, you had to count approximately 60 to 65 characters, including the spaces between words. You can go more than that, but I try to keep it in that range or less. After you were done editing your newsletter, and you knew that you were not going to change things anymore, you went to the end of each line and put a hard return by hitting the enter key. That key forces a definite end to the line. Almost any e-mail program that reads your newsletter will keep it looking nice in a straight line down the left side of the page, instead of getting one long line with one word on the next line. If you put a hard return at the end of about 60 to 65 characters, you'll get rid of the formatting problem.

The hard return trick is still viable if you don't have any of the new programs that do it for you. There is now a way to get out of this pain-in-the-neck necessity for good formatting.

The two programs I know of are: Textpad at http://www.textpad.com and Note Tab Pro at http://www.notetab.com. These programs are handy because they have full editing features like a good word processor, but they can also be set to put in an actual hard return at any number of characters you choose.

Don't think you can just set the margins of your word processor to wrap at 65 characters. Trust me, it doesn't work that way. I have read that it might be possible if you set your settings a certain way, but you are much safer if you put a hard return at the end of each line. If you don't, there will be a pretty good chance that strange formatting will happen depending on the way the recipient's e-mail program is set (which you have no control over).

WHAT YOU NEED TO KNOW

 Even though we're talking about a simple, plain text e-mail newsletter, there are still some things that can make it look terrible to the recipient. The preceding formatting guidelines will make you look good no matter who reads your message.

E-Zine Components

Let's discuss the elements of an e-zine.

Headers

I usually give my headers some bold divider character so it stands out. I insert the title "Great Speaking" and the volume and issue number. After I had a decent number of subscribers, I started putting circulation figures in each issue to brag a little bit. Don't put the circulation figures in there if you have only two subscribers! You can also put your copyright, along with the name of the publisher—which is usually you.

```
###########################################
              GREAT SPEAKING
             Circulation 93,438
        Vol. 6 Number 2—February 6, 2004
        Publisher: Tom Antion tom@Antion.com
              http://www.Antion.com
            (C) Anchor Publishing 2004
###########################################
```

Benefits and Recommendations

In my case, I put in a benefit statement stating that the subscribers will get business leads as one of their perks. Then I put a little statement to encourage them to recommend this e-zine to someone.

```
*** SPEAKER BUSINESS LEADS ***
Your subscription gets you free speaking leads when available.

Please recommend this e-zine to anyone you know who is interested
in being a better presenter or who may want to make money speaking
and training. (It's a good way to stay in touch with clients, too.)
You don't even have to mail them an article.
http://www.antion.com/recommend.html

If you are receiving this issue as a forward and would like
to get your own free subscription, visit

http://www.antion.com/ezinesubscribe.htm
```

Privacy Statement

A privacy statement can be added to let people know you will not be releasing their e-mail address to anyone else.

```
PRIVACY STATEMENT: http://www.antion.com/privacystatement.htm
```

Important note on privacy statements: Don't make the mistake of swearing on a stack of bibles that you won't sell a person's e-mail address or personal information. What if you want to sell your business? You have just violated your own privacy statement, and you are now open to litigation for doing so. A smart buyer would avoid you because of this.

Read my privacy statement for the terminology I use, and consult your attorney if you have any questions.

Table of Contents

Another thing you can add is a table of contents. You've probably seen examples of this if you're on my e-zine list. I also put in a humor section and useful websites. You could put in tips or tricks for any industry that you serve.

Some people put the actual article title next to the section number. I don't do this because I don't want readers to be able to quickly say to themselves, "I don't like the topic of that article." If you do that, then readers will not scroll past the ad I have strategically placed in that section. Try it both ways and see what works best for you.

```
============================================================

                      IN THIS ISSUE
============================================================
        1. Quick Presentation Skills Tip
        2. Advanced Presentation Skills Article
           (Beginners should read this, too.)
        3. Humor Technique Series
        4. Speaker Marketing Tip
        5. Speaker Humor
        6. Websites for Speakers
```

Ads

Advertisers in e-zines are called *sponsors*. The best way to do ads is to spread them throughout the e-zine rather than put them all in one section. If the classifieds are all bunched together, you can simply zoom past all of them quickly and never read them. To prevent that, spread them out and try to make them match the article they're near. I might put an ad for a marketing item near the marketing section and so forth.

Some e-zine publishers put an ad right in the middle of an article to really force you to see it if you are reading that article.

```
********** OUR SPONSOR ***********

DISCOVER "MILLIONAIRE-MAKER" DAN KENNEDY'S
breakthrough strategies for making $20,000 an
hour without a gun for professional speakers and
people seriously interested in the business of
speaking. Earn more speaking PART TIME than most
do full time and stay booked solid with minimum
marketing.

Details: http://kennedysite.com/speaking.co
*********************************
```

To find a sample of my ad rates, send an e-mail to mailto:sponsor@antion .com and get the complete ad rates via autoresponder. You can just copy my guidelines for advertising. You can also visit http://www.antion.com/sponsor .htm to get them.

I don't push ads that hard . . . actually not at all because I can make lots more money with my own products and services than I can from the ad revenue.

Also, you have to test what your market can bear when it comes to the amount of ads in your e-zine and the nature of the ads. I try to keep the ads I'll accept roughly speaker related, but my guidelines are very flexible.

Remove Statement

Always put a *remove* statement somewhere in your e-zine so people can get off the list. At least for my list, the placement of the statement doesn't matter too much.

What does matter now is the wording of the statement. This problem is caused by spam filters recognizing the words *unsubscribe* and *remove,* which are frequently used illegitimately by spammers to get you to click. This proves to them your e-mail address is real so they can sell it to their spammer buddies for more money.

I say, "If you do not want to receive Great Speaking anymore, click the link at the bottom of this e-mail" or something similar. You must constantly monitor what you write because it is easy to innocently, or quite responsibly, as is the case by adding a remove statement to your e-zine, to make your e-mail look like spam.

Miscellaneous Elements

You can have other elements in your e-zine. I have one section that tells about my speaking. I offer a commission if someone refers me. I also put something in about sponsorship, which is basically advertising. This section tells the readers they can get advertising information from my website or by sending an e-mail to my autoresponder. I also encourage links to my website.

Reader Comments

You could put a reader comment at the top, especially if it's negative. I don't mind doing that because many people send me asinine e-mail. It's a letter to the editor as far as I'm concerned, so I put it in. It makes me more credible because I'm not printing just all the great things people say.

Word, WordPerfect, or What?

Some people want to create their electronic newsletter using Microsoft Word and mail it out in that format. As I said before, *don't do this!* The problem is you can't be sure how it will come out. If the recipients don't have Word, they won't be able to read it unless they have the Word Reader from Microsoft. If you simply paste a Word document into the body of an e-mail, they'll be able to read it, but you don't know how their e-mail reader will interpret Microsoft Word codes. For instance, when I first started publishing an e-zine, the apostrophe symbol in WordPerfect turned into some Greek letter and made my entire document look weird.

You're better off using plain text because you know anybody in the world can read it. There is another format called *rich text,* but still a lot of people don't know how to do that either. So, use plain text, or if your target market is sophisticated enough, you can use HTML.

WHAT YOU NEED TO KNOW

 Each e-zine is made up of a series of simple elements. Many of the elements don't change much from issue to issue so you keep them in a template to save time. After you create your first e-zine that includes all the recurring elements, you have very little formatting work to do for each additional issue.

List Management

Backups

You're going to have many e-mail addresses to handle, and you have to make backups. Recently, a major player in the e-zine market lost everything because she did not have backups. Her computer crashed and everything was gone. Poof! Several years of work went down the drain. Don't let this happen to you.

One trick is to e-mail your list to yourself and leave it up on your server. That's a double way to get money out of your AOL or other online e-mail account. Just e-mail files to yourself as a backup. When you have plain text addresses, you could put a whole lot of them on a simple floppy disk because they don't take up much space.

I do backups on CD-ROM because I have the recorder and the CDs are cheap. You can also use tape backups, Zip drives, or even Internet sites to do your backups. Check out these sites:

http://www.recover-it.com

http://www.macbackup.com

http://www.vvault.com

http://www.xdrive.com

http://www.freedrive.com

When you are using a list management company (see next section) to handle your list, you still must do backups. Normally the list management company provides you with a website where you can go to download your subscribers any time you want. You download the list to your computer. I suggest that you then put it on a floppy disk or burn it on a CD. I keep a backup copy outside my office or up on another server, for example, AOL. You could keep a copy in the trunk of your car if you park outside your house or office in case your house or office burns down. That list is worth a fortune to you, and it could take years to re-create if you lost it, so you really must do regular backups.

List Management Companies

One way to handle your list is by using a list management company. I use several so I always have some way to send e-mails even if one of the services is having problems. Here are two:

http://www.savicom.net

http://www.KickStartCart.com

There are big advantages to having this type of company helping you. One, you don't have to attend to subscribes and unsubscribes. People get on and off the list by themselves. Another benefit is that many list management companies allow you to schedule your e-mails in advance so they are sent at a prescribed time while you are doing something else. Two other advantages are that it's cheap and fast to use such a company.

Most good list management companies also allow you to provide custom welcome letters for your subscribers that go out automatically when someone subscribes. This is a nice touch, and you don't have to do anything but write the letter and let them distribute it as people sign up. The flip side of this is a nice automatic letter going out to confirm unsubscribes and to invite the person to sign back up sometime.

A handy use of the automatic welcome letter is that you can use it to deliver special bonus report(s) that are incentives for signing up. You simply put the reports in the welcome letter, and they're delivered automatically when a person signs up. Don't forget to mention the incentives everywhere you have a sign-up button.

If you really want good response from your subscribers, some list management companies put new subscribers into an autoresponse series to get them up to speed so they don't have to wait to hear from you until you put out the next issue, which could be a couple of weeks or more.

I advise you to avoid the free places that handle lists because their service is normally poor. They also tack ads on to your newsletter that you don't control. I don't want the list management people trying to sell things to my subscribers.

To evaluate whether you should use the various free services you find on the Internet, you must scrutinize what you are giving up in exchange for the free service. Anytime you get something free, you have to worry about it.

I suggest paying the small monthly fee to get the services of a reputable company. In addition, if you are paying and something goes wrong, you have at least a little bit of influence because you are a paying customer. If you aren't paying anything, you don't have much recourse if they don't handle your list very well.

Most list management companies require that the people you have on your list fully opt in. That means people have requested to be on the list, and most of the time they won't complain because they chose to get on your list. That's a good thing.

Double Opt In

Double opt in is a method to ensure that people can't get you in trouble by using your list to aggravate other people. If you put your e-mail address into a double opt-in e-zine, you get an e-mail back from the list management company asking you to confirm your subscription by replying to their confirmation e-mail.

This method prevents Joe Jerk from subscribing Tony Nice Guy to my list in an effort to aggravate him and cause e-mail to be sent to him that he didn't request. Before Tony gets an e-zine, he has to confirm that he really was the one who signed up. This virtually eliminates the chance that Tony will think you are spamming him. It's not 100 percent foolproof, but pretty darn close.

The downside of double opt in is that you will not get everyone to reconfirm that they want your e-zine because they might not notice or even receive the confirmation e-mail, or they might not be as hot to get your e-zine when the confirmation comes in.

You must be the judge of whether you want to risk using a single opt-in sign-up method. In most professional markets, you're fairly safe, but you could always get a bad apple that wants to cause you trouble by subscribing other people to your list without their consent.

Don't Trick People to Subscribe

It is clearly spam e-mail to send someone a subscription and then require them to opt out. No reputable firm does this.

Undeliverable E-Mail Addresses

What happens when the list management company tries to a deliver an e-mail that has a bad or undeliverable address? If it's a bad address, the list management company handles it all for you. You have nothing to do. My list management company allows me to pick how many times I want to try to mail to an undeliverable address before they remove it from the list. You generally want to try several times because it might be a good address that was delivered when the recipient's server was down and is called a *soft bounce*. If it is never going to be deliverable, it is called a *hard bounce*.

You don't, however, want to bounce an e-mail address too many times because the receiving ISP will assume you are guessing at e-mail addresses and consider you a spammer. Right now I have my program set at three bounces and you're out.

List Company Disadvantages

Along with being an advantage, opt in is sometimes a disadvantage. You might have access to a list of highly targeted people. They may have even put their e-mail addresses in your guest book at your website. Technically, you have no right to e-mail them if you didn't make it clear to them that you would be sending them something. . . . I know, we are splitting hairs here. If they put their e-mail address in your site, they should know you plan to send them something, right? You would think so, but again . . . technically, you would be spamming them if you e-mailed them. Most reputable list management companies will not accept a list acquired in that way.

In the long run, this disadvantage is a good thing, because one person screaming spam can cause you lots of trouble, but you might want to chance mailing to a list like this because, for the most part, you would have lots of valuable subscribers.

So I warned you. I wouldn't mail to a marginal non-opt-in list because I could get accused of spamming and get kicked off my ISP. You might be willing to take the chance.

If you're not clear on what the disadvantage is, then here it is: I can't put people who haven't clearly asked to be on the list into my list management company. They don't allow it and they'll kick me out. It's not a clear-cut issue. When the visitor to your website just puts an e-mail address in a form trying to get some of my free services, they didn't really agree to get my newsletter. So if I send them the e-zine, technically I'm spamming them.

However, I do have a relationship with them because they gave me their e-mail address, and a one-time mailing inviting them to subscribe could be justified.

To get around this problem, I recently added a privacy statement to the free area of my website that tells people what I plan to do with their e-mail address.

Another disadvantage with a list management company is that it's more cumbersome to keep track of who is on the list and who is asking to get off the list. I like the relationships because that's where I make a lot of the money. When I started, I was willing to talk to people who were new on the list. I might send them an e-mail that says, "Hey, thanks for subscribing." I have far too many subscribers to personally do this now. That's why the process is automated. The old way surely did create some good relationships early on, and if you aren't swamped with business, you might want to add the personal touch . . . at least for a while.

You still have to back up the lists that the list company has. That's not really a disadvantage, but it's something you have to do. If the company disappears or their computer goes down, you have to scramble to get your list out. You have to figure out how to send it out yourself especially when you have an e-mail promotion that must be sent quickly.

Checking Pricing of List Management Companies

Check the prices carefully. They vary considerably:

http://www.KickStartCart.com (combined list management and shopping cart) highly recommended

http://www.lyris.com

http://www.sparklist.com

http://www.biglist.com

http://www.listbot.com/cgi-bin/gold

http://www.listbox.com

http://www.listhost.net

http://www.lsoft.com

http://www.listserve.com

http://www.ismax.com

http://www.skylist.net

http://www.dundee.net/isp/e-mail.htm

http://www.yesmail.com

What You Need to Know

 There are companies that exist only to do a professional job managing the e-mail addresses that belong to you. They handle the people wanting to subscribe as well as those wanting to unsubscribe. This process is all done automatically once you get set up. They do not steal or use your addresses. The exception is that if you use a free service (not recommended), the company will put ads on each e-mail it sends for you. You still have to keep a very secure backup copy of your list.

E-mail Lists

How I Got My List Started

I have been collecting e-mail addresses for a long time. I'm well known in the speakers' association, so I asked the speakers if I could put them on the list. I know thousands of speakers in this country, and many agreed to be on the list. On my website is a sign-up area where several thousand people a month sign up directly.

Handling Your Own Lists

Don't handle your own lists unless you are sending just 10 or 20 e-mails for various small groups. If you do it yourself, make sure you do it right. You can get awfully frustrated and in big trouble for doing it incorrectly.

I keep some of my very small lists (10 to 20 e-mail addresses) in plain text files on disks. You can use Microsoft Outlook or Eudora Pro, which is a popular and good e-mail program. You would simply take your list, click "edit," then "select all," then copy and paste it into the "Bcc:" portion of the e-mail. Don't mess this up!

If you copy your list into the "To:" or "Cc:" part of your e-mail program, everyone on the list will get a copy of everyone else's e-mail address before they get your message. This is extremely bad netiquette and just plain stupid. You have not only violated the privacy of your list but also given your entire list, or worse yet, client base, out to anyone who feels like capturing it. A man in one of the seminars I did for CBS Switchboard.com told me that his competitor sent him an e-mail with his entire client list in the "Cc:" line. What a big dummy!!!

To send your message, paste it into the main part of the e-mail and put your own name in the "To:" line. It would look like this: "To: Tom@antion .com" and "From: Tom@antion.com" with the e-mail distribution list all as "blind carbon copies."

I'm going to repeat this: Do not mess this up! Learn how to use your e-mail program with a very small test with friends. If you accidentally put your list into the "To": line, you are going to cause a nightmare worldwide. My list contains over 92,000 people. You would get 283 pages worth of e-mail addresses before you got to the message. So, learn how to use your e-mail program before you send e-mail.

TIP: You may not see a Bcc area in your e-mail program. If you've never used it before, sometimes it is hidden to save space. Check in your e-mail program's help section to see how to display the Bcc field so you can use it (see Figure 4.1).

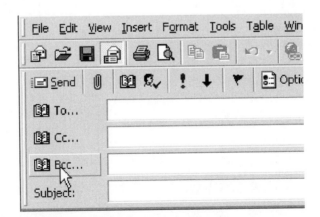

**Figure 4.1   Make Sure You Learn How to Use the
"Blind Carbon Copy" Function of Your E-Mail Program**

Kick Start Cart

You can run your entire e-mail newsletter operation with the Kick Start Cart program. You can even run multiple newsletters. There is a little bit of a learning curve to use all the features, but it is really worth it.

Almost every e-mail I send is personalized by *mail merge*. The program puts individualized information in each e-mail that goes out. For instance, it will put the recipient's name in the subject line and "Dear Tom, Dear Sally" or any other personalized information I want right into the e-mail. It makes it very personal, which raises the response level tremendously.

Mail merge companies include:

http://www.KickStartCart.com

http://www.tugnut.com

http://www.listhost.net

http://www.lsoft.com

http://www.doubleclick.net/us/publishers/e-mail-marketing

Common List Management Problems

You will run into four common problems when you're doing list management yourself, that is, without the help of a list management company or list management software. One problem is that people will give you the wrong e-mail address to be removed and then get mad because you can't find it. Many people have multiple e-mail addresses, and they forget which one they used. Sometimes their e-mail is forwarded from one address to the other and they forget. I get this all the time, especially from MSN. Somebody will have an address like sallypuddy@msn.com, and I search and I can't find it because for some reason MSN changes it to sallypuddy@e-mail.msn.com so it does not match up. Sometimes you have to search for the first name or the first part of it to be able to remove the address because the person keeps getting mad at you because you can't find the address.

Most list management companies eliminate this problem because they have a link in each e-mail that includes the actual address used by the subscriber. All the subscriber has to do is click on the link to be removed.

Another thing I run into is that Sally subscribes, but doesn't tell her husband. Then her husband gets an e-mail, gets mad, and starts calling me a spammer. Therefore, you have to keep track of who subscribed and explain to him nicely that Sally subscribed and let him have egg on his face.

The other problem you might have is old CompuServe addresses. They used to use numbers as your e-mail address, but now you're allowed to change it to your name. I might be sending to a CompuServe number, and the person sends me the name to remove, but I can't match the addresses. I have to send an e-mail back saying, "What was your CompuServe number so I can remove you?" Then they send me the number, and I can get them off the list.

Get them off fast because you want only people who are opted into your list. You don't want to be sending material and angering people who don't want to hear from you. Keep in mind you're never going to be perfect at this. You will have too many addresses floating around, but as long as you're polite to everybody and try to get their names off, you should have very few problems.

What You Need to Know

 You can and should handle parts of your list yourself to do small group mailings and sometimes mail merges (personalized e-mails). You will have some work involved in handling all the e-mail address and weird situations that arise when people can't remember what e-mail address they used. You can buy more sophisticated programs to do much of this list management work for you.

Signature Files for Routine Questions

Another thing you can do to automate yourself is to use your signature files. You'll get many e-mails from people asking similar questions. You use a signature file so that you can pick the response that's appropriate for whomever happens to be asking you something. I have about 30 or 40 signature files for different types of people. All I have to do is pick the appropriate response and I don't have to type it each time.

The method to put in signature files is different for every e-mail program. You'll have to learn how to do it in your e-mail program. If your e-mail does not allow it, you have to cut and paste from a word processing file, which is a nuisance. So, get an e-mail program that handles signatures, such as Outlook or Eudora Pro. The newer versions of AOL (5.0 and above) even have some limited signature capabilities. Netscape may have some capabilities as well.

E-Mail Is Driving Me Nuts

You may already be swamped with e-mail, and this sounds like it's going to generate lots more. Electronic marketing will certainly generate more e-mails that you will turn into sales. But I don't really want to see you driven crazy over this. So here's how you fix it.

One of the reasons you may be having trouble with too much e-mail is that you are probably not using the e-mail filters that are most likely already installed on your computer. If you have a Windows computer, you already have Outlook Express installed. If you are using a version of Microsoft Office, you probably have the complete Outlook program.

I won't go into the "how to" details of setting up these filters because the help section of your program does that. Search for "rules" or "organize" and read through the instructions. You can make your e-mail program work for you so you don't end up in the psychiatric ward of Cyberville hospital.

Let's take junk e-mail first. Did you know you can set your program to recognize certain words or combinations of words so that when it sees them in an e-mail, it automatically deletes the e-mail before you even see it? This will save you from deleting literally thousands of pieces of e-mail in the course of a year. Outlook starts you out with a bunch of words and symbols that it recognizes as spam or junk e-mail. It also has an adult word file you can activate to eliminate pornography.

Now let's use the rules and organization features to put incoming e-mail into specific folders automatically. Let's say you have an important client, John Lion. You make a folder for John and set up a rule that whenever an e-mail comes in from John, the program automatically sends it to John's folder and the sound of a lion roars at the same time alerting you that John just sent you something. Of course, you'll want to get to John's e-mail immediately to see what he needs.

Now let's make another rule for Jerry Jokester. Jerry sends you volumes of jokes, quips, and quotes. You like Jerry so you don't want to offend him by asking to be removed from his list. It's just as simple to make Jerry a folder and make a rule so that when the program sees his name in the "From" line, it sends his e-mail directly into his folder in case he ever asks you about one of his e-mails. You could check the folder once in a while to see if Jerry sent you a real message, or you could use some advanced rules to separate the jokes that he sends out to everyone from personal e-mails he might send directly to you.

What if someone sends you an e-mail order? No problem. Forward it automatically to the orders folder or to your assistant in the next room. People love it when they visit my retreat center at http://www.GreatInternetMarketing.com/retreatcenter.htm and hear my orders go "ka-ching" when they come in. I also make e-mail orders turn red so they are easy to pick out from the voluminous amount of e-mail I get.

There are all kinds of handy things you can do with your e-mail program. Learn to use its functionality to keep your inbox tidy, and you won't go crazy when you start getting more e-mails.

Spam Blocking Services

I've tried about four or five spam blocking services and finally settled on a company called Spam Arrest.

You set your incoming e-mail to go directly to the Spam Arrest company. Spam Arrest then returns an e-mail to senders requiring them to confirm they are a real person.

When the sender confirms by clicking on a link and typing in some text, the original e-mail is released to my inbox. The original sender has seven days to do the confirmation, or Spam Arrest deletes the e-mail. After senders confirm the first time, they never have to do it again. Spam Arrest then recognizes them on future incoming e-mail. This service knocked out 98 percent of my spam e-mail the instant I turned it on.

You can clear an e-mail through manually if you prefer or put in your own list of senders that are okay by you. You do need to watch Spam Arrest closely in the first month or so because you may be getting some automated e-mails such as e-zines that would never be confirmed by the publisher. Once you clear these e-mails through, they will come through automatically the next time.

Another reason I really like Spam Arrest is that the e-mails don't come anywhere near me or my e-mail system or my computer until they are cleared through. This gives me an extra level of protection when it comes to virus-laden e-mail. All the viruses are up at Spam Arrest's servers instead of in my inbox where I could inadvertently click on one.

To try out Spam Arrest, go to the following link: http://spamarrest.com /affl?1997905

Encrypting Your Website E-Mail Address

You can get a savvy Web person to put special coding on your website that keeps automated robots from extracting e-mail addresses. Having this done on your website will reduce the amount of spam you get.

Another strategy for your website is to use throwaway addresses and change them when necessary. You would keep the main address that you really care about for personal correspondence. I wish I had known this long ago because tom@antion.com is pretty much shot as my main e-mail address.

One other website strategy is to use a form on your website that eventually e-mails the visitor's correspondence to you. This is another way to keep automated robots from extracting your e-mail address. The potential drawback is that some people who you really want to contact you don't want to bother filling out a form. You have to balance usability of your site with your need for spam avoidance.

WHAT YOU NEED TO KNOW

 You must learn how your e-mail program can be automated to keep you from becoming buried in e-mails. You can't use AOL for this. You'll have to graduate to a more sophisticated program such as Outlook or Eudora Pro. Add a spam-blocking program such as Spam Arrest. Consider encrypting the e-mail addresses on your website.

E-Zine Strategy

The Bargain

The implied deal I have with my subscribers is that I will give them really great information; in return they will allow me to keep sending my e-zine and marketing to them. If I break my part of the bargain by sending lousy information, people will withdraw their permission for me to e-mail to them by unsubscribing. If I send too much marketing stuff compared to great information, I have again broken the bargain and they will unsubscribe.

People know that I give usable stuff, or I keep my mouth shut. I'm always helpful as much as I can be because I want people to keep coming back. I want to be known as a good source of information. I want them spreading my name. That's one of the ways I use my e-zine. I give good information and let the readers spread the word for me. The best way to maximize the value of this is a one-two punch between your website and your e-zine.

The Website Connection

The strategy is to maximize the value of the connection between my website and my e-zine. I do this by publishing articles and ads that are linked back to my website for more information or compelling ad copy. I can write as much as I want on the website, but I can only fit so much into the e-zine.

I can't advertise all the time so I still might link people to my website or other websites just to keep giving them more great information. This helps solidify their subscription. You just can't forget about giving good information, or you will lose subscribers.

The psychology of the e-zine-website connection is that many people read their e-mail while online. Your enticing links to the website are similar to a person picking up an impulse-buy item at the cash register of the grocery store. The reader figures, "Heck, while I'm here online I may as well pop over to his website to see what it's all about."

If you skipped the previous website section, go back and read it. It shows how once you get them to the website, you can write long copy that really sells visitors. You can't make your sales copy too long in an e-zine. People will go and read long copy on a website, but generally they don't want e-mails that are excessively long.

Make Back Issues Available

Another strategy is to make back issues available at your website so that people can go back and look at articles. They'll also be exposed to the ads again. I have all back issues of *Great Speaking* on the website in a hidden area. You should keep back issues handy and update them once in a while if some of the web pages that have your ads on them have changed. You don't want somebody going to a back issue and finding links that are no good anymore, although that will inevitably happen once in a while.

I used to make the back issue area available before a person signed up for my e-zine. Now I use it as an incentive to get them to sign up in the first place. Check it out at http://www.antion.com.

WHAT YOU NEED TO KNOW

 Your e-zine should not live alone. The combination of a good website and good advertising copy will make the most money. Always give good usable information on your specific topic, and your subscriber base will keep increasing. Use access to your back issues as an incentive to get people to subscribe.

Getting Subscribers

The main way I get subscribers is from a sign-up area on my website. Several thousand people per month put their e-mail address in asking to be on the list. That's great. Plaster your sign-up area on every part of your website. On every important page put a notice to "Sign up for our free magazine." These new e-mail addresses go directly to the list management company, and I don't have to touch them.

Visit http://www.ezineuniversity.com and read its free *Handbook of E-Zine Publishing*. Look around a little bit there and you'll see "listing" or "announcement" sites and directories where you can list your e-zine so people can find it and subscribe. This site will have the most current list:

http://www.ezineuniversity.com/courses/ez601/index.html.

I got 300 subscribers the first day from New List—an announcement list of people who want to hear about new e-zines coming out. Here's a list of all kinds of announcement and directory sites where you can list your e-zine for free. Make sure you check the submission guidelines for each link.

Searchable E-Zine Directories

http://hop.clickbank.net/?powertips/lifestyles

http://www.e-zinez.com

http://www.ezineseek.com

http://www.freezineweb.com/subject.html

http://www.webscoutlists.com

http://tile.net/lists/addlist.html

http://www.ezinesearch.com

http://www.site-city.com/members/e-zine-master

http://www.newsletteraccess.com

http://www.emailresults.com

http://listtool.com/cgi/listTool/addList.cgi (Use only for Listserv, Listproc, and Majordomo lists.)

http://tile.net/lists/addlist.html

http://www.published.com

http://www.etext.org/services.shtml

Announcement Lists

http://www.new-list.com

http://gort.ucsd.edu/newjour/subscribe.html (NewJour)

http://List-A-Day.com

E-Zine Awards

http://www.e-zinez.com/eaward.htm E-ZineZ Excellence Award

http://BestEzines.com

Recommend Scripts

You can get your existing subscribers to recommend your e-zine or website to their friends and colleagues. Their third-party endorsement is worth more than all the bragging you can do about yourself. You make it easy on people to recommend you by giving them a website form to do it. I got mine from http://www.willmaster.com.

You can try out the recommend form at http://www.antion.com/recommend .html.

You can also set one up immediately without any technical help if you have the integrated shopping and e-mail delivery system found at http://www .KickStartCart.com.

I got the version that pops back up already filled in so that people can easily recommend me to several different colleagues. All they have to do is fill in the name of the new person to whom they are recommending me and hit the submit button. One lady recommended nine people to my e-zine using this recommend form.

The marketing tip here is that to get people to take their time to recommend me, I had to do two things:

1. My material has to be good so they would not be embarrassed to recommend me.
2. I gave them a reason that it would be good for them to do it.

If you want people to help you, it is always a good idea to give them an incentive. In this case, I told the people whom I wanted to help me that I had a way to help them keep in touch with their clients and friends. You probably have heard of the marketing ploy of cutting out an article from a periodical and sending it to a client. The article is helpful to the client, and you don't appear to be marketing at all. It's just a nice thing to do for your clients, but it is keeping your name in front of them.

The article idea is a classic and certainly a very good idea, but it is a hassle. You have to cut the article out of the periodical, write a note, find the client's address, make a label, get postage, and so on. However, if you simply type a quick note into my recommend form and ship it off to your client via e-mail, you have no hassle at all. I got about 150 new subscribers the first time I sent this idea out to my mailing list by giving them an easy way to help their client by recommending me.

Buying Subscribers

Warning: You have to be really careful with this one. You will see ads all the time like this:

```
WE'LL SEND YOUR E-MAIL MESSAGE TO 2,000,000 OPT IN
SUBSCRIBERS FOR ONLY $29.95

or

BUY 28,000,000 FRESH E-MAIL ADDRESSES ON CD FOR $49.95
```

Don't try this! You will get hate e-mail and be kicked off your ISP.

There are some legitimate ways to buy subscribers. The process of buying subscribers who signed up for your e-zine at someone else's website is called *coregistration*. The companies that do this send me subscribers, and I pay anywhere from 10 cents to 35 cents each. I've used various companies with some able to send me several thousand subscribers per week.

The people they send have come to their site and specifically requested information on public speaking and asked specifically to sign up for my e-zine *Great Speaking*. Check out the places in the reference section at the end of the chapter. Just be careful and don't spend too much on this until you are sure that the subscribers you get eventually buy something. Also watch the subscribers very carefully at first to make sure you aren't getting spam complaints. Some less than reputable companies aren't too picky about how they get the subscribers they send to you. Your best subscribers will be people who signed up on their own at your website.

Freebies

Giving things away to entice subscribers has its good and bad points. On the good side, many people need that little bonus to move them to action. On the bad side, you may be building your list with people who only want free stuff and will never buy anything no matter how good the deal is. Make your freebies and incentives downloadable informational products so you don't waste time or cash on other kinds of freebies.

Write Articles for Other E-Zines

Another way to get subscribers is for you to write articles for other e-zines. That way other people are spreading the word for you. Sometimes they'll write an article for your e-zine, or you'll swap ads so that you can get subscribers from other people's e-zines. All this can be studied in depth if you read the information at http://www.e-zinez.com and follow all the links you find there.

At http://EzineNewsWire.com and http://www.ezinearticles.com, you can put your article there for other publishers to use in their e-zines. You get a bio blurb and link back to your e-zine subscribe page as payment. It's a great way to get more subscribers.

Another way is news releases to traditional print publications or complimentary Internet websites. I have a good mention coming out in a major article for *Presentations Magazine*. I'm going to be one of the features along with John Cleese to talk about humor in presentations. Part of the deal is that they're going to mention my free e-zine. That will cause a big circulation jump when that article comes out. Try to get in the media.

There are many places that will take free classified ads. You can also pay for ads in selected publications. I'm going to pay for an ad in *Toastmasters* magazine because it has a circulation of 170,000. An ad there obviously makes sense for me because I sell public speaking training information. You should make your own list of publications that make sense for you.

Converting Current Clients to E-Mail

Many small business owners come to me and say, "Tom, I have 4,000 customer addresses, but only two e-mail addresses. How can I do e-mail marketing?"

The first thing I mention to them is *webcards* or *web postcards.* These are postcards with a picture of your website on one side and some type of printing on the other side. I suggest the printing be some type of incentive offer to get the client's e-mail address:

Sign up for our e-mail newsletter and get 15 percent off your next order.

Sign up for our new e-zine and get a free 15-minute consultation.

Sign up for our new e-newsletter and get a free 20-page exclusive report, "Getting Repeat Business."

This is about the cheapest way to reach your entire database. Whatever you spend on the mailing is worth it because once you get that e-mail address, your costs to reach that customer go nearly to zero from then on. You also remind your customers about your website where they can go for current information, so the mailing does double duty for you.

You probably won't get all of your customers to give you their e-mail address, especially on the first try, but you should continue to try to get it every time you have a chance. Some direct mail studies show that two mailings to the same list within two weeks of each other significantly increase your response. Make it part of your preprogram or sales questionnaires with a check box asking if customers would like to have your e-mail updates.

Also, make your e-zine sign-up prominent in your store and even have sign-up forms with incentives on them. Get that e-mail address!

This link will give you lots of ideas for using your postcards: http://www.modernpostcard.com.

An extremely good course on marketing with postcards can be found at http://www.webcontactpro.net/app/aftrack.asp?afid=5478.

Webcard companies can be found at:

http://www.weprintcolor.com/webcards.htm

https://www.web-cards.com

Joint Ventures

Join in with other complimentary e-zine publishers, and put a sign-up area on each of your sites. The sign-up area promotes all the members of the joint venture. The script at the following link can also handle multiple newsletters that you publish: http://willmaster.com/master/subscriberpro/index.shtml

Subscriber Affiliate Programs

Subscriber affiliate programs are another way to buy subscribers. In about five minutes you can set up a program where you pay others to send you subscribers to your e-zine/newsletter. You can set the rate you pay per subscriber with going rates from 10 cents to about 50 cents, or you can pay in free ads for affiliates who send you subscribers. Listpartners at http://list-partners.com has a free service and puts an ad on the subscription confirmation as their payment.

Pop-Up Boxes

Pop-up boxes were mentioned earlier in the discussion on electronic ways to get people to return to your website. They can also be used to encourage visitors to sign up for your newsletter.

Some people get annoyed at pop-up boxes, but if used judiciously, they can be an effective way to increase your number of subscribers. Do you know why every major company and smart small company continue to use pop-up boxes? Because they work.

To take advantage of pop-up boxes and minimize the annoyance factor, you can make the pop-up box show only when someone visits for the first time. After that, it recognizes the visitor and does not display. This method has its pros and cons, too. Some people object to the placing of a "cookie" (file used to recognize them when they return) on their computer, or they have their browser set so it doesn't allow cookies, which will render your one-time pop-up box idea useless.

Unblockable Pop-Up Boxes

New technology allows pop-up boxes that can't be blocked by conventional pop-up blockers. There are two types I use frequently.

First is a *hover ad*. This box uses dynamic HTML scripting language. This language makes a box appear on a page, but the box isn't really a separate page. It is an appendage to the page it's on, so conventional pop-up blockers don't recognize it as a pop-up box.

I've used one for a while that drops in from the top of the page and bounces several times. It really gets your attention. In fact, it doubled my subscription rate the same day I put it on one of my sites.

Hover ads can be used only on entry to a page. They can be delayed before they appear, but you can't use them as an exit pop like I use when someone leaves a page without buying. There are inexpensive generators that help you make these unblockable entry pop-up boxes.

I use one by Corey Rudl at http://www.marketingtips.com/t.cgi/12273/hover.

Unblockable Exit Pop-Ups

I use http://www.amazingpopups.com/power for my exit pop-up boxes. This pop-up generator is not specifically unblockable at the time of this writing. I had a techie guy figure out how to adapt the code for pop-ups made by this generator so that they would be unblockable. This adjustment immediately increased subscribers and sales from my exit pop-ups.

I'm not sure if the code works with any other pop-up generator. If you buy the pop-up generator from the preceding link, I'll be happy to send you the extra code to make it unblockable. (You can e-mail me to request the code at orders@antion.com.)

Special Opt-In Programs

You can get programs that allow your visitors to subscribe by simply clicking "okay" instead of having to put in their e-mail address.

These programs make it easy to subscribe. They automatically use the visitor's default e-mail address, which is usually their "real" e-mail address, not a throwaway address like Yahoo or Hotmail.

Here's where you can get one: http://hop.clickbank.net/?powertips /lightning.

Trade Ads

If you locate and contact other e-zine owners, you can trade subscription ads with them. They get an ad in your e-zine in exchange for your getting an ad in their e-zine. Don't try to trade an ad in your 11-subscriber e-zine with someone who has 12,000 names because they'll laugh at you. You could, however, make a trade offering five ads to one or something equitable to a list with more subscribers. Many of the e-zine resources at the end of the chapter have ad trade sections.

Buying Ads

You can simply purchase classified ads in other e-zines or traditional print periodicals. E-mail the publisher of e-zines that you think would have an audience complementary to your publication and ask for their ad rates. Some publications have autoresponders where you send an e-mail and get the rate sheet back via e-mail. You can try that right here to get my rate card: mailto:sponsor@antion.com.

WHAT YOU NEED TO KNOW

 There are lots of ways to get subscribers. List your e-zine every possible place you can find. Plaster the sign-up button everywhere on your website. Buy subscribers carefully. Advertise for them and trade ads with other publishers. Use automated recommend forms to make it easy for others to spread the word for you. Get your current clients on the list. Use unblockable pop-up boxes.

Getting Content

How do you get content? First, you better be a darn expert if you are going to pretend to be an expert and put out a magazine on a certain topic. You don't have to be. You could simply be the publisher, but if you are the expert, it simply makes sense that you're going to get more business and more product-related sales on that topic if the e-zine matches it.

However, you don't have to do it all yourself. In fact, in one recent issue, I wrote only about three lines in the "Quick Presentations Skills Tip" section. The rest of the information came from guest authors. Heck, I don't mind. I'm still Mr. Big Shot publisher. My name is associated with this magazine. So if I've got a good article that someone else wrote, I'm putting it in there because I want good articles so people stay on my list.

Sometimes people research many different industry publications and boil it all down in newsletters. People make a lot of money doing that in accounting and legal fields. You are putting out information that's necessary but that your subscribers don't have time to read themselves. You condense all the important points and make it easy for them to get the information.

Two article trade sites are http://EzineNewsWire.com and http://www.ezinearticles.com. You just put your articles there and other people take them. Or, you can go there to find articles for your newsletter and all people ask is a link to their website or a link to their e-zine in return. A great place to visit for articles on all kinds of topics is http://www.certificate.net (see more on this later).

You could buy content from professional writers, but it's not necessary. There's so much free stuff out there, so you don't really need to buy material unless you want unique content.

Getting through Spam Filters

If you are going to take all the time to create and manage a great e-zine, I'm sure you would like to get it distributed to your subscribers. There is no sense doing all this work and then having most of your e-zines automatically deleted because they looked like spam.

It's pretty much common knowledge now that ISPs and individuals are heavily scrutinizing e-mail to try to catch spam and virus-laden e-mails before they can do their damage. The primary mechanism to catch spam is called a *spam filter.*

You want to do everything in your power to make sure your e-zine does not look like spam to a spam filter. If it does, it will most likely be deleted immediately and never even get close to the inbox of your subscriber.

The best known standard for spam filtering is the Spam Assassin Database. When Spam Assassin looks at your e-mail, it gives it a score based on its continually updated knowledge of what spam e-mails look like. You never want to send out an e-mail when your Spam Assassin rating is more than 5. (The higher the number, the more likely your e-mail will be filtered.)

Spam Assassin looks at the words and other elements of your e-zine and compares it to the many millions of spam e-mails it receives. Nobody knows the exact criteria Spam Assassin uses to label an e-mail spam because that would tip off the spammers on how to beat the system.

For instance, Spam Assassin might see the word *FREE* in your e-zine in all capital letters. Yes, the word *free* is one of the most powerful words when it comes to writing ad copy, but in an e-mail it will most likely contribute to a bad score and get your e-mail filtered.

All capital letters will also contribute to bad scores. Even innocent and legitimate words such as *remove* and *unsubscribe* can get you a bad score. This is especially bad because responsible e-mailers would always make it easy for people to remove their addresses.

Playing the Game

I have to be very careful and use oddball word combinations so my e-mails don't look like spam. To provide a way for removal, I now say, "If you do not wish to continue receiving Great Speaking, see below." I circumvented using either the word *remove* or *unsubscribe.* You'll have to do this every time Spam Assassin shows you a problem word combination in your e-mail.

The nice thing about Spam Assassin is that when it evaluates your e-mail, it will show you the word combinations that it feels make your e-mail look like spam so that you can fix them before you send out your e-mail to your entire list. Doing this evaluation will give you a much better chance that your e-mails will get through.

Here's a great trick that is effective and has been for some time. If you write out the month in the subject line of your e-mail, you get a good point in Spam Assassin. So any of my e-zines going out in, for example, October would have the actual word *October* written out in the subject line of the e-zine. You can't abbreviate (Oct.), and you can't put in a date format such as 10/2/05. You must write it out. Spam Assassin at the present times evaluates that as, "This must be an e-zine because the date is in the subject line," and it gives you a good point in the overall evaluation. So, if your e-mail normally would get a score of 2, putting the date in the subject line could bring it down to a score of 1.

If you are using the http://www.KickStartCart.com shopping system, access to Spam Assassin is included. This is handy because every time you broadcast an e-zine or create an autoresponder message, you can check your message right in Kick Start Cart.

Another place you can go to check your e-mails is http://www.Lyris.com /contentchecker.

Avoid when creating e-mails for broadcast:

✓ All capital letters (okay to use sparingly)
✓ Repeating dollar signs ($$$$$$$$$)
✓ Repeating exclamation points (!!!!!!!!!!!!)
✓ Words associated with spam e-mail such as *free, Viagra, mortgage, home-based business, MLM, extra income,* and so on.

To get lots of help on what *not* to do in e-mails, type the phrase "spam triggers" into Google and read through the most recent articles that come up. This is a rapidly and ever-changing field, and new word combinations appear all the time. The easiest thing, however, is to simply let Spam Assassin check your e-mail, and then you reword it to get your score down.

E-Mail Promotions

Now that you've got this list of subscribers, let's see how to maximize the amount of revenue you get from them. The best way that I know of is to send them e-mail promotions.

Warning: When you first start out, you may get complaints from people who send you stupid e-mails saying things such as, "Hey, I signed up for free tips, not advertisements."

Do not be swayed by people like this!

How dumb (or at least naive) can someone be to think you are going to benevolently dispense your hard-earned knowledge if you don't at least get a chance to get something back?

Let these tire kickers, freebie seekers, and takers go their merry way. Don't let one or two e-mails change your direction. This can be one of the most lucrative things you will ever do for you, your business, and your family.

Response

To even have a chance to make money with an e-mail promotion, you must keep your e-mail from being deleted, you must get it opened, and you must get it read.

The single most important factor in making sure that your e-mail is not deleted immediately is that the person receiving the e-mail recognizes who it came from.

This means you should use a consistent return e-mail address and name to identify from whom the promotion is coming.

Subject Lines

The single most important factor in making sure your e-mail gets opened is the subject line of the e-mail.

Try to keep your subject line at 50 characters or fewer (including spaces) so that the entire subject line can be read without opening the e-mail. Make it too long and the end will be truncated (cut off).

Your subject line should accurately reflect the content of your e-mail. If you violate this rule, you will really alienate your reader because spammers use this technique to get people to open their e-mails. You've probably seen hundreds of e-mail subject lines that say something like, "Increase your social life today," and when you open the e-mail, it says, "Lowest mortgage rates in your state" or something totally unrelated. Don't do this!

You should, however, write subject lines that entice your readers to open the e-mail. Here are some of my biggest response subject lines and why I think they worked so well:

- For an Internet training product:

  —Subject line:

  "They laughed when I sat down at the computer . . ."

  —Opening line inside the e-mail was:

  "but when I started to Click"

—Explanation: The first part of this explanation applies to all of these examples. You can do certain things with an established e-mail list that you couldn't do with a brand new e-mail list of people who have never heard from you much.

I've established a personality with most of my subscribers because I've been doing my e-zine for six years. If I say something like, "They laughed when I sat down at the computer . . ." the subscribers know I'm talking about me. This creates a curiosity about why someone was laughing at Tom and who was laughing at Tom.

Older subscribers will recognize this subject line as a spinoff of one of the biggest pulling headlines of all time, "They laughed when I sat down at the piano . . . but when I started to play . . ."

- Again for an Internet training product:

  —Subject line:

  "Boy, did I get in trouble . . ."

  —Opening line inside the e-mail was:

  "I wrote a really harsh e-mail the other day . . ."

  —Explanation: I went on to discuss the fact that a lady responded to my e-mail and said that I needed psychological counseling. I asked the readers of the e-mail if they thought I did. Wow! I got an enormous response and a whole lot of sales of the Internet training product I was promoting.

  My harsh e-mail telling people they needed my product and the controversy generated by the return attack on me from the lady created a great sales atmosphere. Controversy sells!

- For a speaking product:

  —Subject line:

  "Joe, where should I mail your Wake 'em Up System?"

  —Opening line inside the e-mail was:

  "Dear Joe: We have a Wake 'em Up Video Professional Speaking System package here with your name on it."

  —Explanation: Some of you probably don't have the guts to do this one. Or, some of you might claim that it's unethical to make people think they have ordered something when they haven't. I'm not burdened with any of those problems.

Not only did this promotion sell very, very well, but also I did not get one single complaint from anyone about it.

You might say that just because people didn't complain doesn't mean they appreciated your promotion. I'll agree to that. You must find the people who like what you do and forget about the people who don't. It's too hard to convert people when there are millions of people out there who would probably love you if you just stuck your face in front of them with your e-mail promotions.

Now, back to why this worked. Yes, the subject line made people feel that there could be some mistake they needed to correct. They are thinking, "I didn't order Tom's speaking system. I better see what's going on here."

That's all I needed to break them out of their mundane e-mail checking to stop and open my e-mail, which was my entire goal with the subject line.

The first line, "Dear Joe: We have a Wake 'em Up Video Professional Speaking System package here with your name on it" was nothing more than the common slang way of saying, "This is perfect for you."

How do I know it's perfect for Joe? Because Joe is on my speakers' e-zine list and is interested in being a better public speaker. He's told me it would be perfect for him just by signing up for my targeted list.

The preceding example is another reason extremely targeted lists outsell general lists. Let's say my e-zine was a general "success"-oriented list. Good speaking skills is just one part of being successful. I don't know exactly why someone is on a general "success" list, so I can't really laser-strike a product promotion to him or her. With a targeted list, I know who they are and can easily send promotions that I know are of interest.

Subject Line Personalization

Testing done by many sources shows that personalizing subject lines gets up to a 64 percent increase in open rates for your e-mails.

You're probably very familiar with a person's first name being inserted into an e-mail subject line. This is extremely easy to do with broadcast tools such as http://www.KickStartCart.com. You simply copy and paste a *merge* code into the subject line, and your recipient's name is popped right in.

One mistake spammers make when doing this is to forget to put a comma and a space after the merge code so that the subject line runs right up against the person's first name like this sample:

Bad subject line format:

```
"TomDon't you think you need Viagra?"
```

Not only does the subject line bang up against the name, but also the spammer capitalized the subject line, totally forgetting that the "D" in "Don't" should NOT be capitalized.

Good subject line format:

```
"Tom, don't you think you need Viagra?"
```

(I wonder how they knew I needed Viagara? . . . Well that's a subject for another book.)

When you have more information on a person (like when you are e-mailing a customer list), you can take subject line personalization even further as I've done in the following subject line:

```
"Sally, pet owners in Cleveland are scared."
```

All I have to do is paste in the merge code for the first name of the customer and the city where the customer lived. Doing something like this really gets high open rates. Here's how it would look in http://www .KickStartCart.com.

```
<$firstname$>, pet owners in <$city$> are scared.
```

Getting Your E-Mail Read—First Paragraph Personalization

If you really want to get your entire e-mail read, personalize the first paragraph. This is easy to do with tools such as http://www.KickStart-Cart.com, which allow you to broadcast e-mail with personalized information added to your broadcast e-mail. Here's an example playing off the pet owner subject line:

```
Dear Sally,

Your pet Foofie is at risk because of the severe flea
and tick problem occurring right now in the Cleveland
area.
```

Here's how it would look with merge codes before you sent it from http://www.KickStartCart.com:

```
Dear <$firstname$>,

Your pet <$petname$> is at risk because of the severe
flea and tick problem occurring right now in the
<$city$> area.
```

Do you even realize how powerful this technique is? There is virtually no way Sally will be able to resist reading the rest of the e-mail.

An absolute must for people who want to make serious money doing e-mail promotions is Corey Rudl's e-mail marketing course, which takes this section and expands it to 400 pages of exact and easy to understand details for doing e-mail promotions. Check it out at http://www.marketingtips.com /emailsecrets/t.cgi/12273.

Types of Promotions

When doing e-mail promotions, you will almost always do better by making some kind of special deal rather than a simple announcement.

Let's say you just wrote a book on leadership theory. You might get some sales by announcing the fact that the book is ready for sale. You will get many more sales on your e-mail promotion if you make some kind of special deal— that's why it's called a "promotion" . . . not an "announcement."

You could do a "prepublication special" offering the book at 50 percent off the regular price if the purchaser is willing to wait five weeks for delivery.

You could offer the book at 25 percent off if purchased by midnight tonight and you'll throw in a 15-minute free consultation.

I don't really care what your deal is, but I want you to get the idea that you must do some kind of deal if you want to get the best results from your e-mail promotion.

Here are a few points to remember when you're doing e-mail promotions:

Most people don't e-mail their customers enough.

If a customer has satisfactorily ordered two or more products from you, you can e-mail that customer just about as much as you want without worrying about complaints.

You'll have to test to find the best days of the week to send to your market.

Current trends are shorter e-mails driving people to a longer copy sales letter.

If you send out an e-mail promotion and get 100 orders, sending out the same promotion to the same list a week later will typically get you another 50 orders.

Here are some e-mail promotions you can do:

- *Birthday sale*
- *Anniversary sale*
- *Oops, I forgot sale:* This is a way to re-send the same promotion to grab that 50 percent increase in sales that was mentioned earlier. The

"Oops, I forgot" is a way to restate the same promotion and add an additional bonus that you "forgot" the first time the promo went out.

- *Last chance reminder:* Maybe you have a Saturday night restaurant special that's not full, so during the day you send out your reminder to catch last-minute reservations.
- *Presidents' Day sale:* There is no reason you can't tie into current events just like a brick and mortar store.
- *FAQ sale:* This is a "frequently asked questions" promotion where your excuse for the e-mail is to "clarify" questions about the promotion you recently sent out. You would say something like, "Many customers were asking me questions about the promotion I sent out last week. If you didn't see it, it was about . . ." You then restate the promotion in the form of questions.

Other Technologies

Three other methods of reaching your subscribers are *direct to desktop, blogging,* and *RSS.*

Direct to Desktop

Direct to desktop technology allows you to use the Internet to send your message directly to the recipient without using the e-mail system. In this case, recipients have agreed to install a reader on their computer.

When you have posted a message, the reader on the recipient's computer alerts the recipient. There are no spam filters to worry about, and there is no need to put goofy spellings of the word F°R#E@E in an effort to beat the system.

This technology has been around for a while, but it has been prohibitively expensive for any but the largest businesses. Now there is a very inexpensive version of this technology, "The Desktop Marketer." It is affordable by even a mom and pop operation. Check it out at http://www.marketingtips.com /desktop/t/12273.

I have mixed feelings about this technology. I think someone who jumps on it right away and uses it will make some great money. What I'm worried about is that when it gets more widespread, people will be reluctant to give up more of their desktop just as they are reluctant to give up their e-mail address today.

Blogging

Blogging is a form of public journaling and is rising in popularity. Blog software is available for free at sites such as http://www.blogger.com.

Blogs are available on all kinds of topics and used for all kinds of purposes from business to political to personal to absolutely bizarre, such as the "Canadian pop culture junkie living in Taipei, dealing with a knitting obsession one day at a time," or the "guy who spends his day leaving messages written on toilet paper in public restrooms." Don't believe me? Visit http://toiletpapermessaging.blogspot.com.

Blogging can help you develop quite a loyal following, and it does allow you to get your message out, but again I fear it has drawbacks that may not suit the small businessperson.

One drawback is the necessity to post often so people will have something to read. Second, you must wait for people to visit before they get their message.

You can send an e-mail telling subscribers there are new postings, but you are back fighting the e-mail system again. At least these e-mails can be very short, which gives you a better chance of getting through spam filters. See http://www.technorati.com/live/top100.html (top 100 blogs).

Check out my blog at http://www.GreatPublicSpeaking.blogspot.com.

One of the reasons I decided to get my own blog is that I found out that I can make updates by telephone. Once you have a blog, which you can get for free at http://www.Blogspot.com, check out http://www.audblog.com. You can call in from any phone an update that will immediately appear on your blog.

RSS

RSS stands for "Rich Site Summary," "Really Simple Syndication," and "RDF Site Summary." It's a special format for syndicating Web content. You create a document in RSS format and register the document with an RSS publisher.

Website owners that can read RSS content can then use the document on their website.

As the three names for RSS ironically suggest, there is more than one format. In fact, at the time of this writing, there are seven different formats, which leads me to believe "Really Simple" is "Really Confusing."

Yes, you can give this a try if you want, but I want to see it more widespread and standardized before I'd spend any valuable marketing time on it.

Here are some links to related resources:

http://www.newsisfree.com

http://radio.userland.com

http://www.feedster.com

http://www.feedreader.com

http://www.daypop.com

To put RSS capability on your site, see http://hop.clickbank.net/?powertips
/rssalizer.

WHAT YOU NEED TO KNOW KNOW

 You should have no trouble finding plenty of interesting content for
your e-zine if you know where to look. Try to put lots of your personal thoughts in the e-zine because the idea is to increase your
name visibility and expert status. Also, people like to feel they are
getting to know the author/publisher. You have to pay attention to
doing e-mail promotions. There are other ways to reach people
who have significant pros and cons.

References for E-Zine Section

Miscellaneous How to Stuff

http://www.e-zinez.com

http://www.ezine-universe.com

http://www.ezine-tips.com

http://www.bestezines.com

http://www.ezineuniversity.com

http://List-Lingo.com

http://www.lifestylespub.com

Buy Subscribers or Send an E-Mail Blast

http://www.list-builder.biz/idevaffiliate/idevaffiliate.php?id=197 (You can
buy subscribers here.)

http://innovationads.com/coregistration.htm

http://www.postmasterdirect.com (safe place to send your e-mail ad, but
expensive minimum orders)

http://www.targ-it.com

http://www.cumuli.com

http://www.webmarketingtoday.com/webmarket/lists.htm (big list of other
places that will advertise to opt-in lists)

http://www.funezines.com (You can buy subscribers here.)

Ad Stuff

http://List-Advertising.com

http://www.ezineadauction.com

http://www.adswappers.20m.com

Free Content for Your E-Zine and/or Website

http://EzineNewsWire.com

http://www.ezinearticles.com

http://www.certificate.net

http://www.anaconda.net

http://www.website101.com/freecontent.html

http://ideamarketers.com

http://www.findsticky.com

http://www.marketingtips.com/emailsecrets/t.cgi/12273 (Corey Rudl's e-mail marketing course—highly recommended)

5

Product Development

Don't skip this chapter because you sell only hardware or gift baskets or some other physical product. Creating other types of products can provide an enormous cash flow when you sell them directly from your website or in your brick-and-mortar store. Other products can also be given away to create a demand for your main line of products.

Products

Because of your line of work, you have expert knowledge that people would pay for if you packaged it properly. In fact, if you've been in your line of work for more than a few years, you probably have forgotten things that a person unfamiliar with your business would pay large sums of money to learn. This person could be either a customer who wants your regular line of products or a person who would like to be in your line of business.

One thing you need to get over is a *protectionism* attitude—thinking that you have tons of trade secrets and telling anyone about them would surely mean you would be put out of business tomorrow. In almost every case, you will make far more money with an *abundance* attitude. Just because you tell people the secret of "what to do" doesn't mean they have the skill or drive to do it. You can make a fortune on this one point alone.

Let's say you have a brisk chimney cleaning business in the Chicago area. You rack your brain and think up every single thing a person needs to know about being in the chimney cleaning business and put it into a business start-up course. You might be able to get $150 to $1,000 for each one of these courses you can sell off your website. You could get even more if you offer a phone consulting package on top of the course price.

Two questions for all you skeptics and protectionists are:

- What is the chance that someone is going to buy this product, go into direct competition with you, and put you out of business in the Chicago area, especially since you already have a client base built up and several year's head start. The answer is: slim to none.

- How much money could you make selling these training courses to business opportunity seekers all around the world? Answer: lots more money than you can make doing the individual jobs in the Chicago area.

A real-life example is Joe Polish. In 1991, he was a broke carpet cleaning business owner who was living off credit cards and eating macaroni dinners. He built his business up and then started teaching others how to build up their carpet cleaning businesses. Now he's a fantastically successful guru of the carpet cleaning industry and has 4,100 carpet cleaning businesses using his marketing techniques around the world. Those 4,100 businesses give him more money every month than he could ever make cleaning carpets.

The problem is that most small business people get so wrapped up in their own local little world of doing the work, they forget to think in terms of how they can sell their expert knowledge around the globe. There is no better time to do this because we can do it for very little cost right from our home or office computer.

I sell things in 40 countries around the world from my home office with one part-time assistant. The neighbors probably think I'm dead because I hardly have to leave the house to do it. I want you to open your mind to the possibilities of how you can do the same thing with your expert knowledge or knowledge you can obtain with a little bit of research.

This chapter gives you a primer on product development so that you can get started in the most efficient manner. Even if you are already in the midst of projects, you can use your material in many different ways once you have created it and multiply your visibility. Once you have finished your product, the product itself multiplies you because you can reach more people. Remember, you can't be everywhere personally.

First, some other good things are related to creating products. One, you receive a passive income. The expression *passive* is kind of a joke. It's still work, but you get an income that can come in if you are sick, if you can't travel, if you want to go on vacation, or whatever.

Second, creating products helps build your celebrity status. When you are the author or the publisher of a tape series or some other product, it builds your celebrity status and makes people want to deal with you or visit your store.

Informational Products

There are all types of products. Low- to high-cost products such as reports, pamphlets, books, audiotapes, videotapes, CD-ROM, and now DVD (digital video disk), which is the fastest growing media ever, are the more traditional products.

Other kinds of products are T-shirts, laminated cards, tote bags, software programs, posters, mugs, and other marketing items that can carry your name. There are many ways you can use products in your mix of revenue sources.

What are some of the benefits of having informational products? You get the passive income and higher credibility, and you can reach more people than you ever possibly could in person.

Also, products like this get you media exposure, which is free advertising. This is part of my media marketing strategy. When you are in the media and people see you in the media, they call you rather than you calling them or you spending a fortune advertising to find them. It is also easier to do business once they call you because your credibility has been established by the media outlet where they saw you.

Recycling

The overall principle of this section is that of recycling your material. Recycling material does not mean that you use just the same things repeatedly and never create anything new. However, it does mean that once you take the time to create something, in the midst of creating it or even before you create it, you want to brainstorm on all the different ways you can distribute it. Think about how many different ways you can package your material and put it out to the public so they will pay you for it or so that when you give it away, it will stimulate sales for your products and services.

In my case, I started out with a five-page report titled, "What to Say When You Get Caught with Your Pants or Skirt Down." The front cover was just a colored piece of paper, photocopied and stapled together. When I was first starting out, I sold hundreds of these at five bucks apiece. This product consisted of funny things to say if something went wrong in the midst of a presentation. I call them "Bomb Proofing" lines. Moreover, those same lines that I wrote 10 years ago are part of the "Bomb Proofing" chapter in my *Wake 'em Up* book.

This original product will be included on a CD-ROM I am making for speakers to use as a humor resource when they are not connected to the Internet. They can use it anywhere while they are working on their speeches and programs.

This product is also in my video systems. Some of the material is in my audio system, and I use some myself in my speaking engagements. I also use some of the material on the media when I am doing interviews. When you include the new DVD version, I am using the same material nine different ways and getting either money or other benefits from it.

How Can a Small Business Use Information Products?

A landscape company could create a downloadable e-book on pond designs or, better still, create a DVD that shows the design and construction details of the pond. Then it would show the emotional impact when all your friends are oohing and ahhing about your pond during a backyard party.

A builder could publish do-it-yourself pamphlets on how to build a deck or remodel a bedroom and offer a consulting deal to oversee the project. You would think that would be a crazy thing for a builder to do, wouldn't you? Not at all. Most people who read pamphlets and books on do-it-yourself projects see how much trouble it is to do the work, and that builder would be the first one they would call to take over the project.

A real estate agent could do a downloadable e-book or special report on increasing the curb appeal of your home to get a higher selling price. That agent will most likely get a shot at the listing and sale of many homes. Another approach would be to sell the report and rebate the price if the agent got the listing. Thus, the agent can make money selling the report around the world, and the cash flow would bring in money that the agent would never have received doing just local listings and home sales.

A golf course (pro shop) could create a multimedia CD-ROM using its own golf pro as the instructor on the CD-ROM. This product could be sold or given away when someone signs up for wintertime lessons, which would provide a revenue stream during slow times.

A lock shop owner could publish home safety information in any number of formats, which would have a checklist of all the potential hazard points where locks are needed. Along the same lines, a lighting company owner could provide information on safety lighting.

I can't think of any business that couldn't profit from simple informational products that are created once and then distributed over and over again.

WHAT YOU NEED TO KNOW

 Selling your knowledge is a very high-profit and low-risk (ad)venture. It builds your credibility and celebrity status. The same knowledge can be sold in many different formats, which multiplies the return on the effort involved in creating the materials (products) that can be either sold or given away to create demand for your main line of products.

Articles

Many people get worried and say, "Oh, my gosh, a book is such a big project." It's not such a big project when it all starts with little chunks of material, special reports, and articles. Articles are relatively easy to create, and you don't even have to write them yourself.

You can get articles published in smaller newspapers, trade journals, and printed newsletters. It's even easier to get articles on lots of Internet sites and in e-zines that are complementary to your topic and product line.

If you can't write or your spelling is terrible, who cares? You can get college students to write the articles for you cheaply. You can put out a bid on Elance.com and have people competing to get your writing jobs. All you do is jot down the ideas for the article or have the person interview you by telephone, and you'll be amazed at the nice work you can get with very little cash outlay.

I used to write for *Successful Meetings* magazine. I wasn't paid for the articles. I am not really a professional article writer, but I want the links to bring people to my website and back to my e-zine to get more subscribers.

Ten-Tips Articles

A simple form of article to write is a 10-tips article. This kind of article is really easy and fast to write. All you do is write an opening paragraph introducing the topic, 10 tips about the topic, and a closing. Editors of print publications love these kinds of articles because they can easily be changed to a seven-tips article if they have less space. These articles are very easily placed in publications.

Your articles end up being parts of book chapters, on audiotapes and CDs, in videos and e-zines, on websites, and everywhere else that you have decided to use them. Once you have created them, you put them in many different places.

Many people wonder about copyrights. When you publish an article, the magazine holds some or all of the rights. Taking a bunch of articles and creating a book works very well, but what happens when you have others owning the copyright? What can you do?

First, there are many different rights related to articles. If I can get away with it, I give publishers only first rights or whatever rights they have to have, but not all of them. If it is a big enough deal, I might give them all. If it is *Newsweek, Inc.* magazine, or other major publication, that is a bigger deal than saving a little bit of writing for my book. I can alter the article significantly to use it in my book anyway. So, don't give up all the rights to your articles unless you absolutely have to. Especially don't give up the electronic rights to a print publication unless you get money.

Publication Rights

Do a search on the following sites for the keyword *rights:*

http://www.authorsguild.org (Author's Guild)

http://www.writerswrite.com/journal/dec97/cew3.htm (A Novice Writer's Guide to Rights)

To buy articles to rebrand under your name, see:

http://hop.clickbank.net/?powertips/bizport

Pamphlets

People are making a fortune on pamphlets. I know a lady who is selling little pamphlets stapled together on how to do a really cool business card. It consists of 100 tips, and she is selling these little folded pieces of paper for five bucks a pop. The production cost is so cheap you can sell them in bulk by the thousands to companies to give away as premiums or goodwill items. In addition, if you are selling your pamphlets in the back of the room at a conference, they are an impulse buy rather than a decision buy because they are so inexpensive. (Watch out that these little sales don't hurt you from selling your big packages of products. You'd be better off throwing them in as bonuses if you sell more expensive packages.)

Books

It is a big jump to finish off a book. Many people ask me, "Tom, was there any big turning point in your career?" I say, "Yes, it was when I was arrested (hahahaha, just kidding)." Actually, when my book came out, I immediately increased my fee and had an easier time getting bookings. My *Wake 'em Up* book is a top-notch trade paperback. You don't have to do one as extensive as mine to promote your business, but it should be a book you can be proud of so it will help promote and sell your products and services.

Simple Steps to Finish Your Book

Many people would like to know how I finished a book with my schedule. The first thing I did was to find a big box. I started saving anything about the book topic. The topic was "advanced presentation skills for speakers and business presenters." I also printed all of the articles that I had written and put them in the box. I gathered information and listened to tapes. In fact, I took over the tape librarian position at our speaker's chapter so that I could have access day and night. I listened to tapes in the car and everywhere else, taking notes and becoming an expert on the topic and throwing the notes in the box.

I read every presentation skills book that is published. I took the best information from all these other books and put it in my book. I didn't plagiarize the books; I just used them for background research.

I watched other speakers, took notes on their good techniques, and put my notes in the box. I searched quotations about speaking, cartoons, newspaper articles, anything . . . and put them in the box. After I had a pretty full box and with a bunch of manila folders in hand, I started putting similar items together, and, at the end of the day, I had a whole bunch—probably 13 or 14 folders. The contents of those folders became the chapters of the book. It is just a simple progression of collecting material and organizing it a little bit. You still haven't written much of anything but little articles here and there.

After I roughed the manuscript out the best I could, I paid an editor to finish it off. These editors have brilliant minds. They can take one sentence 200 pages down, pull it out, and put it in another chapter, so leave that kind of work to the real pros and just pay to have it done.

Then, I came up with the idea for the book cover design and bartered presentation skills training to get the book cover done. The only other thing I paid for was a professional copywriter to write the copy on the back cover.

Another benefit of having a book is that you can sell or trade ad space in the back. Usually a book is made in what is called *signatures.* Sometimes blank pages are left that would just be wasted space. I sold ads, traded ads, or put ads in for my own products and services in the left-over space. There are many benefits of self-publishing. I later discuss the differences between doing it yourself and paying someone else to publish your book.

Ghostwriters

If you have trouble writing simple articles, you can get a ghostwriter. I hired a student at the University of Maryland who can write something in a few minutes that might take me an hour. There is no problem with getting some help, and it is cheaper if you find a college student who wants to earn extra money, so don't be afraid to use others' skills. Students also have an incentive to do a good job so they can put that experience on their resume. Just make certain you both understand the timelines.

Here's an e-book on using ghostwriters: http://hop.clickbank.net
/?powertips/ggmine

Here's an e-book on creating bestsellers online: http://hop.clickbank.net
/?powertips/cbsellers

WHAT YOU NEED TO KNOW

 Getting your ideas down on paper can mean a fortune to you. You
can make articles, reports, pamphlets, and books. Ten-tips articles
are easy to write, or you can hire college students or freelance
writers to ghostwrite.

Publishing

Some helpful publishing links follow.

Publishing resources:

http://www.copylaw.com/new_articles/helpful.html

http://www.ivanhoffman.com/helpful.html

http://www.publaw.com

Let's talk about three different types of publishing: self-publishing, vanity
publishing, and regular publishing.

Self-publishing means that you do everything, or you pay to have it done.
You get the profits, which are much higher than the other ways. It is as quick
as you want it to be.

With vanity publishing, you pay a packaging company or somebody who is
in the business to do the graphic design and the cover and put the whole
book together. It is usually quite expensive, and the company does not sell
the book for you. Whether you self-publish or use vanity publishing, you are
the one who sells the book. Vanity publishing can be as fast as self-
publishing, maybe even a little faster because the packaging company has
been through the process. It will cost you a significant chunk of money just
for the company's expertise rather than your eventual profits, and your unit
costs will be much higher.

In regular publishing, you get an advance and a royalty. An advance can be
anywhere between $3,000 and $1 million. You get the advance, finish the
book, and get a royalty on the sales after the advance is repaid. The average
author brings in $5,000 for the life of the book. But, to give you a bench-
mark, I made more than that before my book was even printed.

Self-Publishing

This section concentrates on self-publishing because that's totally under your control, it's fast, and it's the only way I know to get an 80 percent or better profit margin. When you self-publish, you become a book manufacturer.

High Perceived Value—Low Unit Cost

Many of the tricks I give you about the marketing are based on having a low-cost product with a high perceived value. My *Wake 'em Up* book is a 6 × 9, beautiful book, 336 pages, $24.95 softcover, with a printing cost of $2 each. That difference gives me a lot of leeway to make the deals I tell you about later. At wholesale pricing of a 65 percent discount, which means someone would have to buy 500 or more to get that discount, I still get $8.73 a unit, which is $6.73 profit on each one. So you can see that there is a lot of profit margin in these educational materials if you create and publish them yourself.

If you want to learn more about self-publishing, purchase the *Self-Publishing Manual* by Dan Poynter (Santa Barbara, CA: Parapub, 2003) at http://www.parapub.com. This manual has everything you need to know. I have used many ideas from this book for my tape programs. Poynter's book is about creating books, but the same techniques apply when you create tapes, videos, and other products. It is an excellent $19.95 investment.

What You Need to Know

 Self-publishing is a high-profit way to sell your information. You can make over 90 percent profit on your work. The *Self-Publishing Manual* by Dan Poynter is a must-have in your library.

Marketing Ideas

Let's say you sell computer systems to businesses. You create a quick tips book on how to use the computer and give your customers as many of them as they want. This book would get the productivity with your computer systems up quickly and make you look like a hero.

A mortgage company could give out books about Internet mortgage scams and how to avoid them. Exposing the scams makes this company the "trusted advisor" rather than just another mortgage company.

A furniture store could collaborate with an interior designer and give out or sell a book on designing with furniture. Both the furniture store and the designer would end up with more business, and the furniture store people wouldn't even have to write the book—the designer would.

A bank could give out an investment book as a premium for opening a savings account with $5,000 or more. This book would help people learn how to buy certificates of deposit and other investment instruments from the bank.

A clothing store could give out an image book with purchases over $50. The book would highlight that season's clothes. Although this sounds like a catalog, it's actually a *magalog*, which is a catalog with articles in it like a magazine.

A caterer and a party favor supply company could collaborate on a book that highlights both their wares and cross-promotes each other's services.

A photographer could pitch a deal to the chamber of commerce to get them to finance a photo history of the city. The photographer would shoot and get credit for all the modern-day photos in the book.

A videographer could do the same thing except he or she would distribute on DVD and simply shoot modern footage of the town along with still video of old photographs. Putting the entire project together creatively would certainly show off the videographer's talent and give a great credit to post on his website.

Financing Your Product

When I first had my book printed, I ordered 5,000 copies. The quotes to publish that book ranged from $11,000 to $36,000. Some printers are not set up for book printing, so they have to change their system and charge you a fortune for it. Put out lots of bids to find the right printer, and you can get the price lowered considerably. I had mine down to $11,000, including shipping.

Here's the real cool thing that I made happen to help me finance this. I presold 1,000 copies of the book at $7 apiece. That $7,000 was paid directly to the printer, and it gave extra security to the catalog company buying the 1,000 books because they paid the printer instead of me. Why would they buy 1,000 books? They were going to resell them, but some other company or association might want to do this to get a big discount.

Let's do the math here: I have an $11,000 bill for the printing and shipping. I get $7,000 from another company for 1,000 books. I have 4,000 books left of the 5,000, and it cost only $4,000. I had only $1 in each book, so this is an economical way to do things. I could give away tons of books to promote myself and pay only $1 each. You can't even print a color brochure this cheaply, and a book is kept forever and totally establishes you as an expert on your topic whereas most brochures likely end up on the garbage in short order.

Sponsorship

Let's look deeper into the preceding deal. This deal is a basic *sponsorship*. The company that bought the 1,000 books in effect sponsored my book, and, in exchange, they got their name on the title page. They also had an ad in the back in those pages that would have been blank. I let the catalog company owner write the foreword in his version. It was a great deal for me, and it was a great deal for them. If you are crafty at this, you can get by with a very low investment in your products because of sponsorship.

There are other ways to get sponsorship. If you are interested in sponsorship, that is, if you are tight on cash and you would like to get somebody to sponsor your book, brainstorm on who or what company or associations would be interested in being associated with your message. Also brainstorm on what complementary businesses you could approach that might want to collaborate with you and share the expenses of producing the product. After brainstorming, write a proposal and start shopping it around.

You may not be hard up for money, but you still may want to land a sponsorship deal. You might simply want to make an association with an organization to add to your credibility. Here's a simple deal you might pitch: "For XXX dollars, you will be a sponsor and get a front page ad or a back page ad or your name on the cover that says, 'Thanks to Krunchy Foods'" (or whoever it is).

You could offer to author publications for associations or corporations. Associations provide all kinds of publications for their members for continuing education credits.

Authorship is another good deal that you can try to land if you are in the continuing education market. Corporations create publications to sell or to give to their employees and stockholders. Pitch the deal and see what happens.

The side benefit is that by being the author of such a book, video, DVD, and so on, you have an implied endorsement from the organization that you can use to land lots of other work or product sales in your field.

Splitting Costs

Another way to finance the whole deal is to combine forces with several other businesses to produce a product—called an *anthology*. An anthology is a cooperation among many authors who each write one chapter of a book. It is fast, and they all pay X dollars to get X copies of the book. The product won't totally feature you, but sometimes you can get your picture on the cover of your 1,000 books or whatever number of books you get. The other people get their pictures on the cover of their books. This gets many people contributing the money to a book project.

Let's say you make custom hot rods. You go to your engine manufacturer for a chapter. You go to your upholstery supplier for a chapter. You go to your wheel manufacturer for a chapter, then to the exhaust pipe people, chrome people, tire people, and so forth. You put the entire project together and get each supplier to buy 1,000 books. You make money on the front-end from the money they give you, and you all have an awesome tool to promote and cross-promote your businesses.

The same thing could be done for an audio or video product, and you'll see later how easy these products are to create.

WHAT YOU NEED TO KNOW

 When you self-publish, there are ways to come up with the money without digging into your own cash reserves. You can get sponsorship, presell the product, or create an anthology where several companies share the production costs and cross-promote one another.

Promoting Your Products

A great resource for getting your products promoted is an excellent book titled, *1001 Ways to Market Your Book,* by John Kremer (Fairfield, IA: Open Horizons, 1998, http://bookmarket.com). I read this book, which is about 500 pages, about 20 minutes a night and just check marked all the possible ideas that I might use. Just doing that gave me a two-year marketing plan.

The ideas in Kremer's book will work for all kinds of products. While I'm on the subject of books, though, I don't want you to think in terms of selling or distributing your books in bookstores. Dan Poynter, the self-publishing guru, says, "Bookstores are the worst place in the world to sell books." What he means is that specialty books to promote your business should be sold in specialty stores or on the Internet at specialty websites. You will sell far more hot rod books at hot rod stores, hot rod websites, and car parts stores than you ever would at a regular bookstore or even in giant online bookstores such as Amazon.com.

Recycle to Recycling

Let's get back to recycling your material into audio, video, and TV products. To create my first audio album, I excerpted the humor sections of my *Wake 'em Up* book that I had already created and recycled it by turning it into a six-tape/CD audio album.

All I did, basically, was read from the book. I also threw in my wisecracks that I am able to do when I am on a live recording.

You might think that I would get objections about the repetition from people who read the book and then bought the album. That happened only once or twice in all of these years. An audio album is a different medium, and listeners are hearing me live. It is a little bit different because I am throwing in wisecracks here and there.

Some people are auditory, and some people would rather read. With audio, your business can be promoted while the person is jogging or driving. You can even have the same files as streaming audio on your website.

Even though what you record is roughly the same material as what you have written, it reinforces concepts more than once. Nevertheless, I have had only one complaint from a regular customer, who withdrew the complaint after I explained how important this material was to absorb.

Recycling doesn't mean you never create new stuff. It just means you take the things you create and distribute them in as many places and ways as you can. This process is so simple that I have edited some of my audio products right on my computer because audio is very simple to edit as we see shortly.

Themes

One big thing that will help your marketing is to create themes. *Chicken Soup* is a theme. The *One-Minute Manager* series is a theme. The *Dummies* and the *Idiots* books are themes. Soon there will be a *Dummies Guide to Idiots.* All these are themes, so the synergy effect helps them market one another. If you see a *Dummies* guide and you like that series, you will pick it up. You are more likely to buy it because you recognize it. So, I have the *Wake 'em Up* and *Make 'em Laugh* themes. The *Wake 'em Up* theme could easily be *Wake 'em Up Management* or *Wake 'em Up Customer Service.* Themes are good.

A sporting goods store could have a series of tips books called *The Weekend Bowler, The Weekend Tennis Player, The Weekend Golfer,* and so on.

Tony's Restaurant in Toledo could have a series of recipe pamphlets at the hostess station such as, *Tony's Pastas, Tony's Salads, Tony's Wine Picks,* and so on.

> **TIP:** By creatively using the information from these pamphlets both in the restaurant and on his website, Tony can be the *place* to eat when visiting Toledo. This marketing will steadily increase Tony's out-of-town business over time.

Dreams Jewelry store could have creative and fun booklets on ways to present a piece of jewelry on special occasions, such as *Dreamy Birthdays, Dreamy Anniversaries, Dreamy Engagements,* and so on.

Theme information products promote your business far longer and better than simple ads, and all the same information can be recycled and available on websites.

Systems

When you create these individual products, you put them together in *systems*. You get more money for systems because systems put everything in a one-stop shopping center for people who need information. This is the way I have made loads of money. Before I had the system, each part of it was made individually and sold individually. You can start out small and keep adding the products but keep them on the same theme. Then you package the products as a system and sell at a bigger price point than an individual book or tape. To see an example of an informational product system, visit http://www.antion.com/speakervideo.htm.

A camping store could put together a complete package of equipment for weekend campers that lets them shop faster, spend more money, and be assured they have everything they need. Several different packages could be available.

A gardening store could assemble a complete tool kit to take care of flower gardens along with books, CDs, and DVDs on flowers that do well in the region.

A kitchen supply store could put together a complete baking system for breads, pies, cupcakes, and so on and include all the measuring spoons, baking pans, and everything else needed to bake at home.

These systems could include an interactive CD with hotlinks to websites where more tips, products, and services are displayed.

Videotapes

Videotapes are a completely different level of complexity than audiotapes. If you are speaking on camera, you should be very polished with your material before you make a videotape because it shows up big time when you peek at your notes.

If you are doing a video that is showing you doing something or showing off your product, it is much easier because you can just have someone shoot the video, and you can read a script describing what is being seen on the screen. This technique is called *voiceover*. This method takes the pressure off you because you can read it over and over again until you get it right, or you can have someone else read the script.

Because some things are understood better when they are seen, a video is a good product to put out. The duplication is cheap for videos and DVDs.

Unless you are really willing to invest and if you are really talented with video, you don't want to try to edit videos and make DVDs at home. It takes really expensive computer equipment and the techniques needed to do a good job are very complex. I suggest leaving DVD production to the pros.

Places where you can get good video shot for free or at least cheaply are discussed next.

Colleges

I have two videos that up until lately were my best demo tapes. I did one at a college that didn't have all the money to pay my presentation fee. They had only part of it, but they had complete video production studios and classes on video production. They gave me a three-camera shoot. In that case, they didn't edit the tape for me, but I didn't want them to do that—I just wanted the footage in a big theater setting, so I got that free.

Because I'm a speaker, my video was on stage. The university had a complete studio where I could set up a demonstration and the students would help me produce my video as a class project. If I couldn't have gotten it for free, a donation to the department would have been much cheaper than hiring a company and studio time. Plus, the students working on the job really want to learn and impress you with their talent.

Military

I did the keynote speech at the 50th anniversary of the U.S. Air Force in Leesburg for their worldwide communications conference. They didn't pay me anything, but they did a three-camera beta cam shoot, edited it digitally, and put an F-16 airplane on the front of it. It would have cost me $5,000 to $8,000 to purchase that sort of production. I did one speech.

Cable TV Stations

Cable TV stations have all the equipment, and many have classes that teach you how to use the equipment. You can produce your own show if you want to. In a regular TV station, you will have good quality recordings. You could offer some type of barter deal if they'll do your production.

A restaurant might provide lunches for the crew for a month, or a clothing store might provide clothes for the anchor people.

Charities

I recently did a big charity function. If you tie into a charity, you can make some good deals for yourself and the charity. I made this deal with them:

"I'm going to raise money for you using my name and my clientele base, and I want to get this product out of it."

We did a big event recently. I videotaped it all day. Most of the proceeds went to the charity. The production costs were paid for from the entrance fees, and I have the master tape. I paid my own money to get it edited and put it out to the public as a product.

You could have some type of training event at your store and tape it. Tying to a charity can be a great thing.

Joint Venture with a Video Company

You could make a deal with a video company to shoot, edit, and package your product for a percentage of the profits or, again, on a barter basis if you have something they want.

When doing a videotape, there are strict guidelines that I require because I don't want to have someone say, "Oh yes, we will videotape," and then somebody's husband or wife shows up with a home-grade camera on a little shaky tripod, with no lights or microphones.

Streaming Audio and Video

Streaming means that the audio or video starts playing almost immediately. In the old days, you had to wait (sometimes hours) for a file to completely download so that you could watch a few minutes of video from your hard drive.

Now, with streaming technology, the file can be played as it's being delivered from the Internet or wherever you happen to be getting it. As Internet connections become faster and bandwidth (the size of the cyber pipe that sends information over the net) increases, the quality of the video will keep improving. It's getting better every day, but it's still not the highest quality for most people who try to watch one of these videos. The new, "smart" streaming technologies can recognize the speed of the connection that's being used to watch it and feed just the right amount of data for the best picture at that speed.

The best-known streaming technology is Real Video and Real Audio. Microsoft is blasting ahead with Windows Streaming Media. QuickTime is another. To watch Real Video or hear Real Audio, you need a Real Player, which you can download for free from http://www.real.com. They also have an enhanced version that you pay for, which will do all kinds of fancy things. There are many content providers now that stream all kinds of music, talk, and everything else you can imagine.

I had Real Audio clips on my website long before it was common and, guess what, hardly anyone listened to them. But that's all changed. Many people expect to have access to your material on streaming audio and video, and they can easily play it on their computers.

The process of getting both video and audio on your website used to be complicated. Both audio and video are pretty simple now as you'll see next.

Kick Start Sound

Audio and video is much, much easier than it ever has been. If you visit http://www.KickStartSound.com, you will see programs that will let you record an unlimited number of audio and video clips (up to 30 minutes each) and put them on your website in seconds with virtually no technical knowledge.

One of the programs allows you to get audio testimonials by having your customers call an 800 number. You can even have them call right from your store while they are the most enthusiastic. This is infinitely easier than trying to get people to mail or even e-mail you a letter. It's also very powerful to hear the enthusiasm of a real person who has bought your products and/or used your services.

You can also do audio postcards with the same program. I've sent out audio tips that included an affiliate link to some other product or service and made close to $10,000 each time I did it.

At the time of this writing, the service is only $29.95 per month. Kick Start Sound also has an affiliate program, so every time you recommend the program to someone else who buys it, you get $10 per month. Recommend only three people, and you get the service for free.

Visit http://www.KickStartSound.com to try out both the audio and video programs and to sign up.

Pay Per View/Pay Per Listen

You can even do a pay-per-view streaming (you need a qualified person to figure this out for you) so that you can deliver your content and get paid for it as opposed to using it only as online demo material.

Audio Tape/CD Production

If you go to a digital studio to record an audio product, here is a way to save a lot of money. Write your script out. Practice it quite a bit.

You go into the little sound booth and start recording. Fix any errors you make reading the script at the time you make them.

If I practice enough, I can record a 45-minute tape or CD in an hour and fifteen-minute studio session. This costs me about $40 an hour, so the total is about $50 per CD. That cost is without music, but I can have a saleable CD for about $50 done in a studio if I am not capable of doing it on my PC.

Recording Yourself

You can use a wave (.wav) editor program to edit audio on your computer. Go to any big computer store, tell them you want to edit audio, and they will sell you probably a $60 or $70 wave editor. You can actually see your voice on the screen and cut and paste it just like word processing. You can cut out the umms and aahs, add special effects, or do just about anything you want. It's very simple.

I use Sony Sound Forge (about $69) and virtually never go to a studio anymore. Although you don't have to, I bought a high-quality USB sound card to add to my PC along with a studio-quality microphone (Figures 5.1 and 5.2). to give me a really high-quality sound.

I got the sound card, microphone, and instructions from Mike Stewart (mike@soundpages.com or http://www.InternetAudioGuy.com, see Figures 5.1 and 5.2).

Mike will get you royalty-free music clips if you want to up the production value of your recordings. He also has a program that helps you put the audio clips on your voice recordings.

Figure 5.1   Studio Microphone with Pop Screen

Figure 5.2   High-Quality Sound Card That Plugs into Your USB Port

I went to a music store and bought a microphone stand with a boom on it so that I can keep my microphone handy near my desk. I simply pivot the microphone in front of my mouth when I want to record something.

Dan Janal also has a really great e-book series teaching you how to do teleseminars and how to record great quality sound, and he has a super bonus to go with it. Check it out at http://www.greatteleseminars.com/clickbook.htm.

You can get an e-book titled *Amazing CD Money Machine* at http://hop .clickbank.net/?powertips/cdmoney.

Audio Labeling

I use Avery Label Pro software (http://www.avery.com) to make the labels for my audiocassette tapes. Mac people can rejoice because Avery has a version of the software for you. I have found that Avery audio labels are far superior to the cheaper brands; however, as you'll read later, I use another brand for CD labels.

You can also create an audio business card, the coolest form of business card there is. You can use audiocassette or CD formats. You'll pay more for each one, but you don't give them out as easily as you do your regular business cards. The simplest way to make an audio business card is to get two people together and use an interview format.

For example, Joe the tailor gets together with Pete, who owns the shoe store. For Joe's tape, Pete is the interviewer and Joe is the expert. Pete opens the tape with, "We are here today with Joe Johnson, owner of Joe's Tailor Shop. Joe is the one who makes men look great every time they put on their suits." Pete introduces Joe and asks whatever Joe's written script says. Then Pete and Joe go back and forth with questions and answers that make Joe sound like the expert tailor that he is. When they are done, Joe has an audio business card.

Then Pete and Joe switch roles, and Joe takes over the interviewer role. They record the interview, and now Pete has an audio business card. So, two of you get together and help each other make a recording. The total length doesn't matter too much. Just record enough to make you appear to be the expert.

CD Production

CDs are really easy to produce, and they hold an incredible amount of information (up to 650 MB of audio, video, text, and graphics). Virtually all new computers come with a CD burner, which is a device that lets you play and record on a CD.

CD burners usually come with software that makes it easy for you to pick the files that you want to include on your CD. I happen to use Adaptec Easy CD Creator software by Roxio Company, which is very well known and well supported.

ISO 9660 versus Joliet

A word of caution (and I'm not an expert on this). Apparently, there are two CD formats that you can use when you burn a CD. One is ISO 9660 and one is Joliet. At the time of this writing, ISO 9660 is the preferred format. From what I understand, the Joliet format is newer and won't work on older CD players. When you use the ISO 9660 format, you must use names for your files that are the 8.3 or less method, that is, the main part of the file name must be eight characters or fewer, and you can have a three-character extension, for example: wakeup.wav.

Joliet allows long file names but will create compatibility trouble for you that you don't want. The support people for one of the companies that creates a CD menu program told me that most of their callers are told to switch to ISO 9660 and that solves their problem.

What Kind of Blank CDs Should I Buy?

Don't buy CD-RW, which is rewritable; that is, you can burn something on it and then reburn over it. This is not the kind of CD you will be using for your products. CD-RWs are generally used for office backups, and you'd be lucky if they worked on more than one computer in the same office.

You should use CD-Rs to create your products. They are very inexpensive (down to less than 50 cents when buying in bulk). You'll be throwing some of these away or using them for coasters because when you make a mistake, they cannot be reused.

Buy blank CDs that don't have any printing on the labeling surface. Your local Office Depot will likely have printing on the label side of their CDs that will show through when you put the paper label on.

I get my blanks from Polyline Corp. at http://www.polylinecorp.com. Try to get a name brand because there are manufacturing differences that are likely to get you lots of returns if you settle for the cheapest brand you can find.

Menu Programs

You don't need a menu program if you are doing simple audio CDs, but if you want a more interactive multimedia CD that is designed to be used on a computer, I use AutoPlay Menu Studio from http://www.indigorose.com. It allows you to make a really nice menu to help people navigate your CDs. It also creates the files automatically that make the CD start by itself when it is put in a Windows computer (see Figure 5.3).

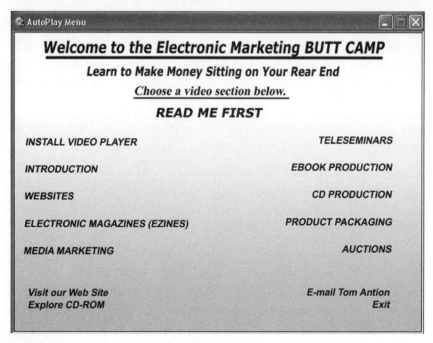

Figure 5.3   Put a Professional Finishing Touch on Your CD Products with an AutoPlay Feature and Menu

Some of the techies out there will argue that there is no need to buy a program for this task. That's easy to say if you're a techie. For the rest of us, the $200 is well spent because most of us would never figure it out on our own.

CD Menu Programs

http://www.indigorose.com

http://www.autorun-autoplay-tools.com

http://www.moonvalley.com/products/romwithaview/default.htm

CD Labeling

I use Sure Thing CD Labeler from http://www.surething.com. There are plenty of others out there. I've tried them all, so don't waste your time. Get this one. It's a program that has 3,000 gorgeous color backgrounds to pick from and lots of preformatted text layouts and fonts. I had my first CD label coming off my inexpensive color inkjet printer within about 15 minutes from the time I installed the program.

Figure 5.4   You Can Make Terrific CD Labels in Minutes with the Labeling Software

Figure 5.5   This Handy Carrying Case Slides Down Nicely Next to a Laptop

Besides being the best and easiest program to use, the labels cost about half the price of the major competition. I order them from http://www.label-gear.com. The Sure Thing program also has the capability of using other name brand labels and importing your own custom graphics to use as backgrounds (see Figure 5.4).

You can buy special printers that will print right on your CD, but really good ones start at over $1,000 and go up from there. You also have to get printable surface CDs to go along with the printer.

CD Printers That Print Directly on the CD

http://www.ioproducts.com/cdprinlab.html

http://www.mainstreetcd.com

http://www.ram-peripherals.co.uk

CD Packaging

In my packaging, I usually include a flexible plastic clamshell for several reasons. The plastic doesn't crack like hard plastic jewel cases, and because it's transparent, the label on the CD serves as the label for the product. It is so thin that it fits in a laptop case and takes up virtually no space. The only thing the clamshell lacks is a spine, which is handy for labeling your CD so it can be found easily in a CD rack (see Figures 5.5 and 5.6).

If you want to include more documentation in the form of a small booklet, you can use the jewel case to hold the booklet snugly inside. Some jewel cases hold many CDs, which is handy if you have a multi-CD set.

Figure 5.6 Jewel Cases Tend to Get Scratched and Crack, but Are Good for Organizing CDs in the Home or Office Because You Can Label the Edge

Figure 5.7 Clear DVD Case Holding Two CDs

I like DVD cases better. You can still use them for CDs, and they usually have a built-in document area. I still use clear ones so the CD label acts as the label for the entire product. Most of the time, I use these for my lower priced (up to $39.95) one- or two-CD sets (see Figure 5.7).

For bigger and more expensive CD or DVD programs, I use either a vinyl case with a clear overlay to add a printed insert or a nice quality, zippered case. The vinyl albums usually have a literature pocket on one side or room for additional CDs or DVDs. I use vinyl albums because they have a higher perceived value than most smaller cases do.

The zippered case isn't quite as big physically as the vinyl albums, but it does hold 12 CDs. I like them for some jobs because I know that customers

Figure 5.9 This Case Holds 12 CDs/DVDs

Figure 5.8 Zippered CD/DVD Holder

**Figure 5.11   Large Vinyl Album with
Literature Pocket**

**Figure 5.10   Large Vinyl Album with
Clear Overlay**

will put their own music CDs in the case and have my name in front of them all the time as they drive around in their car (see Figures 5.8 through 5.11).

You can get CD holder inserts to fit in three-ring binders. You can also get little stick-on devices so you can store a CD anywhere there is a clean, flat surface. I get all my CD packaging from http://www.polylinecorp.com (see Figures 5.12 through 5.13).

The Sure Thing program mentioned earlier will also create jewel case inserts.

**Figure 5.13   Plastic CD Holder Inserts
for Three-Ring Binder**

Figure 5.12   Three-Ring Binder

To get a great packaging catalog, call Polyline Corp., http://www.poly-linecorp.com. Another company's website is http://www.cdsleeves.com.

Types of CD Products

You can put all kinds of files on a CD. The easiest thing to do is to put your e-book on CD. The same file that you use as a downloadable product can be put on a CD.

Audio files can be put on CD. You can take a cassette product and use the same information to make a CD product. Remember, we want to put our information out in as many formats as possible to maximize the return. Here's an e-book all about this topic: http://hop.clickbank.net /?powertips/w4994c.

Video can easily be put on CD. You can put your videotape on CD, or you can make video products on CD. My Butt Camp on CD (http://www.antion .com/buttcampcd.htm) is a special video product made with a screen capture program. The program records anything that is displayed on your screen. It also records simultaneous audio as you narrate what's being seen on the screen, or you can add voiceover or music audio later (see Figure 5.14).

The screen capture program I use is Camtasia. Websites for Camtasia and others are:

http://www.techsmith.com (Camtasia)

http://www.hyperionics.com/index.asp (Hypercam)

http://www.bbsoftware.co.uk/BBFlashBack.aspx (BB Flashback)

You must watch your file size when using screen capture programs. The file size can become enormous unless you set the settings properly. Although

Figure 5.14 "Butt Camp CD" Version 1.0

you can string many videos together for a longer production, these programs are designed only for fairly short screen capture videos. The longest one on my Butt Camp CD is about 10 minutes. I have 50 of these shorter videos on one CD. The Camtasia "producer" allows you to string shorter videos together. See http://www.antion.com/buttcampcd.htm.

Making a screen capture video program is a great way to showcase your website. You can give the CD to customers or even mail it to them. When they put it in their computer, they can learn how to use your website. If they are connected to the Internet, they can click directly to the areas of your site where you want them to go.

CD Duplication

You can start out simply duplicating your CDs one at a time on your home or office computer. You can burn the same file over and over again onto CDs and do the labeling right there, too.

When you get a little volume going, you might want to purchase a CD duplicating machine. These machines are now under $200 (see Figure 5.15).

You can always find duplicating companies (check your Internet or local yellow pages) that will do all the work for you. They can do the artwork, labels, duplication, and packaging. Going this route will send your unit price up a bit, but your savings in labor and time should more than make up for it.

I use Sam Silverstein at http://www.SamSilverstein.com for most of my CD duplication.

Here are some sources for CD duplicating machines:

http://www.cdrecorders.com

http://www.ioproducts.com

**Figure 5.15   This CD Duplicator Turns Out $200
Worth of Product Every Two Minutes**

http://www.essential-data.com

http://www.discmakers.com

Fancy Discs

You can get discs shaped likes stars (our customers are the stars), saw blades (this would be great if you sold saws), and a bunch of other fancy designs. You can even get transparent discs. One of the best references for all kinds of CD stuff is Disc Makers (http://www.discmakers.com). They have a free catalog and a free, informative CD production guide.

Here are more CD references:

http://cdduplication4less.com/shaped.htm

http://www.multishapecdrom.com/cd_price.html

http://www.cdfx.com/newsite/shaped.php

http://www.crystalclearshapedcds.com/index.shtml

http://www.morphius.com/manufacturing/shapedcds.cfm

http://www.eastcomultimedia.com/replication/cdrep/shaped

Mac Stuff

The appropriate terminology for discs that work in both Macs and PCs and other computer platforms is *hybrid disc*. I haven't developed any products that will play on a Mac because the market is just too small and it isn't worth my limited time. I may someday make Mac products, but certainly not until it is really easy and can be done at the same time as the PC version. I highly recommend that you get the free CD production guide from Disc Makers mentioned earlier. They have a good explanation of the challenges you face in creating Mac CDs and hybrid CDs.

DVD

I just tackled my first in-house DVD production, and I wish I hadn't done it. It is a DVD set for public speakers who want to learn how to add magic tricks to their presentations (http://www.Magic4Speakers.com). It's just not easy enough yet to do it without someone who knows what he or she is doing. We struggled every inch of the way, and a project that should have taken a week ended up taking months.

All the production equipment and authoring software that are really good are high priced compared to any other product development tools we've discussed in this book, and the learning curve for the good stuff is enormous. Trust me, the cheap DVD software just won't cut it.

My main suggestion is to find a company to do the video editing and DVD production for you. This method may still have its own frustrations but for now is the better alternative.

It doesn't seem to be too much trouble to make DVD copies. For software to do so, see http://hop.clickbank.net/?powertips/iprogress.

Other Packaging

For books, it is most likely that you will need professional design work. If you are making products specifically for mail order, the cover design is not as critical.

However, I always suggest making the nicest looking product you can afford because you never know who will see it after it is sold. You would hope that it would look enticing enough to encourage someone else to buy it.

Even in brick and mortar stores, many specialty topic books don't have tremendously intricate cover designs. Some have no text on the back cover. Because it doesn't cost you any more to have text on the back cover, I think it's a good idea to put good advertising copy there.

Creating the Cover

I now create the cover in a file on my computer. If the product is $8\frac{1}{2} \times 11$ or smaller, I make one master on my color printer, which is a very high-quality printer. I have duplicates made at Kinko's or Insty-Prints on a color copier. Then I cut them to fit the album. I can make them one at a time for about 79 cents apiece.

If it is larger than $8\frac{1}{2} \times 11$, most of these more modern places such as Kinko's will take a file off your computer and output it directly to a beautiful color copy. In that case, I just let the copy shop print it directly from a disk.

Any graphic designer could make a suitable file for you. Some use Adobe Photo Shop, Harvard Graphics, or Adobe Illustrator. The main thing is most of these programs will "save as" some other kind of file. You'll find the Adobe PDF is readily accepted just about everywhere. So you want to check with the place that will duplicate them and ask what kind of files they need to use for their color copier. Then you create the file. They print it out and cut it down to size, and you shove it into the vinyl album. Then you have a gorgeous-looking product.

If you want to see the packaging for my video system, go to http://www
.antion.com/speakervideo.htm. All this packaging except for the printing of
the book was created right on my computer, and I don't have any graphics
talent whatsoever. In addition, I can print each piece one at a time if I wish.
This is really the cheapest and best way to do it.

What You Need to Know

 You can create all kinds of high-quality informational products on
a very small budget. CDs, audiotapes, videotapes, and DVDs can
all be made and packaged quickly and inexpensively.

Dropkick Your Self-Publishing Fears: How to Create and Distribute E-Books

How much easier can this get? People go to my website and enter their credit
card number. In about 15 seconds, the money is heading toward my bank account. They download the *Wake 'em Up* e-book to their computer. I get an e-
mail saying that I had a sale, and I don't even have to go to the post office
anymore.

The e-book is no longer the wave of the future—it is what savvy information marketers are doing right now to make a fortune using the Internet to sell
digital products. I am pulling out books, reports, and other information that
wasn't worth reprinting, updating them, and putting them out in downloadable electronic format. I'm also hiring writers to write other e-books for me.

The naysayers out there may be saying, "But, Tom, all the major media reported a long time ago that e-books just didn't make it. Why should we waste
our time with them?"

Here's what you have to remember. The major media reports pretty much
on major companies. They are clueless as to what the little guy is doing. Yes,
it's true that across the board e-books have not been accepted in a major
fashion. You don't see 100 people on your subway car reading e-books on
their handheld readers. That doesn't negate the fact that little guys like you
and me are making millions by selling e-books and other digital products to
little niche markets.

Smart small businesses are cleaning up on the fact that there is an
information-hungry, worldwide audience with little patience and short attention spans. They want information on a myriad of relatively obscure topics,
and they want it now.

That's why you can sell an e-book titled *How to Buy a Used Motorcycle* on
Saturday night at midnight to a person who wants to go out looking for one
Sunday morning.

That's why you can sell a *Kidney Stone Relief* e-book to someone who is dreading the next trip to the bathroom.

That's why you can sell a *How to Start a Hot Dog Vending Kiosk* e-book to someone who is looking for a fast and easy way to make some extra money.

None of these books would have an easy time finding a major publishing house and would most likely never see widespread distribution. But each one has the capacity to make $10,000 to $50,000 per year for the publishers (that's you) when selling them on the Web. And when you sell an e-book, the money you get represents virtually pure profit!

So, ignore the major media and read on to see how to make an e-book that will either give you direct cash flow or can be used to promote your other products and services.

Speed to Market

Now, literally five minutes after you create a document, it can be converted and on the Internet for sale to the world. The first night I had the *Wake 'em Up* e-book out there, which was about seven years ago, I got two orders. I didn't even announce it to anybody, and $40 was in my bank account. That's not a million, but I'll take it, and I think most of you would, too.

One of my e-books, *101 Nice Things to Help Out after the Funeral* went from concept to market in less than eight hours. This is the kind of speed that can make you a fortune while servicing your information-hungry customers.

No Fancy Website Needed

Another thing that is cool about e-books is that you don't even have to have a fancy website. I use mostly one-page sales letter sites and bring in tons of money. Or, if you don't want to make a new website, you can simply use a page in your existing site to promote the e-book.

Another cool thing is that because of the simple methods you will use to create your e-book, you incur almost zero production cost.

Content That Sells

You will find that nonfiction or "how to" e-books are by far the best sellers. It also gives you a big boost if your e-book represents a topic that has a natural sense of urgency.

For instance, my wedding toast and wedding speech e-books sell better than my wedding reception e-book. The reason: People wait until the last minute thinking about toasts and speeches and then realize they are going to be on video the next day doing a wedding speech. They don't want to look stupid for all eternity, so they rush to the Internet for help. Wedding receptions are normally planned months in advance of the wedding, so the urgency factor is not there.

Scarcity

Just as with advertising copywriting that was discussed in another section, scarcity is a big motivator. If you have information on a tightly niched topic and the person searching can't find the information easily anywhere else, you have a great chance to make the sale.

I got an e-mail from the guy who wrote the hot dog vending e-book. This guy makes from $400 to $1,400 a day setting up his hot dog kiosk in front of stadiums. He told me he had seen me at a speech the year before and went right home and wrote the e-book. I really laughed and was thrilled when he told me about the e-book and how well it was selling. I'm sure opportunity seekers don't see too many hot dog vending books.

E-Book Security

Many people who write and publish e-books are worried about security or somebody stealing their e-book and selling it on the black market (the black cyber market, I guess you'd call it).

Here we go back to that protectionist attitude. No, I don't agree it's right to steal your e-book and distribute to all my friends, but guess what? In many cases, you'd be lucky if someone stole your e-book because that means they've heard of you.

However, there are some measures you can take to protect yourself from wholesale theft of your e-product. First, if you use a good shopping cart system such as Kick Start Cart, the download links the customer gets are good for only 24 hours and then they disappear automatically.

This prevents someone from posting the link on some discussion board where hundreds or even thousands of people could download your book for free.

Another great tactic, which is perfectly acceptable in this type of publishing, is to have links inside the e-book going to your web pages, your other products, and all kinds of things. You can make hyperlinks that people, if they are connected to the Internet, will jump directly to wherever you want them to go. So, if someone does pass your e-book illegally on to someone else, that someone else might have the courtesy to buy something.

Adobe PDF

The following sections discuss a simple document conversion from Microsoft Word to Adobe PDF format. Don't worry if you don't use Microsoft Word. Most major word processing programs will convert easily to Adobe PDF.

Most computers now come with the free Adobe Acrobat Reader already installed. You will experience far fewer problems (customer headaches) with PDF than with any other format. Both Macs and PCs can read PDF files, and they can be read on many handheld devices.

There are all kinds of other formats that, in my not-so-humble opinion, will cause you customer service nightmares. Angela Adair Hoy from Book-locker.com, one of the largest e-book sellers on the Internet, told me that when she accepted all the fancy formats for e-books, her customer complaint and confusion rate was more than 30 percent. When she went exclusively to Adobe PDF format, her complaint and confusion rate went below 2 percent.

Unless you've got nothing better to do than field calls from customers and prospects who can't figure out how to use your e-book, I suggest you stick with the simple Adobe format.

How to Do It

To do the conversion from Microsoft Word to Adobe PDF, you can buy the Adobe Acrobat program. Don't confuse this with the free Adobe Reader. You must buy the full program if you want to do the conversion yourself.

You'll have a little bit of a learning curve with Adobe Acrobat, and you'll have to experiment a little bit to get all the conversion settings right for your type of e-book. After that, it's pretty much clear sailing. I hardly think about it now because when you have both Microsoft Word and Adobe Acrobat installed on your computer, an Adobe button shows up in Microsoft Word. All I do now is create the document in Word, click the button, and a few minutes later the conversion is done.

If you don't like the sounds of any of this, simply hire someone to do the conversion for you.

Links

If you want hot links in your e-book, you have to type out the entire URL including the "http://" because it's safer and easier to make sure your links are clickable. Also, if someone prints out the e-book, the entire link is there for them. So, you need "http://www" and whatever the URL is.

For e-mail addresses, you must put "mail to:" in front of the address, for example: mailto:tom@antion.com. Don't put any spaces in until after the .com.

Split Screen

For those of you who haven't read an e-book through the Adobe Acrobat Reader, you can have a split screen where the left-hand side of the screen is a clickable outline of your book and the chapters, and they are all hot-linked to their respective places in the book. The whole thing will sit on one screen. You click where you want to go, and it will take you to Chapter 14, subheading 2, for example.

When you are trying to put in a heading tag, the heading tag has a certain font size associated with it. Don't let that worry you. Just make it a heading, and then you can go back to the point size and change it to whatever size you want. As long as your chapter and subheadings have a heading tag associated with them, you'll be okay. Make sure you do that so your conversion is easier.

Preparing Your E-Book in Microsoft Word

I asked the guy who gets me out of trouble when I make formatting blunders to give me a checklist of things to do to prepare a Word document for conversion to Adobe. Many of the tips are simply good formatting practices that will help you in any program.

David Hogan's tips for preparing your e-book for conversion to Adobe are:

✓ Use heading tags, and make sure they are not mingled with other text. A heading should be by itself and *not* in the middle of other text. Do not make the mistake of using heading tags for the sake of appearance. Headings play a vital role in the bookmarks of the Acrobat file. Structure should be the prevailing thought.

✓ Be certain there are regular paragraph returns (return or enter key) after the heading. These should not take on the properties of the heading. For example, if you use Chapter 1, Chapter 2, and so on, they should all be the same heading type and nothing else in the book should have this type of heading.

✓ To change the appearance of a heading:
—Select text and make it a heading.
—Make changes to the font, size, type, and so on. Then reapply the heading to the selected text. This step will prompt you to update the heading you choose instead of using the existing heading style.

✓ Give thought to where you want the table of contents. Resist inserting it until you have completed your book. Then insert pages where you want it to go and let Word create it.

✓ Many people prefer to create Word indexes at the completion of a chapter to minimize the work involved and review time. Wait until you are finished with your work to mark index entries. It then becomes part of the review process and aids you in finding mistakes.

✓ When inserting pictures, consider first inserting a text box. Then insert the picture in the text box so there is better control of the picture's placement.

✓ If you want a caption box to go along with the picture, group the caption box with the main box by holding down the Shift key while you choose both the picture box and caption box. Right-click your mouse and choose the grouping option.

✓ For precise placement of pictures, learn to place your pictures into tables. Then set the border shading of the table to "none." A 3 × 3 table, for example, can give you precise placement of four pictures next to one another with a caption between them. See the following table:

Picture here		Picture here
	Caption here	
Picture here		Picture here

Drag the borders of the table as needed for placement, and remember to turn off the table border shading by right mouse-clicking the table and choosing borders and shading; then mark the box for "none."

✓ Make sure you have space between different styles. For instance, if you apply a border or a font change, you should have space between that style and the next different style text.

✓ Use page breaks when necessary (Ctrl+Enter). This keeps text together without weird text flow errors. This step is critical, and main heading or chapters should begin on new pages where possible.

✓ *Do not use the space bar* to try to move or align text. This creates absolute nightmares upon conversion. Use tabs, tables, or text boxes to control the placement of text.

✓ Always make text entries for bulleted and numbered lists first before you apply the bullets or numbers. Also, make sure you have a blank line after the list before you apply the bullets or numbers.

✓ Avoid extra large headings in electronic documents because people resent having to click too much and to waste a whole page (if they print out the document) on a large font.

✓ You might consider using only the top two-thirds of the page so that the end user does not have to scroll to see the entire page. This is a matter of preference, and printing should be considered when doing such.

✓ Lots of white space is desirable because too much text tires the eyes.

✓ Finally, the biggest mistake is to format as you go. Type your text first, then hit your enter key a couple times to leave space for a heading. Wait until you are finished with the entire book to fill these spaces with your headings. This recommendation is usually ignored more than anything else, and it will cause more grief than any other item.

Here are four e-books about e-books:

1. http://hop.clickbank.net/?powertips/digishine (*PDF Secrets*)
2. http://hop.clickbank.net/?powertips/ebksecrets (*E-Book Secrets*)
3. http://hop.clickbank.net/?powertips/warmsnow (*Your Guide to E-Book Publishing Success*)
4. http://hop.clickbank.net/?powertips/higher (*How to Get Higher E-Book Profits*)

Additional Adobe help and resources:

http://www.adobe.com/epaper

http://www.adobe.com/products/acrdis/createbooks.html (step-by-step instructions for preparing and converting e-books)

TIP: The downloads at the Adobe site have more detail than you need to create simple e-books for online distribution.

Screen Captures

If you want to add visuals to your e-book right from your computer screen, you can use screen capture programs to do the job. The book you are reading right now has screen captures sprinkled throughout to add clarity.

Many Windows computers have a basic screen capture utility called Paint. You use it in combination with your Print Screen key to capture and edit images from your computer screen.

Here's the quick course on using Paint and your Print Screen key:

- Display what you want to capture
- Hit the Print Screen key
- Open Paint
- Paste
- Click on "Select" button
- Highlight what you want to capture
- Copy
- File New
- Paste
- Save

Check here for some more advanced screen capture programs:

http://www.screencapture.com (Capture Eze Pro)

http://www.hyperionics.com/index.html (HyperSnap-DX)

http://www.techsmith.com (Snag It)

http://www.creativesoftworx.com (Capture LITE and Capture PRO)

http://www.captureexpress.com (Capture Express)

http://www.stclairsoft.com/ScreenCatcher/index.html (for Mac)

E-Book Pricing

E-book pricing can be all across the board and depends largely on the topic and scarcity of the information.

Moneymaking stuff is mostly at the top of the list. I can't tell you how many downloads I've paid $37 or $97 for because it was highly specific, moneymaking stuff. If you have something highly specific and it's on a hot topic, you can make it into something like a business start-up kit, a moneymaking kit, or system. There is no set number, so don't feel that you are limited to the pricing if you have the hot topic that people want and it will make them money.

My e-book *Wake 'em Up! How to Use Humor and Other Professional Techniques to Create Alarmingly Good Business Presentations* is an awesome, 300-page book. Its paperback counterpart is pretty much the bible of the professional speaking industry when it comes to onstage performance. It's a $17 e-book because people pretty much hate public speaking, and most people who don't hate public speaking value the moneymaking aspect of speaking rather than the "art" of speaking. That's why I can get $97 for an e-book on making money as a speaker and only $17 for one on being great on stage.

In addition, my classic 300-page book sells for the same price as my 60- to 70-page wedding and eulogy e-books. So you can see that pricing can go all across the board.

What this all boils down to is testing. It's so easy to do a split test on the Web that in a day or two you could absolutely know which price for your e-book makes you the most money. Sometimes raising the price will get you more sales (and possibly more returns), and sometimes lowering the price will get you more sales.

You also have to consider why you are doing the e-book in the first place. Are you trying to get the maximum number of people exposed to your material so you can sell them back-end products? Or, are you trying to make the most cash flow the quickest from the e-book sale itself? All this factors into what price will be best for your e-book.

Special Reports

One of my students, Joan Stewart, aka "The Publicity Hound," sells PDF special reports on microniche topics about getting free publicity. These are somewhat shorter than a 50-page e-book, and she sells tons of them for $9 each.

Think about that. For $9 you could come home with 36 hardcover Shakespeare books from any respectable yard sale or flea market in America, but you get only 15 or 20 pages on how to write a press release from Joan. Is that fair? You're darn right it's fair because Joan has built a system that provides what small business owners need to get free publicity. And she's there with the information when they need it.

Delivering the E-Book

If you have a shopping cart or if you are considering a shopping cart, you need to know whether it will handle "soft goods." Soft goods are these downloadable e-books that we are talking about, or you might write computer programs and sell them, which is a soft good.

A hard good is something that you end up shipping, such as a printed book or a tape. I had to jump through some extra hoops to find http://www.KickStartCart.com, a shopping cart that I could make do both in one order. So if you are shopping for a shopping cart, make sure that you can do both hard goods and soft goods in the same transaction. That way, somebody could order a CD and a downloadable product at the same time.

This information applies when you sell your software or your e-books from your own website as opposed to someone else's website. There are places that will sell your e-book for you, but I can assure you more money can be made handling the transaction yourself and building up a list of loyal followers as we've discussed throughout this book. The exception is placing your e-books with Amazon.com or Barnes & Noble online.

> **TIP:** http://www.LightningSource.com is the company that handles
> Amazon's e-book sales.

You can and should be ready to e-mail a backup copy to someone who has muffed the download or suffered a computer crash, but only as a last resort. You must have the tools available to let people purchase and download immediately.

Free E-Book Distribution

Let's say you are using your e-book as a purely promotional tool and you don't require payment for it. How do you distribute it?

There are several ways I do this. First, the e-book can be simply put on a web page in your site with a hyperlink on it. You tell people where the link is, and they visit the page and download the e-book themselves. They can be totally anonymous and take the book at will and pass the link on to their friends.

The second way to distribute your e-book is to put it into your shopping cart system and make it a "zero price" product. In this case, the person downloading would have to put in name, address, e-mail address, and so on, but not credit card information. In this case, you get more information about the person, but most likely fewer people downloading because of the request for all the personal information. Make sure your merchant account allows zero price products before you try this.

The third way I distribute is on CD. The same file that can be downloaded from Kick Start Cart can be burned on a CD. I do this frequently at live events because people like to have a physical product to take with them rather than a link written on their handout.

E-Book Length

My main focus when it comes to e-book length is not exactly how many pages I am providing, but whether the customer perceives the product as a good value. I spend lots of extra time when creating e-books to be sure I add everything I can add to the book to make it better. In addition to simply being a good thing to do, adding checklists, resources, and helpful links add pages to the final count.

My shortest e-book at this point is 21 pages. That's the *101 Nice Things to Do After the Funeral* book. My longest is titled *Click*, and it's a 656-page Internet marketing book for professional speakers. My wedding and eulogy e-books go from 50 to 70 pages.

Your final page count can be varied considerably by changing the font size and adding or subtracting graphics, text boxes, and white space.

I use a 14-point or 16-point Times Roman font for almost all of my body text. These sizes are easier to read on a computer screen but not too large if someone wants to print out an e-book.

Here's another tip: Don't make your chapter headings gigantic because people get mad if they try to print the book and it takes a whole page for the words "Chapter One."

Adobe's free guidebook, *How to Create Adobe PDF Files for E-Books* (http://www.adobe.com/products/acrdis/createbooks.html), suggests making a page size of 6 × 9 inches (15.24 cm × 22.86 cm), which displays nicely on a monitor and still prints out okay on 8½ × 11 paper. I just leave it at 8½ × 11 because it's easier.

Audio E-Books

There are two ways to add audio to your e-books. First, you can embed the audio files right in your PDF file. Second, you link to the audio file, which is housed on a website. Each method has pros and cons.

Embedding

The problem with embedding the audio file in the PDF file is that your overall file sizes can become enormous. This makes automatic downloads more difficult especially for those who don't have high-speed connections.

The upside to embedding your audio is that the person can listen to the audio without being connected to the Internet. He or she could be on a plane listening to your audio book on a laptop.

You could even burn a PDF file with embedded audio to a CD where you would have 650 megabytes of storage capacity and plenty of room for lots of audio. You would have a nice, self-contained package that, again, would not require the person to be connected to the Internet.

Linking

Linking is nice in that you can distribute your PDF e-book easily because the file size will be really small. The person receiving the PDF file clicks on a link that takes him or her to the audio file or a page where the audio file link is, which would either be streaming off your web server or available for download to the person's computer or mp3 player. Visit http://www.GreatInternetMarketing.com/backups.htm to hear Tom sing a parody song about backing up your files.

The bad part about linking to a streaming audio is that the person must be connected to the Internet to listen to your files. The bad part about letting people download an mp3 version of your file is that they now have to keep track of the mp3 downloads and your PDF file.

E-Book Covers

E-book covers (like the one you see in Figure 5.16) are simply graphic representations of your e-book. Obviously, there is no physical book cover or physical book.

Figure 5.16   Sample E-Book Cover

Figure 5.17   Sample One-Page Website Graphic

E-book covers are typically used to advertise the book and give someone something to relate to even though an e-book is quite different from a physical book. People seem to get the message that they are buying a "book" with information in it.

For a handy tool that allows you to make beautiful e-book covers in minutes, without having any graphic arts experience, see http://www.ecovergenerator.com/x.cgi?adminid=814&id=22663.

I also use the Header Generator program to make simple, one-page websites and to make the first page of many of my e-books. Again, I was up to speed in no time. Figure 5.17 is a sample.

A variation of this header was used at the main website for this product (http://www.Great-Speeches.org) and inside each of the four volumes.

To try out this software, visit http://www.ecovergenerator.com/x.cgi?adminid=814&id=22663&pid=2160.

The following e-book tells you how to create e-books quickly: http://hop.clickbank.net/?powertips/chiaewen.

How to Create and Distribute an E-Course

E-courses are credibility tools, and they are also great sales tools. You can easily create a course in your field of expertise and either sell it as a product or give it away as a give-before-you-get sales tool.

If it's a free course, you give good information, but you don't give all the information. It's designed to be helpful to people and not a blatant sales pitch, but if you gave them everything, there would be no reason to buy anything from you. If you are selling the course, make it very comprehensive and don't hold back. You want the recipients to really feel that they are getting value.

E-courses are even easier to create than e-books. You don't have to do any fancy formatting or heading tags or conversions. You just create it in plain text e-zine fashion. For a sample of my seven-day mini course, send an e-mail to: mailto:minicourse@aweber.com. A blank e-mail is fine. You'll get the first part of the course back within a few minutes. Then each day for seven days, you will get the next section of the course.

AOL users, beware. I had about 100 complaints that parts of the course were never delivered. Every single one was someone with an AOL address! One thing you can do to be sure you get an e-course that you ordered is to check your spam filter to see if the email got caught. You can then set the filter to recognize the sender and clear the future parts of the course through to your inbox. If you are creating e-courses, you might want to remind the buyer about this in your sales copy. You certainly don't want to get complaints that people didn't get the course they paid for.

Here's a checklist to create an e-course:

✓ Pick your topic.

✓ Gather your material into related sections. Each section will be one lesson in the course. Five sections means five days to the course. If your material is complicated, you could do one lesson per week, but on a free course I would recommend against it because it will take you too long to get people to buy.

✓ Write a welcome and introduction to the course along with a list of all the upcoming lessons.

✓ Don't skimp on any of the lessons. People can unsubscribe from this and either ask for their money back or just disappear from your list and then you won't have a chance to sell them anything.

✓ If it's a free course, you should weave subtle hints into the course that make people want to know more. You'll see examples of this in my mini course. My goal was to show you that you don't even know what you don't know about Internet marketing and that not knowing these things will hurt you and your family and give you warts or whatever the consequences are. This is just one technique to make people want to buy.

✓ Once the course is written, set up an account with one of the sequential autoresponder companies listed earlier to distribute the course for you. If you have http://www.KickStartCart.com, you can do unlimited numbers of these courses with no extra expense. Each company has its own set of instructions for setup, but basically you'll cut and paste your e-mail into their system so they can send it out upon request.

Don't forget what you learned about putting hard returns at the end of each line of your course or use an inexpensive program such as Text Pad to do it for you. If you don't, you will likely have a lousy looking e-course.

✓ Now, promote the course to your e-mail list, put a notice about it on your website, and put up a sign about it at your retail store. Generally, tell people about it anyway you can. I put it out to a list of about 11,000 and got over a 10 percent response in the first three days. Those 1,200 or so people spent about $7,000 with me after taking their "free" course.

TeleSeminars and Webcasts

Another very profitable way to sell your knowledge and promote your business is via telephone seminars and webcasts aka webinars.

With teleseminars, all people have to do is call into a telephone bridge line, which is a low-cost conference call technology. Don't bother asking your long distance provider about it because they will probably tell you they never heard of this technology. It's most likely they'll try to sell you a 65 cents per minute per person conference call line. A listing of telephone bridge companies follows this discussion.

You can use these calls to make money directly by selling your information and answering questions for people on the call, or you can use the calls to give user tips for people who already own your product. These calls can really create increased loyalty toward your products and services and can create upsell situations where these loyal customers will buy more of your stuff or upgrade to bigger products.

If you have a more technically sophisticated audience, webcast technology can do the same types of seminars, but add real-time graphics and interaction that you can't do over the phone. (See the following list for webcasting companies.)

Telephone Bridge Companies

Judy Sabah

mailto:judy@judysabah.com 303-777-1765

Fax 303-733-8288, http://www.JudySabah.com

Full Service TeleSeminar Company

Dan Janal at Great TeleSeminars (This company will handle all the details for you, or you can pick from a menu of services so that they handle only the parts that you don't want to.)

http://www.kickstartcart.com/app/aftrack.asp?afid=157849

TeleSeminar Audio Training

http://www.antion.com/teleseminarkit.htm

Conference Call Companies

http://www.actionconferencecall.com

http://www.calleci.com

http://www.uconference.com

http://www.contactcall.com

http://www.vialog.com

http://www.event-telemarketing.com

http://www.conferencecall.com

http://www.conferencecallusa.com

TeleClass Companies

http://www.teleclass.com

http://www.teleclass4u.com

http://www.teleclassinternational.com/main2/training.html?aid=41

http://www.teleclassleader.com

Webcasting Companies

http://www.vialog.com

http://communicast.com

http://www.webcasting.com

http://www.playstream.com

http://www.presentplus.com

http://www.you-niversity.com

Web Conferencing Companies

http://www.astound.com

http://www.mshow.com

http://www.placeware.com

http://www.webex.com

http://www.web-conferencing-central.com

Video Conferencing Companies and Software

http://www.webex.com

http://www.inview.net

http://www.mivnet.com

http://www.proximity.com

http://www.cuseeme.com

http://www.microsoft.com/windows/netmeeting

6

International Website

This chapter is by no means a comprehensive treatise of international website operations. It's no more than a "here's where to stick your toe in the water" chapter. I haven't done much of any of the things in this chapter because I can barely get the work done to reach all the potential business in my own backyard. I will be doing more and more international optimization in the future, and will be sure to report on it in the updates page for this book.

Websites by definition are international. If you have a website, then anyone, anywhere in the world can view it. This doesn't mean, however, that they can use it. That's what this chapter is about.

I'm going to give you a resource right up front: *How to Build a Successful International Website* by Mark Bishop. Even though the book is a few years old, I highly recommend it because it brings up issues that you probably wouldn't think of when it comes to usability in a non-English speaking country. To be honest, I didn't understand half of the content in this book, but giving it to your webmaster will probably save you quite a bit of money because the webmaster won't have to do as much research to make your international site happen.

For instance, do you know what graphic depictions and colors might be offensive to people in Uzbekistan? Did you know that Katakana is the Japanese script used to spell out foreign words. Believe me, I never even thought about this stuff. The book I recommended doesn't give you these answers either, but it sure makes you think about them so you don't alienate the people you are trying to attract.

You might correctly assume that many people around the world who are serious about doing business globally, learn to speak English. That is true, but many people don't. Many people who could buy your products and services can't speak English. You might say, "If I'm a management consultant and produce products in English, people who can't speak English couldn't use them anyway." I answer, "Not so!" English-based products are in demand around the world. We in the United States tend to think that we are the center of the Universe and we don't go out of our way to buy information products from other cultures because we feel we know it all. People from other cultures are a little more open minded and willing to learn, so don't think

"Flags courtesy of www.theodora.com/flags used with permission"

Figure 6.1   International Web Sites Sometimes Use Clickable Flags to Help Foreign Visitors Navigate the Site

you can't sell in other lands. They can get the information translated and/or use it to help their own study of English.

Sometimes, it doesn't take a lot of work to make a site more user friendly for those from other cultures. It's a little easier if you concentrate on one culture and go through the method. Then adding additional cultures will be a little easier.

Don't think you have to create an entire website for your international visitors. In many cases, all you have to do is put a link on your main page with their country name on it. If you want to get fancy, you can add their flag. From that link you can have as little as one page that describes what you do and invites them to look at your products. They can then e-mail you to help them order. If you have many countries, you are better off using a drop-down box because you don't want to take up your entire home page listing all the countries (see Figure 6.1).

The page you create for each country (or language) is pretty important. You can't simply use an online automated language translator to create this page. You need a real, live person to do it, and preferably one who is native to the country in question. This person will do the translation for you. You can also recruit them to be available via e-mail to translate e-mail orders and inquiries that are too complicated for a web-based translator.

If you give people from other lands a chance to read something about your company in their own language and an e-mail link, you'll be tapping an entire segment of the world population that your competitors are most likely ignoring.

Right now the bulk of Web usage (about 75 percent) is in the United States but other countries are continuing to increase their usage of the Internet and it will obviously continue to grow. Making an internationally friendly website wouldn't necessarily be my first priority but more and more potential business will be available from non-English speaking countries. You can easily get your website ready to grab your fair share.

Pay Extra Attention to Bandwidth

In my travels I have used Internet Café and hotel computers in many foreign countries. High speed Internet access has extremely limited accessibility and when it was available it was expensive.

When constructing the international portion of your site pay particular attention to the fact that many people still pay for Internet access by the minute or quarter hour. They generally don't have the latest and greatest of anything when it comes to hardware and software.

You must keep graphics very small and don't do anything that would keep your pages from loading quickly on a slow connection—14.4 and 28.8 modems are still commonly in use in many places around the world.

Language and Culture Differences

Avoid obscure references that would confuse a foreign visitor. Get your translator to help you with this.

You probably want to convert any measurements to the metric system and when in doubt list both. If you want people to fill out forms, then use their language and conventions. For example, in the United States we have zip codes in our address. This might be a postal code or some other name in another country. Again, get a native to review even small points like this.

How about time zones? Don't say customer service will be open from 8:30 A.M. to 5:00 P.M. Tell them what time zone that is.

Look in any major search engine for translation services or get started with the links below:

http://www.translationplus.com

http://webideas.com/translations (Russian translation)

http://www.webtranslation.com/cecindex.htm
(Chinese language conversion)

Here are a few things to think about when constructing a global user friendly site:

✓ Do you make it impossible for someone outside your country to order through your shopping cart by making certain fields in the shopping cart mandatory? Example: I think the United States is the only country that has a zip code. If the shopper's country calls it something else or they don't fill in that blank, will your system refuse the order? What if their postal code has letters in it and your form only accepts numbers?

✓ Do you make your visitors read a long sales letter and then tell them at the end the offer is only good in the United States?

✓ Is it extremely clear where non-English speaking visitors should click for assistance or information in their language?

Promoting Your International Website

You will use the same techniques you learned earlier in this book to promote your website to non-English speaking countries. You could certainly do all the off-line methods described in this book too, but it will be significantly more difficult if you don't live in the country or countries you are targeting.

Each country-specific web page should have it's own title bar/tags, META tags, keyword density, heading tags, and body text that are customized for the particular country you are targeting on that page. It's really no different than customizing a page for an English-speaking visitor. You are just using the language of the targeted country rather than English:

http://www.glreach.com (specializes in search engine optimization for different languages)

http://webdoctor.oregon.com/searchengines.htm (large listing of international search engines and directories)

Some of the top regional or country-specific foreign-language search engines and directories are listed next. Notice how Google seems to be just about everywhere:

Asian Search Facilities

China

http://chinese.yahoo.com

http://www.beijixing.com.cn/bjx01/start.shtm (business search engine)

Japan

http://www.goo.ne.jp

http://www.google.co.jp

European Search Facilities

Germany

http://web.de

http://www.altavista.de

http://www.google.com/intl/de

France

http://www.ecila.fr

http://www.voila.fr

http://www.google.fr

Italy

http://www.virgilio.it

http://www.arianna.it

http://www.google.it

Russia

http://www.rambler.ru

http://www.yandex.ru

http://www.google.ru

Spain

http://www.ole.com

http://www.google.es/intl/ca

United Kingdom

http://www.searchuk.com

http://www.ukplus.co.uk

http://www.google.co.uk

Latin American Search Facilities

Argentina

http://www.grippo.com

http://www.google.com.ar

Brazil

http://www.cade.com.br

http://www.google.com.br

Colombia

http://www.conexcol.com

http://www.google.com.co

Mexico

http://www.iguana.com.mx

http://www.mexicoweb.com.mx

http://www.google.com.mx

Peru

http://www.adonde.com

http://www.astrolabio.net

For more foreign search engines and directories check these links:

http://www.allsearchengines.com/foreign.html

http://www.searchenginecolossus.com

Additional International Resources

http://www.exim.gov (export insurance)

http://globaledge.msu.edu/ibrd/ibrd.asp (international business resources)

http://www.irwa.org (International Webmasters Association—tips and resources for making a multilingual website)

http://www.odci.gov/cia/publications/factbook/index.html (handy and current information on any country in the world)

http://www.languagemasters.com

mailto:drussell@languagemasters.com

http://www.globallanguages.com

Ranking Manager: http://www.websitemanagementtools.com (This site is great for international reporting of how your website is doing in search engines around the world. At the time of this writing, it supports 448 search engines listed at http://www.websitemanagementtools.com /ranking-manager/engines.php.)

7

Cool Internet Stuff

Don't go crazy with this chapter. You could easily negate all the sales process and sales psychology you learned throughout this book by cluttering up your website with lots of crazy stuff. Use these items sparingly or in a novelty/specialty area of your site. Some of the items are simply tools to help you be more productive and save money and some of them can really be great for sales. Pick wisely what is best for your situation.

Keyword Searches

This first item isn't really something you put on your website, but I thought it was a cool and powerful tool you should know about. I used to use a paid service a long time ago that was part of CompuServe. It would search the Internet for articles based on keywords. Well, that service is back and it's **FREE** (http://www.Google.com/newsalerts).

If you want to land a sale for your products and services with a certain company, put their company name in the news alert and you'll get free research coming to your computer every day. Use the research to impress the heck out of your prospective client.

Here's a couple more services you can try out:

http://www.tracerlock.com

http://www.customscoop.com

http://www.cyberalert.com

http://www.ewatch.com

CGI Scripts

I don't have a clue as to how to define this term that anybody reading this would care about. All you need to know is that CGI scripts can make your site do cool things (like the "recommend" script you saw in the e-zine section). Go to the sites listed next to find tons of examples:

http://www.willmaster.com (I use these people. I really like them.)

http://www.scriptarchive.com

http://cgidir.com/Scripts

http://www.freecenter.com/cgi.html

http://dreamcatchersweb.com/scripts

http://www.cgi-world.com (custom scripts for your website)

http://www.cgi-works.net (custom scripts for your website)

Productivity Stuff

http://www.speed411.com (Find high-speed Internet access in your area so you can work faster.)

http://www.gator.com/ads.html (Tired of filling out forms? Tired of forgetting passwords? Gator is free software that does the typing for you. Gator eliminates frustrating web chores like filling out forms and remembering passwords and it's free.)

http://www.bookmarktracker.com (keeps track of all your bookmarks)

http://www.stamps.com. (No more waiting at the post office. Buy your stamps online.)

Clean Up Text

http://www.customsolutions.us/cleanup/index.htm

http://www.westcodesoft.com/ungarbleit/index.html (for Mac)

Fax from Your Computer

http://www.efax.com

http://www.symantec.com/winfax

Interactive Maps

http://www.mapquest.com

http://www.mapblast.com

http://www.MapsOnUs.com

Online Phone Books

http://www.switchboard.com

http://www.bestyellow.com

http://www.411.com

http://www.bigyellow.com

http://www.bigbook.com

http://www.fedworld.gov (government stuff)

Meta Search Engines

They search many other regular search engines at once.

http://www.askjeeves.com

http://www.metacrawler.com

http://www.dogpile.com

http://cyber411.com

http://www.metafind.com

http://www.copernic.com (You must install their free software.)

http://www.debriefing.com

Sound File Search Engine

http://www.findsounds.com

Graphic Search Engine

http://www.ditto.com

Legal Search Engine

http://www.findlaw.com

Money-Saving Stuff

Telephone

http://www.mediaring.com

http://www.freewebcall.com

http://www.dialpad.com (United States only)

http://www.net2phone.com (not free but really cheap)

Internet Call Waiting

Saves you from getting two phone lines.

http://www.buzme.com/default.asp

http://www.pagoo.com

http://www.faxcube.com (web faxing)

http://www.hotvoice.com (free phone)

http://www.j2.com (Get fax and phone sent to your e-mail inbox.)

http://www.trac.org (nonprofit organization with lots of moneysaving phone tips)

E-Mail Stuff

Check your pop3 e-mail from any computer attached to the Internet using:

http://www.pandamail.net

http://www.mailstart.com

http://www.mail2web.com

http://www.mail-inspector.de (Germany)

http://www.pop3now.com

http://www.twigger.com

http://www.bluetreesoft.com/mail_features.html

Conversion and Calculator Stuff

Currency Converters

http://www.xe.net/ucc

http://www.accu-rate.ca/converter/acconv.htm

http://www.moneyextra.com/rates/currency/converter

http://www.x-rates.com/calculator.html

http://www.bloomberg.com/analysis/calculators/currency.html

Time Converters

http://www.timezoneconverter.com/cgi-bin/tzc.tzc

http://www.worldtimeserver.com/?locationid=MX2-1

http://www.timeanddate.com/worldclock

http://www.timeticker.com

Metric Converters

http://www.metricconversion.ws

http://www.worldwidemetric.com/metcal.htm

http://www.onlinedconversion.com

http://www.chinaimporters.com/metrical.htm

http://www.convert-me.com/en

All Kinds of Calculators

http://www.webwinder.com/wwhtmbin/javacalc.html

http://www.aba.com/aba/cgi-bin/autoNT.pl (calculator for buying a vehicle)

http://www.autosite.com/new/loanlse/calc.asp (calculator for leasing a vehicle)

http://www.hsh.com/calculators.html (financial calculations)

http://www.bankrate.com/brm/calc_home.asp (mortgage and cost of living)

http://www.btimes.co.za/calc/calc.htm (tax return and expense)

Language Translators

http://babelfish.altavista.com (Online language translator—just pop in text from an e-mail or an entire website and get an instant translation.)

http://translation.langenberg.com (web page translator)

http://www.tranexp.com (software)

http://www.translation-experts.com (software)

http://www.alis.com/en/indexfl.html

http://www.freetranslation.com

http://www.shortbus.net/dialect.html (funny dialect translator—jive, Buckwheat)

http://www.rinkworks.com/dialect (funny translator—redneck, Elmer Fudd, moron, etc.)

Printing Stuff

http://www.mimeo.com (prints and delivers really high-quality handouts)

http://www.kinkos.com

http://www3.notesonline.net (custom sticky notes)

Miscellaneous Stuff

Books

http://www.webpagesthatsuck.com

Clocks

http://www.panaga.com/clocks/clocks.htm#sun (massive number of cool clocks and countdown meters you can put on your website)

http://javascript.Internet.com/clocks

http://www.dynamicdrive.com/dynamicindex6

http://simplythebest.net/scripts/perl_scripts/clock_scripts.html

http://www.arachnoid.com/lutusp/worldclock.html

Copyright, Trademark, and Legal

http://www.tmexpress.com (trademark site)

http://www.nolo.com/category/tc_home.html (trademark and copyrights)

http://www.benedict.com (copyright website)

http://www.ilrg.com (Internet legal resource guide)

http://www.findlaw.com

Free Software for Websites

http://www.bignosebird.com

http://www.tucows.com

http://www.tudogs.com

http://www.reallybig.com

Home Business

http://www.homebusinessworks.com

http://www.aahbb.org (American Association of Home Based Businesses)

http://www.hoaa.com. (Home Office Association of America)

http://www.nase.org (National Association for the Self-Employed)

http://www.soho.org (small office/home office)

http://www.NetAim.Info (Internet Association of Information Marketers)

Reminder Services

Be reminded by e-mail of important dates like birthdays and anniversaries.

http://www.pcreminder.com

http://www.iflowers.com

http://www.candor.com/reminder/default.asp

http://www.memotome.com

Other Miscellaneous Stuff

http://www.babylon.com (Build your own glossary of information and show your expertise off to the world.)

http://www.cyberangels.com (Internet safety and security information)

http://www.ipl.org/ref (the Internet Public Library—lots of resource info)

http://www.webtrends.net (lots of helpful stuff for people working on websites)

http://www.m-w.com (lots of dictionaries)

http://www.submitcorner.com (more helpful web stuff)

http://www.KickStartDomains.com (tool to check out if your domain name is available with suggestions of other possibilities)

HTML and Other Tutorials

http://www.htmltutorials.ca

http://www.newbieclub.com/?newbie_heaven

To stay motivated by reading about what other Internet businesspeople are doing I highly recommend Corey Rudl's site Secrets to Their Success: http://dynamic.secretstotheirsuccess.com/t.cgi/12273.

Glossary

Active X: Controls created by Microsoft that will make your web browser "active." For instance it will allow it to show animation.

Administrative Contact: In essence the owner of a website. Make sure it's you whenever you buy a domain name.

Adobe Acrobat: Program used to convert files to PDF format for use in e-books. Can be read by both Macs and PCs.

Adobe Reader: Free program used to view PDF files.

ADSL (Asynchronous DSL): is a cheaper version of DSL Internet access where your download speed is faster than your upload speed.

Ad Swap: The act of trading classified ads with another e-zine publisher.

Affiliate Program: Software that allows other people to sell your products on their website for a commission. The software tracks what you owe them. See also Associate Program.

Algorithm: A mathematical ranking method used by individual search engines. These are secretive and changed frequently by the search engines to prevent webmasters from "beating the system."

Alias: A different name for the same e-mail account. You could have ordersantion.com, customerserviceantion.com, and tomantion.com all going to the same e-mail destination. You could then use the e-mail filters of your e-mail program to organize the different addresses into folders for you.

Alternative Description (or Alt Text): An HTML area related to a graphic that in days past was used to describe the graphic to those surfing the Web with their graphics turned off. Now used by savvy web marketers as an area to put keywords related to the page.

Anchor Text: The clickable text in a hyperlink. This is now very important when it comes to link popularity.

Animated GIF: A graphic that simulates the effect of motion by using two or more different images that display in sequence.

Announcement Lists: Lists of people who want to hear about new e-zines coming out. You submit to the list and they tell everyone about your new e-zine.

261

Antialiasing: A technique for smoothing out jagged edges on text and graphics.

Antivirus Software: Updateable software designed to recognize and protect you from damage due to computer viruses.

AOL (America Online): The largest online services provider. Generally considered a place that makes it easy for an Internet beginner to get e-mail, visit the Web and to take advantage of its many forums and services. Not recommended for commercial ventures and large scale e-mailing, but still a handy subscription to have especially if you travel a lot. They have local toll free numbers in many cities and countries.

Applet: A small Java program that adds special effects to a web page.

ASCII (American Standard Code for Information Interchange): I know that's more than you want to know. More commonly known as "Plain Text" that can be read by just about any computer.

Ask the Expert: An area of a website designed to solicit questions from visitors to be answered by an authority on the subject.

ASP (Application Service Provider): A company that provides software for your use. You do not need to have the software run on your computer. It runs on theirs. A common example of an ASP would be your web host. You simply rent the computer and software needed to host your website.

Associate Program: See Affiliate Program.

Audio Business Card: Promotional cassette tape given out instead of a traditional business card.

Autoresponder: Software that automatically responds via e-mail to someone requesting information. See Infobot and E-Mail on Demand.

Avatar: A 3D representation of you in a chat room. It normally doesn't look like you unless you look like count Dracula or a cute little puppy.

Backbone: The central network that ties lots of other networks together. Used frequently when evaluating how good of a connection your web host or ISP has to the Internet.

Back Button: A left-pointing arrow button usually at or near the top left of a browser that takes you back to the last page you looked at. To view the page you viewed before hitting the back button, click on the "Forward" button that is a right-pointing arrow.

Back End Sales: Subsequent sales made to the same person. They are generally considered easier to make and much cheaper than the cost to acquire a new customer.

Backup: A copy of your computer files and/or programs usually kept on computer discs, CD-ROM, or magnetic tape. Website based backup facilities are also available.

Bandwidth: The amount of data that can be transmitted in a fixed amount of time, that is, the size of the cyber pipe that sends information over the net.

Banner: A graphic, usually rectangular and usually displaying an advertisement. Viewers can click on it to go to another web page.

Barter: Trading of goods and services without exchanging money.

Baud: Bits per second. The measurement of the speed of a modem. A 56K modem has speeds up to 56 kilo bits per second.

BBS (Bulletin Board System): A computer and other hardware that can serve files and other types of messages. Some are connected to the Internet and some are only accessible via modem over a telephone line.

Bcc (Blind Carbon Copy): The area of your e-mail program to paste your e-mail address list when doing a multiple recipient mailing so that no one sees anyone else's e-mail address.

Beta Testing: Before a software program is released to the public it is tested for bugs and crashes. In many cases volunteers test the software in real-world environments.

Big Butt Camp: Advanced content Butt Camps by Tom Antion.

Big Target Theory: Tom's Internet theory of having as many good web pages as possible to give you a better chance of being found on the Internet.

Blacklist: A list maintained by ISPs and spam organizations that identifies suspected or known spammers.

Blog, Blogging: Chronological online posting of personal, business, or web related information and links. This term has caught on faster than "Weblog" because it avoids confusion with "web server logs," which is unrelated. See Weblog.

Bluetooth: A short-range (about 30 feet) communications technology that allows Bluetooth compatible devices to communicate with each other without wires. Example: a Bluetooth printer would not have to be wired to your Bluetooth computer to operate.

Body Text: The text on a web page that is readable by the public.

Bookmark: A quick retrieval method for web pages, or a place holder on a web page or word processing document that you can jump to immediately via a hyperlink from elsewhere on the page.

Bot: Short for robot. An automated piece of software sometimes called a spider or crawler that searches the Internet and helps develop the catalogs for search engines. Also, just about any automated piece of software.

Bounce: When an e-mail is returned. A "hard" bounce generally occurs if the e-mail address is no good. A "soft" bounce generally occurs if the recipient's inbox is full. In either case you may not get notice that the bounce occurred.

Brick and Mortar: Term used to describe a store or business that has a physical location.

Broadband: High-speed data transmission on a single cable like cable modems and DSL.

Browser: The software that allows you to see World Wide Web pages. This software reads HTML scripting language and interprets it for you so that you can see web pages. Common browsers are Internet Explorer and Netscape.

Butt Camp: Title, coined by your friendly author, for my electronic marketing seminars. Idea came as a spin-off to the much overused term "Boot Camp" because I sit at home on my rear end and make money.

Byte: One character of information.

Cable Modem: The device that allows you to access a high-speed Internet connection through your local cable TV company. Speeds are really fast for both upload and download, but slow down when lots of people are on at one time.

Cache: Information storage on your computer so you can access it very quickly. When you visit a web page, the page and associated graphics are stored on your hard drive of your computer so that the next time you visit that page it loads quickly instead of waiting for the page to travel across the Internet again. Disk cache allows things to be stored in your superfast RAM instead of on your hard drive for the same reason . . . fast access.

Can Spam Act: Legislation passed in 2003 and taking effect in January 2004 to regulate commercial e-mail in the United States.

CD Burner: Device used to record on CDs.

CD-R (Compact Disc, Recordable): A computer disc that can hold up to 650 mega bytes of data that you can write to by means of a CD-R drive.

CD-ROM (Compact Disc, Read Only Memory): A computer disc that will store and playback up to 650 mega bytes of data.

CD-ROM Drive: The device used to play back information from a CD-ROM. The drive can be installed in your computer or as a plug in device that stands alone outside your computer.

CGI (Common Gateway Interface): The rules for running an external program on a web server.

CGI-Bin (CGI Binary): When you see this in a url that means you are accessing an external program. Also a common name for a directory on a web server where CGI scripts are kept.

Chargeback: A debit to a merchant account because of a bad charge card or dispute.

Chat Room: Specialized software that lets people communicate in groups in real time. More advanced software allows avatars or graphical representation of each person and really advanced software allows actual voice conversations.

Clickstream: The path a visitor takes through a website.

Click Through: The number or percentage of visitors who click on a link or banner advertisement.

Common Misspelling: A misspelled word purposely put in the keyword META Tag to attract traffic who have misspelled a search term.

Conference Call: A telephone call where three or more persons in different locations participate.

Confirmed Opt In: Someone has to reply to an e-mail before their e-mail address is added to your list. See Double Opt In.

Conversion Rate: The number of responses you get as compared to the number of total visits. Example: 100 visits to your sales page that result in 3 sales is a 3 percent conversion rate.

Cookie: A small file placed on your hard drive when you visit some websites. This file is used to track things like the last time you visited, your password, what pages you visited, and so on.

Copywriting: The term used to describe the art of writing advertising text for a website, print, or broadcast medium.

Coregistration: A method of getting other websites to offer your e-zine to their visitors. You pay that website owner for each subscriber who signs up at his site.

Cutaways: Shots of the audience or other shots inserted into the main production when recording video.

Cyberspace: Term from the 1984 novel Neuromancer by William Gibson. The term was used to describe a world of interconnected computers and the society that used them.

Cybersquatter: A person who registers an Internet domain name with the intent of selling it to someone who would be very likely to want it.

Database: Customer or prospect information stored for retrieval. It is most often organized into fields of information that can be merged into your e-mail correspondence by means of a "mail merge" e-mail program.

Dedicated Server: A computer that has only one website on it, or only the sites owned by one person, that is, it's dedicated to serving that website as opposed to having hundreds of websites using up it's resources. Since you control it, you can have as many of your own websites on the server as will fit or you can rent out space to others if you want to.

Defrag: A computer maintenance operation that should be done regularly to improve the performance.

Designer: See Web Designer.

DHTML: A fancy HTML language that allows unblockable pop-up boxes and other advanced elements on a web page. See Dynamic HTML.

Dial-Up Connection: A temporary connection between two computers over a phone line. This is the most common method of accessing the Internet.

Digital Camera: Camera requiring no film that creates images immediately usable by your computer.

Digital Cash: A method of paying for something by transferring numbers between computers.

Digital Certificate: A way to send digital messages securely and used to verify that senders are who they say they are.

Digital Studio: Where audio or video is recorded and edited on computer instead of on tape.

Digital Wallet: Encryption technology for e-commerce transactions that holds things like a real wallet and more, like digital cash, digital identification, and shipping preferences.

Direct to Desktop: A technology that permits publishers to send messages directly to the desktop of those that have opted in. This technology does not use e-mail and therefore does not have the associated delivery and spam filter problems.

Directory: With regard to Internet searches, this is a search facility where websites are put into categories by real people, not automated robot spiders.

Discussion Board: An area where people can post questions, answers, and comments, usually about a particular subject.

Distance Education: Catch all phrase for learning that is not done face to face. It may be done face-to-face over video conferencing, telephone conferencing, via e-mail, snail mail, or any other medium that is not face-to-face.

DNS (Domain Name Server): Special servers located around the Internet to route e-mail and Internet connections.

Domain Name: Strings of letters and/or numbers used to name organizations on the Internet. Antion.com is a domain name. Speak4Money.com is a domain name.

Doorway Page: A page optimized to get a high ranking in a search engine. Modern day side door pages must be readable by a visitor, that is, they can't be simply random text like they were in the old days. See Side Door, Splash Page, and Gateway.

Double Opt In: Requiring a confirmation from someone requesting to be put on a mailing list to be sure the person really wants on the list.

Download: Copying a file or files from the Internet to your computer as opposed to upload, which is copying a file or files from your computer and sending it to the Internet.

Downloadable Product: An information or software product that travels in the form of a computer file, not a physical product like an audiocassette tape or printed book.

DPI (Dots Per Inch): In printers and scanners it is the measure of the number of pixels that can fit into an inch of space. A 600 dpi printer will produce sharper images than a 300 dpi printer.

Driver: a small file that helps the computer communicate with hardware devices like printers and your mouse.

DSL (Digital Subscriber Line): A high-speed Internet connection that allows you to have both voice and data on the same line, which allows you to talk on the same line you are using for your Internet connection. ADSL (asynchronous DSL) is a cheaper version where your download speed is faster than your upload speed.

Dubs: Copies of tapes. Example: I'm going to get 50 dubs of my tape.

Dupes: Short for duplicates and similar to dubs.

DVD (or Digital Video Disc): The next generation CD ROM. A DVD disk holds 20 times the information that a CD ROM can. You can use this to watch movies on your computer. Don't confuse this with DivX, a brand new and already obsolete DVD impostor.

Dynamic HTML (DHTML): A powerful scripting language giving more control of positioning on web pages.

Dynamic IP Address: The IP address of your computer will change each time you access the Internet.

E-Book: A book that is contained in a computer file.

E-Booklet: A short e-book, normally under 100 pages.

E-Commerce: Conducting business over the Internet.

EDI (Electronic Data Interchange): Data transfer between different companies using networks like the Internet.

Educational Materials: Another name for your "product" so that it more easily aligns with terminology used in budgets, which makes the sale of such material easier.

Electronic Clipart: Clipart that's delivered as a computer file as opposed to being printed on paper.

E-Mag: Abbreviation for electronic magazine.

E-Mail: Electronic mail. Mail sent computer to computer.

E-Mail Client: The program you use to get and send e-mail. Common ones are Outlook, Eudora, Yahoo

E-Mail on Demand: See Autoresponder.

Emoticon (emotional icon): Used to convey extra meaning when sending an online communication. To interpret them tilt your head sideways to the left and look at them. Compare what you see to a facial expression.

Encryption: Changing data so it is unreadable to anyone that doesn't have the decrypting key so the information can travel safely over the Internet.

Entry Page: A page, not necessarily the home page, where a visitor enters a website.

Ethernet: A connection standard for Local Area Networks. See LAN.

Exit Page: The page where a visitor leaves a website.

Extranet: Outside access network so specified groups can gain access to information on an Intranet.

E-Zine: Modern abbreviation for electronic magazine.

E-Zine Directory: Directory comprised only of e-zines arranged by topic along with descriptions and subscription information. Usually providing a free listing to the e-zine publisher.

FAQ: Abbreviation for frequently asked question.

Fee Credibility: A consistent and believable speaking fee as opposed to "I'll take whatever I can get."

Field: A space in a web form where a visitor to your site is required to put in information, like their name and e-mail address.

Filters: In e-mail programs these are helpful parts of the program that cut down on junk e-mail and organize other e-mails automatically.

Firewall: A device or software that limits Internet access to your computer to protect you from unauthorized intrusion by hackers or mischievous computer users.

Firewire: A very high-speed connection that allows quick transfer of files. Commonly used for putting video files on your computer from a digital video camera and for transferring lots of date to portable hard drives and so on.

Flame: A nasty e-mail directed at one person.

Flash: A web animation technology that uses very small file sizes.

Floppy Disc: A storage disc that can be inserted in and removed from your computer and carried with you (no current discs are actually "flexible").

Font: A typestyle.

Frames: A website design technique that splits a web page into independent sections. The navigation buttons may be in their own frame and the heading may be another frame and the content area of the page may be in yet another frame. This technique is extremely detrimental to good search engine positioning and is never recommended by marketing experts. The only exception is if you do an intensive doorway page strategy.

Freeware: Software that's available for free.

Front Page Extensions: Special software the Web host must have installed on their server to be able to take advantage of all the features of the Web authoring program Microsoft Front Page.

FTP (File Transfer Protocol): An older method (still used quite frequently) to transfer files between computers or archive sites.

Gateway (or Doorway Page, Side Door, Splash Page): See Doorway Page.

Ghostwriter: Person who writes for hire and gives the credit for the work to someone else.

GIF (Graphics Interchange Format): A compression format for graphics.

Gigabyte (GB): 1,073,741,824 bytes, Slang—I've got a 12-gig hard drive.

Graphic: A picture or nontext item on a web page.

Hacker: Someone skilled in accessing (hacking into) computers that don't belong to them.

Hallway Page: A page that links to all your doorway pages so that search engine spiders can find the doorway pages easily. See Site Map.

Hard Bounce: An e-mail that will never be deliverable, that is, a bad e-mail address.

Heading Tag: An HTML code that is given a higher relevancy than regular body text when a search engine spider looks at the words within the tag.

Headset: A headphone with a microphone attached.

Hidden Page: A page that resides on your website server, but isn't linked "from" your main site but may have a link or links "to" your main site. These are typically used as side door pages and for pages you do not want the general public to see.

History List: A drop-down menu on a web browser that lets you go quickly to a page you have already visited without having to click your back button repeatedly. The list keeps track of all the places you visited.

Hit: A file downloaded from the Internet. Example: When a page that has five graphics on it is requested from your server that counts as six hits—one for the page and five for the graphics.

Home Page (or Index or Default): The main page of your website.

Host: The place where your website is stored so it can be viewed on the Internet.

HTML (Hypertext Markup Language): The formatting language of the World Wide Web. Web browsers read this hidden-from-view language and show it to you as a web page.

HTML Editor: A program like Microsoft Front Page or Dreamweaver that allows you to create and edit web pages. With these programs you need virtually no knowledge of HTML.

HTTP (Hypertext Transfer Protocol): The main method used on the Web to allow linking to other web pages. Web address begin with http://.

Hub: A piece of hardware used to connect multiple computers.

Hybrid CD: A compact disc that will play on more than one computer system.

Hyperlink: Underlined words or phrases on a web page that take you to another web page when you click on them. They usually change color for a while to remind you that you have already clicked on them.

Hypertext: Text that is linked to other web pages. You activate the link by clicking on it with your mouse.

Icon: A small picture or image that represents something else. You can double-click on icons to start programs, or open folders or windows.

Identity Theft: A criminal activity where the perpetrator uses your personal information to make purchases and do other criminal acts.

Image Map: A web page graphic that is linked to another location. Sometimes a large graphic is linked to several other web pages. Each link is called a hotspot.

Impression: The number of times a specific web page, banner or ad has been downloaded from the Internet. This is used as a measure in advertising, but it doesn't necessarily reflect how many times a person has actually seen the page or ad.

Inbox: Where your e-mail is received.

Index: A search engine's collection of web pages.

Infobot: See Autoresponder.

Information Product: A product that is instructional in nature.

Intranet (Lower case): Connecting two or more networks together.

Internet (Upper case): The totality of enormous numbers of networks in the world. The largest Wide Area Network.

Internet Café: A business that rents computers and Internet connections. These businesses are found in many countries that do not have widespread home computer use like we have in the United States.

Internet Explorer: Most popular browser software.

Internet Time: Term used to describe how fast things move on the Internet. Example: Five traditional years equal five months on the Internet.

Intranet: A network that is within a single organization and not available to the Internet.

IP Address: A unique number assigned to every individual computer linked to the Internet.

IRC (Internet Relay Chat): A method that allows users to converse in real time.

ISDN: A fast Internet connection that uses phone lines.

ISP (Internet Service Provider): Company that provides a connection to the Internet.

Java: A programming language.

JavaScript: Another language developed by Netscape that has nothing much to do with Java.

Jewel Case: A hard plastic case for a CD ROM.

JPEG (Joint Photographic Experts Group): A compression format that works well with color graphics and can usually allow graphics to be read by both Mac and pc. You can control the amount of compression, which is important because the more you compress, the more color that is lost.

Junk E-Mail: Just like junk mail you receive in your regular "snail mail" box, except it is delivered via e-mail. See SPAM.

Keystroke Analyzer: A software device designed to either overtly or covertly record all the keystrokes of a computer.

Keyword: A word that someone would type into a search engine or directory when looking for information on the topic of the keyword.

Keyword Density (or Keyword Weight): The ratio of the number of keywords on a page to the total number of words on a page.

Keyword Phrase: Several words typed together into a search engine or directory when someone is looking for information on the topic of the keyword phrase.

Keyword Prominence: The closeness of a keyword or keyword phrase to the beginning of a section of a web page. Example: If a word is at the top of the page it has a relevance of 100 percent, at the bottom of the page it is 0 percent, and 50 percent if it is found in the middle of the page. If a word is at the beginning of a link or the title bar of the page it would have a relevance of 100 percent in that particular area, and so on for other areas of the Web page.

Keyword Stacking/Stuffing: Adding gibberish or too many keywords to a page to try to trick the search engines into giving you a high ranking.

Kilobyte (KB): A measure of the size of a file; One thousand bytes. Example: Keeping your e-zine below 20 KB will keep it from turning into an attachment on AOL.

LAN (Local Area Network): Two or more connected computers that are in close proximity to one another.

Landing Page: The page where a person ends up after clicking on a link. Usually associated with pay-per-click or other ads that drive people to your website.

Link: See Hyperlink.

Link Farm (or Link Exchange Program): A web page consisting of nothing but links. This is a very negative thing when the links go to unrelated websites.

Link Popularity: A measure of the number AND quality of links coming INTO a site from other websites.

Link Reputation: What inbound links to your web page say about the page. Your inbound links are generally more valuable if the page they are coming from has keywords in the actual clickable part of the link. This clickable text is known as Anchor Text.

Link Text: See Anchor Text.

Link Trading: Linking to another website in exchange for a link back to yours. See Reciprocal Links.

Linux: A type of operating system.

List Management Company: A company that handles your e-mail list and takes care of subscribes and unsubscribes. They usually have varying amounts of additional features to save you work and time.

Listserve: A trademark of L-Soft International. A very common mail list.

Login: Verb—Connecting to a computer or website using your user name and pass word. Noun—The account name used to access a computer or website (usually not a big secret).

Lurking: Listening in on a public discussion without contributing. This is a good idea so that you get a feel for the nature of the group before you jump in and make a fool of yourself.

Mail Bomb: An extremely large file maliciously sent to try to crash someone's e-mail server.

Mail Lists: A group e-mail discussion on a particular topic. Everyone on the list gets a copy of each message.

Mail Merge: E-mail that is personalized for each recipient.

Mail Server: A computer and software that sends, receives, and stores e-mail.

Mall: A collection of Internet stores linked together and supposedly sharing traffic. Not recommended in this course.

Megabyte (MB): 1,048,576 bytes.

Megahertz (MHZ): This is a unit of measurement that tells how fast your computer can do things. A 700 MHz computer is a little less than twice as fast as a 366 MHz computer. There are many other variables that affect the overall system speed.

Mega Links: Normally used between several domains controlled by the same organization to increase traffic and link popularity.

Menu Program: Software that allows you to put a professional looking navigation system on an informational product.

Merchant Account: Normally refers to the merchant's ability to accept VISA, MasterCard, and various other credit cards as a form of payment.

Meta Search: A search of multiple search engines all at once.

Meta Search Engine: A search engine that does meta searches, that is, that searches multiple other search engines when you type in a search query.

META Tag: Special HTML tags that are not seen by people viewing a web page, but that give information about the page. Two primary META Tags of concern to web marketers are the KEYWORD META Tag and the DE-SCRIPTION META Tag. Many search engines use the information in the META Tags of a page to help them decide how to index the page and when to bring the page up when someone is searching for a particular topic.

MIDI (or Musical Instrument Digital Interface): The mechanism to connect a musical instrument to a computer.

MIME: Common usage is that one computer communicates with another computer to see the requirements to "talk" to one another. An example would be a multipart MIME e-mail that finds out if the receiver can read plain text and HTML e-mails or just plain text.

Mini Disc: A recordable disc made by Sony that is smaller than a CD ROM.

Mirror Site: An exact copy of a website usually needed when the traffic to the site is too much for one or multiple servers to handle.

Modem: This is the device that allows your computer to connect to the Internet through phone lines.

Moderator: Person who controls what messages are allowed to be distributed to a mail list.

MP3: A compression format for audio that allows near perfect quality, but a very small file size.

MPEG: A compression format for video and audio files that allows them to be transmitted quickly over the Internet.

Multiple Domains: More than one website owned or controlled by the same person or organization.

Navigation: The means by which a visitor travels (or navigates) to the different pages on your website.

Netiquette: Etiquette on the Internet.

Netizen: A term derived from citizen or citizen of the Internet. Implies a responsible use of Internet resources.

Netscape: Former very popular browser software. Does not have much market share now.

Network: When you connect two or more computers.

Network Card: This piece of hardware for your computer allows you to connect several computers together so they can all share data. Commonly known as an Ethernet card.

Newbie: Slang term for someone new to the Internet.

Newsgroup: Discussion groups on USENET.

New Window: A second or subsequent browser window that is opened on your computer.

Noise Canceling: An electronic method to reduce background noise and enhance the main signal. Usually used with regard to microphones.

OCR (Optical Character Recognition): Software that allows you to scan text into your computer so that it is actually text in nature instead of graphical. This allows you to edit the text.

Online Press Kit: A web based or e-mail based press kit.

Onsite Search Engine: A search engine that only searches the pages in one website.

Operating System (or OS): The software that communicates with hardware on your computer. Examples: Windows XP, MAC OS, Linux.

Opt In: Someone specifically asks to be included in a mailing list.

Optimize: Prepare a web page so that it has the best chance of getting high rankings in search engines.

Outbox: Where your e-mail resides until it is actually sent.

PageRank: A measure of the overall importance of a page on the Internet as reported by Google's ranking system.

Page View: A complete page (including graphics) retrieved from your server.

Paid Inclusion: A search engine deal where you must pay to be included in their index. This gives no guarantee that you will get a good ranking on your keywords.

PAL: A television broadcast standard in Europe. If you create a video by U.S. standards (NTSC), you will have to convert it before you sell it to someone in Europe, however, many people in Europe have VCRs that play both.

Password: A secret word or combination of letters and numbers used to gain entrance to a protected area. Passwords are usually case sensitive.

Pay Per Click: An advertising or search engine method, where you pay each time someone clicks on your ad, link, or search engine listing.

PC: Personal Computer, but usually used to refer to IBM compatible computers as opposed to Apple Macintosh.

PCMCIA (or PC Card): A credit card sized device that plugs into a laptop to give the laptop extra functionality. You can add RAM, modems, network adapters, hard drives, pagers, and even global positioning to your laptop with the appropriate PC Card.

PDA (or Personal Digital Assistant): Handheld electronic device to keep phone numbers, take notes, and so on.

PDF: A document format by Adobe that requires a reader software on the computer reading the document. Both PCs and Macs can read this format.

Perl: A popular programming language.

Permission Based: As in e-mail marketing, when someone gives you permission to e-mail them.

Ping: To check if a server is running. Comes from the sound sonar makes in the movies when searching for a submarine.

Pixel: One dot on a computer monitor.

Plain Text: A simple format where no formatting is allowed. This format is readable just about everywhere.

Plug-In: An add-on to a larger program to give it special capability. Example: Real Player is a plug-in to a browser to allow the browser to play Real Audio and Real Video.

PNG: A graphic format for the Web.

Pointing: Having more than one domain name access the exact same files on a server. This is usually an inexpensive way to use more than one domain name, but from a marketing standpoint a less effective use of multiple domains.

POP3 (Post Office Protocol): Current access standard for Internet e-mail. You will need to know the POP3 setting (given to you by your e-mail provider) to set up your e-mail program to retrieve your e-mail. While you're at it, you'll also need your SMTP setting for outgoing e-mail (doesn't apply to AOL, CompuServe, Prodigy e-mail).

Pop Up Box (or Pop Up Window): A smaller browser window that "pops up automatically" on a web page. They are usually promotional in nature and some surfers find them annoying.

Port: Typically the place where information goes in and out of a computer. Example: parallel port or serial port.

Portal: Term to describe a website that is intended to be the first stop when entering the Web or their "point of entry." They typically have a search engine and some have free e-mail to keep you coming back. Yahoo is a portal.

Pre-Loaded Graphic: An advanced website trick used when you MUST show a large slow-loading graphic.

Prepublication Sale: Selling an informational product before it is actually finished.

Press Kit: A promotional packet containing information about a person, product, or service. May contain testimonial letters, photos, program descriptions, product specification sheets, business card, press clippings, articles, and so on.

Privacy Policy: A statement of what you will and will not do with someone's personal information.

Prominence, Keyword: See Keyword Prominence.

Publication Rights: Permission given to another party for use of intellectual property. Example: I'm selling the print publication rights to a major publisher, but I'm retaining the electronic publishing rights.

Queue: A line of waiting people as in, "Your hold time in the queue will be approximately six minutes," or data stored to be processed in sequence.

QuickTime: Originally developed by Apple Computers as a method of storing sound, graphic, and movie files. QuickTime player software is now available for both Mac and pc. QuickTime movies have a .mov extension.

RAID (or Redundant Array of Independent Disks): This is a back up and protection method that writes the same information to multiple disks to protect against failure of any one disk.

RAM (Random Access Memory): Usually expressed in megabytes (MB) it is the temporary memory needed to operate programs. The more RAM you have the more programs you can operate at one time. If you try to operate many programs and you don't have enough RAM your computer slows down tremendously and may even quit (lockup or crash).

Real Audio (http://www.real.com): A streaming audio format.

Real Names (http://www.realnames.com): A way to type a regular name like Sony into a search facility so you don't have to remember the actual URL. Real names cost $100.00 per year. Not highly recommended unless you are a household name or have a household name product.

Real Player (http://www.real.com): Browser plug-in to play real audio and/or video.

Real Video (http://www.real.com): A streaming video format.

Reciprocal Links: See Link Trading.

Recording Control: Inexpensive device to adapt your phone line so you can plug it into a tape recorder.

Redirection: A web page script or program that sends the visitor to another page automatically. Definitely not recommended and becoming considered spam to many search engines.

Referrer Logs: Website traffic logs that tell you from where traffic is coming into your site.

Relevancy: How well the information you provide matches the information a searcher was looking for. The more relevant, the better.

Remove Link: See Unsubscribe Link.

Resolution (Monitor): The higher the resolution the more that can be displayed on the monitor. Small monitors are typically 800 pixels × 600 pixels. Larger monitors are 1,024 × 768 and you even have 1,280 × 1,024.

Resolution (Printers and Scanners): Measured in DPI—Dots per inch. The higher the DPI the sharper the printer can print.

Return on Investment (ROI): The amount of return as compared to the amount of effort or money spent.

Robots.txt File: An instruction placed in the HTML code of your website that instructs search engine spiders to not index the page. A good article discussing this advanced concept is available at http://www.1stsearchranking .com/robots.htm.

Router: A hardware device that only allows authorized computers to connect to each other.

RSS (Rich Site Summary): A format for syndicating web content. If a site wants others to be able to use some of its content, it creates an RSS document. The document is registered with an RSS publisher that makes the document available to others who can read and use RSS documents.

Scanner: Hardware device used to digitize artwork or text and make it ready for use on a computer.

Screen Capture Program: Software that records information that is displayed on a computer monitor.

Search Engine: Robot spider that searches for web pages that meet the criteria of a keyword search done by a searcher.

Secure Server: A server that has the ability to use encryption software to protect information from being understandable if intercepted.

Self-Publishing: Publishing in a fashion whereby you are totally responsible for editorial and production guidelines for your own informational product. This includes the financing of the project.

SEO (or Search Engine Optimization): Preparing a web page so that it has the best chance to get high rankings in a search engine.

Sequential Autoresponder: Software that automatically responds via e-mail to someone requesting information and then follows up with additional e-mails at prescribed intervals, which you set.

Server: A computer that "serves" your web pages to whoever logs on to the computer and asks for them.

Shareware: Software that you can have for free to try out and then pay for if you want to keep it. Many run on the honor system, but some quit working after the free trial period or "nag" you into paying by having pop-up reminders.

Shopping Cart: Software that displays products, pricing, and shipping charges designed to make the shopping experience easier for customers.

Side Doors (Doorway Page, Splash Page, Gateway) See Doorway Page.

Signature File: A contact information and promotional file appended onto an e-mail message. Slang: Sig File or Sig.

Site Map: See Hallway Page.

Site Popularity: The number of people visiting a site from a particular search engine coupled with the length of time they stayed on the site.

Small Butt Camp: Shorter version of a Butt Camp Seminar.

Smart Card: A credit card size device containing an electronic memory that could hold information like medical records, identification, and digital cash.

SMTP (Simple Mail Transfer Protocol): A standard to keep e-mail operations working smoothly. You'll need the SMTP setting (provided by your e-mail provider) to send e-mail and you'll need the POP3 setting to retrieve your e-mail (doesn't apply to AOL, CompuServe, Prodigy e-mail).

Snail Mail: Slang for mail that is sent through the Post Office.

Soft Bounce: An e-mail that is not deliverable now, but may be deliverable in the future. This could be because the e-mail server of the recipient is temporarily down or the e-mail box is full.

Soft Goods: Products that can be downloaded from the Internet. Products that do not require shipping.

Source Code: The HTML code of a page that is read by a browser. If you are in the Internet Explorer browser, you can look at this code for most people's websites by clicking on "view" then "source."

SPAM: (1) Unwanted commercial e-mail or (2) cheating a search engine.

Spam filter: Software designed to recognize and intercept unwanted e-mails before they arrive at your inbox.

Spider: An electronic program used by search engines that searches for keywords and collects information about websites in the search engine's index.

Spider: A robot that searches the Web to find web pages and searches the links on those pages.

SPIM: Unwanted commercial messages coming through your instant messaging system.

Splash Page (Doorway Page, Side Door, Gateway): See Doorway Page.

Split Testing: Comparing the results of one ad against a different ad. This is critical to maximizing your sales.

Spyware: Software that surreptitiously gathers information from your computer and transmits it to a third party for advertising or other sinister purposes.

SSL (Single Socket Layer): A security standard to allow secure online commercial transactions.

Statistics: Information about a website like number of visitors, time on the site, where they came from, and much more.

Stickiness: A website's ability to keep a visitor in the site usually by having engaging content.

Streaming: Data moving quickly from one place to the other without the need for it to be completely at one place or the other before you can start using it. For instance, you can listen to a streaming audio file while it is being sent to your computer as opposed to waiting a long time for it to completely download before you can listen to it.

Submit: Entering your website/web page information into the index of a search engine or directory.

Submitters: Software designed to submit your website to many different search engines automatically. DO NOT USE! (A new submitter is being tested that may simulate submitting by hand. Watch update website for further reports on this.)

Surfing: Slang term for looking around on the Internet.

Surge Suppressor: Protection device for computers and other electrical hardware.

Sysop: Systems operator. A person responsible for the operation of a physical computer.

Systray (or System Tray): A collection of small icons usually on the right side of the Widows toolbar.

T1, T3: EXTREMELY fast Internet connections.

Table: A web page design tool that assists in alignment of text and graphics.

Tape Drive: A tape recorder for backing up data.

Techie: Slang for person adept and fascinated with technology.

Technical Contact: Normally the webmaster, or technical advisor of record associated with a website domain.

Technogeek: Slang for a techie who is also nerdy.

Telephone Bridge Line: An inexpensive technology used for conference calling.

TeleSeminar: A seminar or training session conducted on the telephone.

Template: A self-contained layout for a website that makes it easy for you to have a professional looking website running quickly and at low cost. Also, a layout for a web page or e-zine.

Text Editor: A software program that handles only plain text. It will not handle graphics or fancy formatting of any kind.

Text Format: See Plain Text.

Theme: The graphical look and feel of all the elements of a website. Also, the topic of a collection of web pages.

Three Prong Attack: Tom Antion's marketing approach consisting of Website Development, e-mail List Building, and Product Development.

Title Bar: Usually thin blue bar that runs horizontally at the top of a web page when viewed in a browser and contains the page's title.

Title Tag: The HTML tag that contains the contents of the page title.

Top Level Domain: This is the extension after the main domain name. Examples: .com, .org, .edu, .info.

Traffic: Term describing how many people visit your website.

Traffic Analysis: Observing traffic patterns as visitors navigate through your site for the purpose of making changes that would increase conversion ratio or response rate.

Transparent GIF: A graphic that lets the background show through so it appears that the graphic is floating on the page.

Trojan Horse: A computer program that hides inside another computer program and tries to trick you into running it.

Truncated: To shorten by cutting off characters at the end.

Turnkey Store: An Internet shopping tool either on or connected to your website that is ready for business as soon as you plug in your products. In some cases you don't even need a website.

UCE (or Unsolicited Commercial E-Mail): Spam.

Undeliverable: With regard to e-mail, an e-mail that could not be delivered to it's recipient. Reasons might be that the recipient's inbox is full. The e-mail may be larger than the e-mail provider allows or the e-mail address may no longer be valid.

Unique Visitor: A person visiting a website in a certain time period.

Unsubscribe Link: A link in bulk e-mail that allows someone to click on it to be removed from your list.

Update: Term to describe distributing more current information than what you previously distributed.

Upload: Sending information from your computer to another computer or to the Internet.

UPS (Uninterruptible Power Supply): A battery that provides electricity when normal electric power fails.

URL (Uniform Resource Locator): The unique address of a web page.

USB (Universal Serial Bus): An easy way to plug things into a PC.

USENET: A world-wide system of discussion groups.

Vanity Publishing: Paying another company to take care of production details of your informational product that is usually a printed book.

Video Conference: A conference held where the participants are in different locations and connected via phone line. Each participant can see the others by means of a video monitor.

Viral Marketing: Getting your advertising message to spread "like a virus" from person to person.

Virtual PC: A program for Apple Macintosh computers to allow them to run Windows programs.

Virus: A piece of programming code designed to do mischievous or malicious things to a computer or network.

Visitor Session: Hits to a website by a single visitor within a certain time frame. A single visitor is not counted again unless he or she has left a website for a minimum period of time.

Voice Recognition Software: Software that learns your voice and turns what you say into text on your computer.

Vortal (or Vertical Portal): An entry point to the Web that focuses on only one topic or group of people.

VPN (or Virtual Private Network): A private network that you can connect to from the public Internet. The information transfer between the two networks is encrypted.

VRML (Virtual Reality Modeling Language): Programming language for 3-D application on the Web.

WAN (or Wide Area Network): A network that spans more than one building or group of buildings that are in close proximity to one another.

Web: Short for World Wide Web.

Web Casting: Broadcasting over the Internet.

Web Conference: A meeting of three persons or more using the Internet.

Web Designer: A person who knows how to put a web page on the Internet. Most don't have a clue how to do it properly from a marketing point of view.

Web Form: A part of your website that collects information and is usually connected to a program that sends the information to you and wherever else you want it to go.

Web Host: A company that keeps your website on a computer they control and makes the site available to be seen on the Internet.

Web Log: A collection of all the activity of your website. This is typically interpreted by a "Statistics" program to make the results more user friendly.

Web Log: See Blog.

Webmaster: Fancy name for a person who maintains a website.

Web Page: A document designed to be looked at in a web browser.

Web Ring: An interlinking of many websites that are on the same topic.

Web Safe Colors: Colors that look okay in any web browser.

Website: A collection of web pages.

Web Trends: A popular, advanced website statistics program.

White Paper: An article that explains something.

WHOIS: An Internet program that allows you to search out ownership of domain names.

Wi-Fi (or Wireless Fidelity): A term for a popular form of wireless connectivity.

Windows: Made by Microsoft, this is the most popular operating system (OS).

Wizard: A program that leads you through certain steps in sequence to accomplish something like creating a certain type of document or installing a program.

Worm: Form of a virus.

WWW (World Wide Web): Graphical part of the Internet that allows you to link to other areas in the Web.

WYSIWYG (What You See Is What You Get): Abbreviation for software that shows onscreen what your finished page will look like.

XML: Another more powerful successor to HTML.

Yahoo: What I say because I'm near the end of working on this glossary. Yahoo is probably the most well-known and successful search directory on the Internet.

Zip: A very common compression format to make large files take up less space and travel faster when being sent to another computer.

Zip Drive: A storage device made by Iomega Corporation. Many are portable allowing you to back up or carry large amounts of information and use the information on another computer.

For Ongoing Help

If you've gotten this far, I'm sure you can see there are a tremendous number of details to learn to be highly successful selling your products and services on the Internet.

I can assure you that questions will come up as you begin to implement all of the strategies you learned about in this book.

I've got several resources to assist you in getting help as you continue to improve your web operation.

For website work you can contact:

Jason at http://www.Saeler.com or

Harold at http://www.HaroldHingle.com

Internet Association of Information Marketers

NetAim provides an inexpensive way to learn on an ongoing basis and network with Internet marketers of all levels. NetAim.Info also has a discussion board where you can post questions and make comments any time day or night 365 days a year. Check out all the benefits of joining at the link.

Immersion Training in the Lap of Luxury

You can visit me at the Great Internet Marketing Center in Virginia Beach, Virginia. This is the only facility of its kind in the world. You'll be picked up by limo at Norfolk International Airport. You'll spend a long weekend living at my home where you'll be immersed in real-world Internet marketing: http://www.GreatInternetMarketing.com/retreatcenter.htm.

Mentor/Joint Venture Program

This is the most intense program I offer where I am with you over the course of a year training you, answering your questions, giving you ideas, and smoothing your way to riches on the Internet.

Oh, . . . and when I say you'll speak to me, I MEAN YOU'LL SPEAK TO ME. I want you to think of the biggest name people you can that have mentor programs and compared to them I'll blow you away with the amount of personal attention you get from me. Yes, I will have other experts under my supervision helping you, but you won't be left out in the cold for important stuff.

This is a very serious program and I understand that it is definitely not for everyone. Check it out at http://www.GreatInternetMarketing.com /mentorprogram.htm.

Good luck and I wish you the very best in your efforts to harness the power of the Internet for your business success.

Index